Salcombe, Kingsbridge, and Neighbourhood, a descriptive and historical guide ... Second edition. [With illustrations and a map.]

James Fairweather

Salcombe, Kingsbridge, and Neighbourhood, a descriptive and historical guide ... Second edition. [With illustrations and a map.]
Fairweather, James
British Library, Historical Print Editions
British Library
c 1897])
264 p. ; 8°.
010368.aa.45.

The BiblioLife Network

This project was made possible in part by the BiblioLife Network (BLN), a project aimed at addressing some of the huge challenges facing book preservationists around the world. The BLN includes libraries, library networks, archives, subject matter experts, online communities and library service providers. We believe every book ever published should be available as a high-quality print reproduction; printed on- demand anywhere in the world. This insures the ongoing accessibility of the content and helps generate sustainable revenue for the libraries and organizations that work to preserve these important materials.

The following book is in the "public domain" and represents an authentic reproduction of the text as printed by the original publisher. While we have attempted to accurately maintain the integrity of the original work, there are sometimes problems with the original book or micro-film from which the books were digitized. This can result in minor errors in reproduction. Possible imperfections include missing and blurred pages, poor pictures, markings and other reproduction issues beyond our control. Because this work is culturally important, we have made it available as part of our commitment to protecting, preserving, and promoting the world's literature.

GUIDE TO FOLD-OUTS, MAPS and OVERSIZED IMAGES

In an online database, page images do not need to conform to the size restrictions found in a printed book. When converting these images back into a printed bound book, the page sizes are standardized in ways that maintain the detail of the original. For large images, such as fold-out maps, the original page image is split into two or more pages.

Guidelines used to determine the split of oversize pages:

- Some images are split vertically; large images require vertical and horizontal splits.
- For horizontal splits, the content is split left to right.
- For vertical splits, the content is split from top to bottom.
- For both vertical and horizontal splits, the image is processed from top left to bottom right.

Staunton
Uppfield
Stroud

MARINE HOTEL,
SALCOMBE (near Kingsbridge),

The best Winter Resort undoubtedly in England.

———◆———

THIS strictly family Hotel, with Gardens and Terraces to the water's edge, replete with every modern convenience, and perfect sanitary arrangements. Stands in its own Grounds on the shores of the Kingsbridge Estuary, half a mile from the open sea and the magnificent promontory of Bolt Head

The walks in the neighbourhood are romantic and beautiful in the extreme, as is also the boating on the picturesque Creeks of the Estuary. The Climate, within the influence of the Gulf Stream, is almost semi-tropical; the mean temperature is that of Venice. Year after year sees the same visitors return to the neighbourhood.

For those staying at the Hotel arrangements will be provided for FISHING, BOATING and SAILING, which can be enjoyed with perfect safety at all times.

Yachtsmen will find perfect anchorage in any weather for Vessels of any tonnage under the windows and within fifty yards of the Hotel. Free Harbour.

Visitors can book direct to Kingsbridge, thence by Steam Launch (4 miles), Coach (twice daily), or Carriage to Salcombe (6 miles).

Winter Terms, £3 3s. 0d. per week.
Summer Terms, 10s. 6d. to 12s. 6d. per day, by arrangement.

Fast Steamers from Plymouth to Salcombe two or three days every week, landing within a few yards of Hotel.

Address:—

      MANAGER, Marine Hotel,
            Salcombe, Kingsbridge.

Telegraphic Address: "Marine, Salcombe."

SALCOMBE BUILDING ESTATE.

Any part of this valuable

Freehold Building Estate

(Called by Visitors "The Riviera of England,")

To be Sold in Plots for Building.

WATER LAID ON FROM MAINS.

SANITATION PERFECT.

The Scenery is amongst the Best in the Kingdom.

Hunting, Fishing, Shooting, and Yachting

(In one of the best Harbours of Great Britain) may be indulged in.

For Plans and Particulars, apply to

JAMES FORD, Civil Engineer and Architect,

1, George Street, Plymouth.

HAMMETT'S

LADIES' AND GENTLEMEN'S

HAIR-CUTTING, DRESSING, AND SHAMPOOING ROOMS,

42, FORE STREET, KINGSBRIDGE.

Artist in Hair. Ladies' Combings straightened or made up in all designs.

Human Hair Plaits from 2/-. Families and Schools promptly attended to.

A Large Assortment of Hair, Tooth, Nail, Clothes, and other Brushes. Dressing, Small Tooth, and Back Combs. Razors and Razor Strops, Hand Mirrors, etc.

H. HAMMETT'S GERMINATIVE LIQUID, a sure Preventive from Hair falling off. This Lotion is guaranteed as one of the best ever offered to the public. Sold in bottles at 1s., 2s., and upwards Prepared and sold only by the Proprietor.

Cigars and Tobacco of superior quality. Pipes, Pouches, etc.

BOLT HEAD HOTEL,
SALCOMBE, SOUTH DEVON.

THIS HOTEL is charmingly situated near the famous Bolt Head, and stands in its own grounds; overlooks the English Channel, and commands magnificent views of the surrounding Coast, and inland scenery. A Verandah and Balcony, each 80 feet long, form pleasant resorts, from which are obtained beautiful sea and inland views.

Spacious and well-lighted Billiard Room

EXCURSION & PICNIC PARTIES CATERED FOR

Capital Boating and Sea Fishing.

Good Sands near for Bathing, and safe for Children.

Carriages meet Trains when requested.

For particulars and terms apply to

R. TRINICK, PROPRIETOR.

J. W. COOK,
Baker, Confectioner, Grocer
GREENGROCER, FRUITERER,
AND
FORAGE DEALER,
57, Fore Street, 1 & 2, Market Street,
SALCOMBE.

:o:

GAME AND RABBIT DEALER.

Poultry killed to order at the shortest notice.

Wholesale and Retail Potatoe Merchant,

NEW LAID EGGS.   FRESH BUTTER.
CLOTTED CREAM.

Pony Carriage and Invalid's Donkey Chair on hire.

All Orders promptly attended to.

ERNEST CALKIN,

Dispensing and Family Chemist,

34, Fore Street, Salcombe.

Physicians' and Surgeons' Prescriptions and Family Recipes carefully and accurately prepared, only with the Purest Drugs and Chemicals.

SURGICAL AND SICK-ROOM APPLIANCES.

Toilet Requisites, Perfumery, Sponges, Sponge Bags, Tooth, Nail, and Hair Brushes, Bathing Caps and Sandals, etc.

MINERAL WATERS, SODA, SILTZER, POTASH, LITHIA WATERS, AND LEMONADE IN SYPHONS.

PHOTOGRAPHIC PLATES AND CHEMICALS.

Any article not in stock obtained at the shortest notice.

Agent for W. & A. Gilbey's Wines and Spirits; Henessy's Brandy; Jameson's Whisky; Coate's Plymouth Gin; Burgoyne's Australian Wines, etc., etc.

J. FAIRWEATHER,

Newsagent, Stationer, &c.,

Respectfully informs Visitors and Residents that the

LONDON MORNING DAILY PAPERS

Are supplied by him daily, at the published prices.

ALL MAGAZINES AND PERIODICALS REGULARLY SUPPLIED.

BOOKS & MUSIC OF EVERY DESCRIPTION OBTAINED TO ORDER BY RETURN.

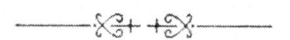

A PARCEL FROM LONDON DAILY.

"TIMES" OFFICE, SALCOMBE;
"JOURNAL" OFFICE, KINGSBRIDGE.

☞ TEA A SPECIALITY

Pure, Rich, and Delicious, at Popular Prices.

Specially blended to suit the water of the district.

A Perfect Tea, our leading line — WHITE'S CHAMPION BLEND. **1/6 lb.** usually sold at 2s

Other Blends of extraordinary merit, 10d., 1s., 1s. 2d., 1s. 4d. and 1s. 10d., no higher prices.

Taken fresh from the chest. Weighed as required.

The Cash Supply Stores,

75 AND 77, FORE STREET, KINGSBRIDGE,

E. WHITE, Proprietor.

We make a Special Study of Provisions.

This is The Place for General Groceries, Patent Medicines, Tobacco and Snuff, Brushes, Brooms, etc., etc.

ALL GOODS AT LONDON STORE PRICES FOR CASH ONLY.

Carriage Paid on 5s orders.

W HATCH,

COAL MERCHANT.

STORES:—FORE STREET, SALCOMBE.

Only Best Quality House Coal supplied, and delivered to any part of the District.

F. HATCH,

Baker and Confectioner,

ISLAND STREET, SALCOMBE.

FAMILIES WAITED ON DAILY.

CAKES OF EVERY DESCRIPTION.

PRINCIPAL DEPOT FOR

Photographs & Souvenirs

OF

Salcombe, Kingsbridge, and Vicinity.

Jas. Fairweather,

PRINTER, STATIONER, & BOOKSELLER,

"Times" Office, SALCOMBE,

Invites the attention of Visitors, Tourists, and others
to his large stock of

PHOTOGRAPHIC VIEWS,

Which comprises the Finest Series of Views of the District.

Salcombe,   The Old Castle,   The Bolt Head,
    The Harbour and Estuary,   Kingsbridge,
South Pool,   Hope Cove and Bay,   Thurlestone,
    Bantham,   River Avon,   Loddiswell,
Stokenham,   Torcross,   Start Point,   Hallsands.

Embracing over

200 Different Views of Magnificent Scenery.

BEAUTIFUL NEW COLOURED VIEWS OF THE DISTRICT.

Views of Local Scenery

In a great variety of Articles, from 6d. upwards.

Albums of Local Views, 6d. & 1s.

Novelties, both in shape and design, in
PHOTOGRAPH FRAMES AND ALBUMS.

Circulating Library.   New Books constantly added.

HILLSIDE SCHOOL,
KINGSBRIDGE, S. DEVON.

Established in 1875 by the present Head Master.

THE Education imparted is thoroughly sound and comprehensive, and such as to qualify the pupils for professional and commercial pursuits.

The School-room is high and well ventilated, with Class-room, Spacious Dormitories, Perfect Sanitary Arrangements, and Covered Playground.

All the exercises to make up real boyhood are indulged in, viz. :—boating, fishing, swimming, and the various sports of the playground and field.

Without exception, boating, fishing, and swimming are under the close personal supervision of the Principal.

Parents may feel assured that in sending their boys they are placing them under the immediate care of a Master who gives his whole life to his work.

Cambridge Local Examination and Civil Service Successes.

W. R. GAY, Principal.

ROBERT M. STEWART, A.P.S.,
Dispensing and Family Chemist,
KINGSBRIDGE.

Physicians Prescriptions and Family Recipes carefully prepared with the purest Drugs and Chemicals.

ELASTIC STOCKINGS, ANKLETS, TRUSSES, BANDAGES.

R. M. S. would specially bring to your notice the large Stock he holds of Sponges for Bath and Nursery, Sponge Bags, Bathing Caps, Kent's Hair, Nail, and Tooth Brushes, Surgical Appliances, Abdominal Belts, &c.

Special attention to orders by Rail, Post, or Boat.

Agent for the Devon and Exeter Savings Bank, Sun Life and Fire Insurance Office.

THE SALCOMBE GROCERY STORES.

Established 1865.

W. S. ELLIS,

42, Fore Street, SALCOMBE,

TEA,

Coffee, and Provision Merchant.

TEAS AND COFFEES
Of the Finest Quality
FROM 1/- PER LB.

Sole Agent for Salcombe and Neighbourhood for:—
Carr & Quick's, Ltd., Wine Merchants, Exeter, Celebrated Wines and Spirits.

Carr's No. 1 Blend Scotch Whisky, a speciality, 3s. 6d. Per Bottle; 2d. Per Bottle off by taking 6 Bottles.

COLEMAN'S WINCARNIS.

Holloway's Meat and Malt Wine and Coca Wine, 1s. 6d. and 2s. 9d. Per Bottle.

Sole Agent for Salcombe and Neighbourhood for:—
Rogers' Celebrated Pale Ales and Stouts, in Cask and Bottles, from 1s. per gallon and 2s. 6d. Per Dozen Imperial Screw Stoppered Bottles.

Patent Medicines at Co-Operative Prices for Cash.

N.B.—Any article not in Stock will be obtained at the Shortest Notice, and sold at the Lowest possible Prices for Cash.

SALCOMBE FROM PORTLEMOUTH.

SALCOMBE, KINGSBRIDGE,

AND

NEIGHBOURHOOD,

A

𝔇escriptive and 𝔋istorical 𝔊uide

TO ALL PLACES OF INTEREST BETWEEN

START BAY AND THE RIVER AVON.

BY

JAMES FAIRWEATHER.

SECOND EDITION.

SALCOMBE AND KINGSBRIDGE:
JAS. FAIRWEATHER, PRINTER AND STATIONER.

PRINTED AND PUBLISHED BY
JAS. FAIRWEATHER, PRINTER AND STATIONER,
SALCOMBE AND KINGSBRIDGE.

PREFACE.

IN passing a second edition of this Book through the press, the author is grateful for the kindly reception the former edition met with from the public. The aim has been not only to make the book descriptive of the varied scenery of the district, but also to give a historical record of the chief places of interest, and in doing so liberal use has been made of books previously published on the subject, especially Abraham Hawkins' history published in 1819, a valuable but now rare book, it having been out of print for a great number of years.

Liberal use has also been made of the numerous appreciative articles on the district that have appeared in magazines and newspapers published in various parts of the country during the past few years, written by persons who have visited the neighbourhood.

The book is considerably enhanced in value by the numerous illustrations that now appear in it for the first time, and for which the author is greatly indebted to the many kind friends who readily placed their photographic views at his disposal, for reproduction, sveeral of them being very choice presentations of the unrivalled scenery to be met with in this district. Many of the views were taken specially for this work. Among those who have placed their photographs at the author's disposal, are the Rev. R. A. Morris, lately of Salcombe, but now of Bideford; Mr. Graham Smith, of London; and Mr. W. Beer, Kingsbridge. Most of the views of Kingsbridge, together with the Avon Valley, Bantham, the Start,

Prawle Point, etc., are from the excellent and varied stock of views of Mrs. Haynes, of the Studio, Kingsbridge. The illustration of an extraordinary cluster of Foxgloves that appears on page 248 is from a photograph taken by Mr. Gay, of Kingsbridge, in the month of June in Courtenay Walk, near Bolt Head. The author's son also took several views specially for this work.

For the exhaustive list of Plants to be found in the neighbourhood, that appears on pages 241 to 255, the author is indebted to the Rev. W. Bevil Browne, formerly of Salcombe and Kingsbridge, but now residing at Shaldon; also to Mr. G. May, of Bexley; Mr. Prideaux, of Wellington; Mr. J Lawson, a frequent visitor to Salcombe; and to the Rev. W. S. Wyle, of Salcombe, who very carefully revised the list.

For the list of Birds that have both bred in and visited the district the author is indebted to Dr. Edmund Elliot and Mr. R. Nicholls, of Kingsbridge, and for the list of Domesday names to Mr. W. Davies, Kingsbridge.

This new edition is now offered to the public as a handy, and the author believes, trustworthy Guide to Salcombe, Kingsbridge, and the neighbourhood.

CONTENTS.

	PAGE.
EARLY HISTORY	9
RIGHT TO WRECKAGE	22
SALCOMBE—THE TOWN	27
„ PLACES OF WORSHIP	49
„ AS A WATERING PLACE	55
WHAT OTHERS HAVE SAID ABOUT SALCOMBE	67
SALCOMBE—THE HARBOUR	78
SALCOMBE CASTLE	85
SALCOMBE TO BOLT HEAD	98
BOLT HEAD TO BOLT TAIL	117
SEWER MILL COVE	118
SALCOMBE TO HOPE COVE	127
HOPE COVE TO BANTHAM	142
SALCOMBE TO KINGSBRIDGE	152
KINGSBRIDGE AND DODBROOKE	165
THE KINGSBRIDGE RAILWAY	198
SALCOMBE TO SOUTH POOL	200
SALCOMBE TO HALLSANDS AND START	207
START POINT	217
SALCOMBE TO TORCROSS AND SLAPTON	230
SLAPTON	237
LIST OF PLANTS	241
FERNS	254
BOAT FARES AT SALCOMBE	255
BIRDS	256
DOMESDAY NAMES OF PLACES	259
TABLE OF DISTANCES	260
INDEX	261

SALCOMBE, KINGSBRIDGE,

AND

NEIGHBOURHOOD,

SALCOMBE AND NEIGHBOURHOOD.

EARLY HISTORY.

GENERAL history should always be a subject of great importance in the education of our race; it tends to widen our sympathy and interest, by bringing us into closer relationship to that world which is outside of ourselves. The history of our own country will always, necessarily, be of most importance, and each locality can offer its own quota of information to make that history complete.

We shall also find that our greatest interest clusters around the place of our birth and of our adopted home, our thoughts travelling back over the past, desiring to know something of its early history; but how frequently are our longings to peer into the past baulked at the outset by the paucity of information we can glean concerning it, our ancestors either thinking that matters occurring immediately around them, and appearing by their very familiarity of no importance to them, could be of no importance to posterity either; or by the lack of the knowledge of writing, events that would have formed subject-matter for history were unrecorded, and thus buried in oblivion. We must, however, quiet our curiosity with the thought that School Boards and School Attendance Committees were not then in existence, and consequently the art of caligraphy had not reached the state of proficiency it has with us.

In the lack of more definite knowledge, much can be surmised respecting the early history of a place by the name which it bears. It may be taken for granted, generally, that the name bestowed upon a place by its original occupiers would continue in force through successive ages, each succeeding generation being satisfied therewith. In this way we can tell pretty accurately how the first settlers in this country spread themselves over it, by finding where Celtic, Roman, Saxon, or Danish place-names predominate.

Respecting the early history of the locality that we are now considering, we have little or no definite knowledge to depend upon; but, taking its place-names for our study, we may come to some tolerably correct conclusions.

We have evidence that both Celts and Saxons gathered around our shores, as well as signs that the Norsemen alighted on our coast to carry on their piratical and predatory deeds. We can trace the Celts at Prawle from PRAL a "skull," a name given to the place, doubtless, from some dark and mysterious deed enacted there; also at Kellaton in Stokenham parish, and Killeton, in East Allington parish, from CELLI, a "grove," deriving their names probably from being situated in pleasant wooded vales. In Ringmore again, we have a name of Celtic origin, from RHYN-MAUR, meaning the "great promontory," evidently showing that it was not originally given to the parish that now claims it, for it would be altogether inappropriate, as it is situated in Bigbury Bay. Let us, however, take a map of our county, and notice how the tract of land stretching from the Bolt Tail to the Start Point juts out into the sea, and we shall at once perceive how very appropriate would be such a title to it, as RHYN-MAUR, the "great promontory." It is more than probable, therefore, that the name was first applied to this tract of land, and not to the parish that now bears the name, but that that was bestowed in after years. Here, then, we have traces of the Celts, the original occupiers of our country.

EARLY HISTORY.

But what shall we say of Salcombe; is it of Celtic or Saxon extraction, for the Celtic CWM and the Saxon COOMBE mean one and the same thing—"a valley," and it evidently was selected for its sheltered position, and the name applied accordingly. We incline to the belief that it is of Saxon origin, and that its prefix "Sal," which no doubt was formerly written "Salt," was given to it from its proximity to the sea, meaning as a whole the salt valley. It is probable, however, that the earliest occupiers of this neighbourhood settled first on the other, or eastern, side of the harbour; or at all events that Portlemouth was of more importance than Salcombe in very ancient times, shewn by the fact of the harbour supplying it with a name, Portlemouth meaning the mouth of the port, a name that it would not have taken unless it was first established or of greater importance than Salcombe, a place that has, however, outgrown it in recent years.

While the Saxons were thus gradually locating themselves along our shores, and up our beautiful valleys, they would by-and-by be molested by the Norsemen alighting on the coast to carry on their acts of piracy and plunder.

There is an old tradition that Stare-hole Bottom was at one time a Danish encampment, and to substantiate this there is much circumstantial evidence. Much of the land about the Bolt is called the Sewers, and in this name has been recognised SEA-WARE, or sea folks, and this would point most decidedly to the settlement of the Norsemen in the neighbourhood. The name of the parish in which this land is situated, as well as at least one hamlet in the parish, would imply their being used as places of defence, for both BURY and BURGH bear this meaning; the former especially being given to places of encampment for warlike purposes. We have thus Malborough and Bolberry, the former with the prefix "Mal" signifying a meeting place, showing that Malborough must have been in former days a place of some considerable importance. Coming nearer home, we have also a high tract of land, eminently adapted for defence, called the Berry. These names would imply that the places had been used for warlike purposes, and all point to the Norsemen having taken up a position on our coast, the inhabitants gathering on these high and commanding positions, to offer a stout resistance to the incursions of their Danish foes. The place where the Danes landed and took up their abode, has generally been fixed by tradition at Stare-hole Bottom, it being just such a place, too, as we should imagine a horde of pirates would select

COPY OF AN OLD PRINT OF BAKER'S WELL, SALCOMBE.

Taking, then, the various place-names about here, together with the traditions relating to the neighbourhood, we have strong circumstantial evidence that the Danes once resided in this locality.

But to pass from these times and trace events in the history of the locality of greater certitude, we find that in 1347 the harbour was known by the name of Kingsbridge, in which year it was called upon to provide a naval subsidy. The next trace that we can find of Salcombe, is in connection with a very laudable act on the part of the inhabitants. Included, as they then were, in the ancient parish of Malborough, the residents of Salcombe were more than two miles distant from their parish church, and we can well conceive that their attendance at Divine Worship would be very limited indeed, the old and infirm being entirely debarred from this privilege. We find, therefore, the inhabitants raising amongst themselves, by public subscription, funds sufficient to erect a Chapel-of-Ease. It stood on the site which the Public Rooms now occupy in Market Street, and was dedicated to St. John the Baptist. The register of Bishop Stafford, preserved at Exeter, states that it was licensed by that Bishop in the year 1401. The record is in Latin, and may be thus translated:—

"A License for celebrating Divine Service in a Chapel. Also, on the last day but one of the said month (January 1401-2), his lordship granted that in a certain Chapel, situated in the village or hamlet of Salcombe, under the parish of Alvington, and in the diocese of Exeter, erected and constructed anew, divine service may be celebrated by certain fit Presbyters, to be procured at the expense of the inhabitants of the said village or hamlet of Salcombe, without prejudice to the mother church, provided the consent of the Vicar of Alvington be obtained thereto."

Although Salcombe was then in the parish of Malborough, yet it will be seen from the above license, that West Alvington was regarded as the mother church, forming until recently, with Malborough, South Huish, and South Milton, one vicarage. The people of Salcombe at that time must have been animated by a fine, religious spirit; for not only did they themselves build this chapel, but as it had no land or other endowment attached to it, they undertook to support their minister at their own cost, an example of religious liberality worthy of imitation by people of modern and more wealthy times.

Very little is heard of this Chapel afterwards; but in 1601 the Rev. Thomas Moore was curate, who had a daughter, named Johanna, baptized at Malborough, which would seem to indicate that there was no font in the Salcombe Chapel, and that all baptisms as well as burials took place at Malborough. On January 6th, 1646, there was interred at Malborough the body of the Rev. Walter Pearce, who had been Curate of Salcombe, and this was only a few weeks previous to the visit of the Parliamentary Forces to besiege Fort Charles. This was apparently the last curate appointed to the Chapel, and it was probably then allowed to fall into decay. The widow of Mr. Pearce evidently continued to reside at Salcombe, for her interment is registered as having taken place at Malborough on January 27th, 1652-3. No minister would be appointed to the chapel during the Commonwealth, and doubtless the chapel got into a ruinous state through neglect. At the beginning of the nineteenth century it was in a very dilapidated condition, not having been used for divine worship for some considerable time previously. Its subsequent history will be referred to later on.

At the latter end of the 15th century Salcombe was thus described by Leland in his "Itinerary":—

"Saultcombe Haven, sumwhat barrid, and having a Rok at the entering into it, is about vij miles by West South West from Dertmouth; and about half a mile within the mouth of this Haven, longing to the Privileges of Dertmouth, is Saultcombe, a fishar towne, and a three miles upper at this Haven Hedde is Kingesbridg, sumtyme a praty town. The Est Point of Saultcombe Haven is a great Foreland into the Se, caulled the Sterte."

This description cannot be called very graphic, neither is it very long, but yet it is suggestive; miles must have been in those days longer than they are with us, or else they must have been what are commonly termed "Cornish" ones, to make it only 7 miles to Dartmouth and 3 miles from Salcombe to Kingsbridge. We learn also that the etymology of the name was at first "Saltcombe," but we suppose that someone in after years thought the 't' was superfluous and accordingly left it out. Kingsbridge is said some time to have been a pretty town, its beauty, probably, being more marked at that early period, than it is now, whilst Salcombe, from the nature of the employment followed by its inhabitants, would have a very fishey smell, detracting from the natural beauties by which it was surrounded. Leland calls Salcombe a "town," perhaps here is the foundation for the old tradition, that at one time it was a large place.

The harbour, doubtless, was taken advantage ot at a very early date by shipping, notwithstanding the entrance to it was somewhat barred. Times were when pirates prowled around our own shores, and committed their depredations, as well as on more barbarous coasts; and Salcombe, from its comparatively defenceless condition, and also its isolation, would become a harbour of refuge for these marauders, who could take up their quarters here with perfect safety, ever and anon putting out to sea to plunder passing ships, and when booty failed them on the high seas, then they would molest the inhabitants, and rob them of all they could. So extensive and annoying had this practice become, that in the year 1607 the County Justices complained to the Government that Salcombe harbour was infested with pirates, who often landed armed parties to the great danger of the inhabitants. We must not, however, understand that these pirates were all foreigners; they were mostly Englishmen, who carried on their robberies on the high seas making use of such harbours as Salcombe for shelter.

The following extracts taken from Hamilton's "Quarter Sessions under James 1st" show the unpleasant state of things which existed at Salcombe at that period:—

Piracy was practised at this time by Englishmen as well as by Turks. A letter was sent to the Council representing that the inhabitants of the haven town of Salcombe, in the County of Devon, were sorely oppressed and endangered through the insolence of sundry dissolute sea-faring men, who often come into the town in great numbers, two hundred armed men at one time, and threaten, when they are denied such things as they would have, that they will burn the town. It was represented also that they often foraged and stripped the country adjoining of sheep and other commodities, and took from poor fishermen their boats and barks. Moreover, as it is somewhat inaccurately expressed, they "murdered each other, and buried them in the sands by night," and committed daily sundry other outrages. The authorities of the County felt quite unable to suppress them, as they could

THE HARBOUR MOUTH FROM DEVON ROAD.

always take refuge in their ships lying off the harbour. The justices therefore called upon the Council to send down his Majesty's forces to subdue them. They give the names of some captains or chieftains among the pirates. It may be supposed that their advice was taken, for we afterwards find a charge of £6 for conducting "pyraths" to gaol from Salcombe. It may also be inferred that the pirates showed fight, for there was a payment made to the surgeon for curing them. But the fair harbour of Salcombe still continued to be a favourite haunt of such characters,

In the reign of Charles 1st, as we learn from Walter Yonge, Sir William Courtenay's castellated mansion of Ilton, near Salcombe, was robbed, and much of his plate and household stuff was carried away. It was done by certain pirates which came up in boats from Salcombe, and fled the same way they came without apprehension.

As far back as 1605 frequent references are made in State-papers to the town and shipping of Salcombe; and in that year an agreement is noted as to Spanish prizes driven into Salcombe and sequestered by Sir Richard Hawkins. In 1628 there is an examination of one John Roche, of Salcombe, who came from Wales in the *Jonas*, with twenty-three or twenty-four other ships, all of which were taken by the French. To show the importance in those days of Salcombe over other places, we may mention that certain towns had to lend ships to other towns which could not find them for themselves; and we see in 1634 the *May Rose* being lent by Salcombe to Barnstaple; and in the assessment of the town for a ship of 400 tons under the King's writ, Salcombe and Malborough were rated at £156 2s. 0d., whilst Plymouth was rated at £185 0s. 8d. One of the strangest facts in these entries, and one that brings home to us the high value of our supremacy on the seas, is that of the examination of a John Daniel, of Salcombe, in 1636. This mariner came out of Tenby, in his ship the *Swan*; when off Padstow they saw two big ships, which they took to be the King's ships; but off Mounts Bay a Turkish man-of-war of 100 tons gave them chase and ran them ashore. All in the Salcombe ship escaped except one man, who stayed on board and was taken by the Turks, who rifled and destroyed the ship.

To show what a large fishing trade was carried on here two or three hundred years ago, we have but to mention that the customs of the port for one year, from January, 1644, to January, 1645, taken by order of Sir E. Fortescue, of Fallapit, then Governor of Salcombe Castle, amounted to £5,000. We must not suppose that the whole of this sum was received from vessels laden with fish, but a considerable portion of it must have been; for great many of the vessels which cleared out in that year were stated to have been freighted with pilchards. The fishing trade of Salcombe in those days, evidently, must have been very remunerative; but in the lapse of time it was neglected for the more exciting, and for the time more profitable, trade of smuggling, and fishing was thus left to such places as Plymouth, Dartmouth, and Brixham, which continue to benefit thereby, whilst the trade is well-nigh lost to Salcombe. These extracts, taken from many sources, show the importance of Salcombe as a shipping port within the last three centuries.

The number of inhabitants in Salcombe at the census of 1791 was only 271, and the number of inhabited houses about 50; but in the next ten years it was nearly doubled, as the number is then given as being about 500.

The fair which at present lingers out its existence at Whitsuntide, has an old history, and was formerly held on the Tuesday only in Whitsun week; but towards the close of the eighteenth century it was extended to the Wednesday, and later still, it was further extended.

The progress of Salcombe from the commencement of the nineteenth century was fairly rapid. At that time, like many other similar places, the inhabitants obtained their livelihood principally by fishing and smuggling. A regular trade was carried on in the latter, and that in the most business-like and systematic manner. Large boats were built and fitted out expressly for this purpose, making occasional visits to the Channel Islands, and returning laden with tobacco and spirits, hiding it in all kinds of places, till an opportunity offered of disposing of it. Sometimes parties would go over to the opposite coast of France, freight vessels with spirits, and come over and land the kegs at Salcombe or some place near. Being pure spirit, they would dilute it with water and colouring matter, until they got it to a certain per centage, when they would sell it to the neighbouring publicans, or hawk it about the country, and as soon as it was disposed of, the party would meet together to dine, and afterwards settle their accounts and divide the profits. There can be no question but that the traffic was very successful, many individuals accumulating considerable sums of money by their participation in it, for it was a very rare circumstance for a boat to be captured with contraband articles on board. The effectual working of the coastguard system has entirely abolished the traffic.

There was no regular post to Salcombe at the beginning of the nineteenth century, but a woman used to proceed daily on foot to Kingsbridge, executing numerous petty missions, and returning at night heavily laden, charging a penny for each letter conveyed to or from the office at that place.

This woman was called Mrs. Sarah Stone, generally known in the neighbourhood at that time as " Poor Sally Stone." At the time of which we write she was getting old, and had previously seen better days; but her husband had dropped down dead on board the small vessel he was master of, and she was left entirely dependent on her own exertions for support. She had two children, both fortunately grown up. The one, a son, was a sailor; the other, a daughter, became the wife of the late Mr. Edward Cole, who afterwards became sub-postmaster of Salcombe. Poor Sally latterly used a boat for her mission to and from Kingsbridge. She managed this so skilfully, and was such an excellent sailor, that she not only conveyed the letters, but also passengers and parcels daily between the two towns; and so great was their confidence in her integrity and skill, that she used to take large sums of money to and from the banks at Kingsbridge, for many of the inhabitants; and many persons preferred her boat to any of the others that daily plied between the two towns.

In 1821, Mr. Yeats, of Woodville, applied for a Post Office at Salcombe, Sally Stone being appointed postmistress at a salary of £5 per year. She afterwards

SALCOMBE FROM ILBERTSTOWE POINT.

applied for an increase. It was represented, in a memorial drawn up for her, that her father, Joseph Jarvis, was on board of one of the ships when the Channel Fleet became embayed in Bigbury Bay in a fog, and knew not where they were. Jarvis informed the officers that he knew the place well, and could pilot the Fleet safely out, which he did; and, having had no reward for that service, it was prayed that this augmentation of salary might be given to his descendant, partly as remuneration for services rendered by her father. Her salary was then increased to £10 per year, and so continued to the time of her death.

'It happened that a very old acquaintance of Sally's, who had shared her small cottage for some years, died, and left her the little trifle she possessed. To obtain this, advice and assistance were, of course, necessary; and in all her difficulties the late Rev. Thomas Young was the person she applied to. As clergyman of the parish he was happy and ready to give his assistance to all who solicited it. The present case was attended with much trouble. Documents were to be procured, copied, and forwarded to various parties; and ultimately the will had to be "proved." All this was satisfactorily managed. The little money was obtained, and put into Sally's possession, the Rev. T. Young positively refusing to accept any fee or remuneration for what he had done. This made poor Sally feel very uncomfortable, as she could not reconcile to herself the idea of not paying for what had been done for her. One evening, a short time after this event, Mrs. Young was informed that Sally Stone wished to speak to her, but it must be in private. She was sent into the dining-room, and on Mrs. Young entering, Sally burst into tears. She hoped it would not be thought she had taken a liberty, but she could not rest until she had shown her feelings in some other way than by words, for the service Mr. Young had rendered her; she must implore and intreat that they would do her the favour to accept a patchwork quilt, which she had begun in her youth, and occasionally added to. She entreated that it might be used on the bed of their eldest son, then a boy of five years, that they might, when they looked at it, think of her, and say "there is at least one grateful person in the world, and that is poor Sally Stone." Her proffered gift was accepted. Some years afterwards, poor Sally was seized with an apoplectic fit; and as the Rev. T. Young was passing along the street, he found her lying speechless on the ground with the letters in her hand (she was just about to deliver them). He assisted to get her to her home, and was afterwards a constant attendant on her. This appeared to give her great satisfaction, until she breathed her last, although she was unable to express her feeling. A few days subsequently she was buried by the side of her husband. She died in 1841.

RIGHT TO WRECKAGE.

WE have now to refer to an old and very curious custom, as to the rights of the late Earls of Devon to all wreckage on rather an extensive coast-line. The rights to unclaimed wreckage was originally vested in the Crown, but in very many cases it was made over by special grant to lords of manors whose lands abutted on the sea. It is not known at what date this right was granted to the Courtenay family, but they can show a very ancient claim. It existed as early as the year 1416, and it was confirmed in the reigns of Edward VI. and Elizabeth, and the late Lord Devon fully established his right thereto at the Court of Inquiry held at Plymouth soon after the passing of the Merchant Shipping Act of 1854, to inquire into the claims of the lords of manors on the Devon coast. Lord Devon's right extended from Dartmouth Castle to the eastern shore of the river Avon, below Aveton Gifford, and extended so far out to sea as a man on horseback could see an umber barrel. At stated periods, and also on the occasion of any wreck, Lord Devon held Admiralty Courts at the various places on this coast-line, but it is probable that they were generally held at Salcombe from its importance. All matters connected with the sea and this harbour were under the jurisdiction of this Court, a code of laws being drawn up for the regulation of the same by them, and for any infringement of which they could administer what punishment they chose, and it is even probable that at one time the Courtenays had the right to inflict capital punishment. The Court was composed of thirteen respectable men, and these had to settle all matters respecting salvage, pay the amount, and preserve the property for the owners till claimed, when the same was delivered over, deducting only what was paid the salvors.

From the following will be seen the nature of these Courts, and some of the Rules and Regulations in force:—

"What is enquireable in this Court is as follows:—The Court is a Royal privilege granted from the Crown to the subject.

Wherein are inquirable all matters relating to the seas as wreck, which are three sorts—as 'Flotsam,' 'Jetsam,' and 'Lagan,'

'*Flotsam*' is when a ship sinks, and the goods that swim.

'*Jetsam*,' when a ship is in danger, and the goods are cast into the sea to lighten the ship.

And '*Lagan*' is when the ship is in danger that they cast out the heavier goods into the sea to lighten the ship, and put a buoy or a light thing that swims to it to take it up again—if they are saved, and find it again.

Whosoever finds any wrecked goods ought to carry it to the chief inhabitants of the town or place next to where it was found, and there to remain until a claim be made to it, either by any person saved alive belonging to the ship, or their wives, children, or executors, owner, merchant, or such a good title to the land.

And if no claim be made within a year and a day, then it must be delivered to the Admiral, or such as hath the Royal privilege of the Royalty, paying reasonable for their trouble for salvage.

If any man or living thing escape to shore alive, it is no wreck.

If any one should have a lanthorne or make a light in order to subject them in danger of shipwreck (if no harm happen), yet it is felony.

If any one convey secretly any of the goods, if it be the value of a nail, it is felony. Wrecked goods do not pay customs.

If any cast out any ballast from any ship or boat within the port of Salcombe contrary to the statute forfeits 3s. 4d. (and by an order formerly made in this Court). If it be let lie there forty-eight hours, shall forfeit 40s.

VIEW ACROSS THE HARBOUR TO SUNNY COVE.

If any one fineth another out of this Court, if it be here determinable, forfeits 40s.

If any one doth labour within this Royalty between sun and sun on the Sabbath-day forfeits 40s.

If any one ashore salt pilchards, and suffer the guts to be thrown or go into the salt water forfeits for each offence 3s. 4d.

If any one launch any boat within this Royalty on a Sunday before midnight forfeits 40s.

If any one forceably takes another's hale (haul), or disturb him therein, forfeits 40s."

The persons who drew up these Regulations were evidently strict Sabbatarians, and, perhaps, it is in no small measure due to their influence that there has been in the past so little Sabbath desecration by way of boating in Salcombe harbour, where, from its pleasant and sheltered situation, it must ever be a great temptation, especially during the summer months.

In by-gone days, before lighthouses were established, wrecks were plentiful, and the coast-line on which the Earls of Devon exercised their rights, was noted for the frequency of shipping casualties. We can well imagine, therefore, in the olden days when beacon fires lit on some prominent head-land were the only guide to mariners, and wreckers were numerous and eager to light false fires, that many in this locality would be out about the Bolt to ply this nefarious traffic, and with false lights in their hands draw hapless mariners to a cruel and bitter fate, caring little for human life, provided they could obtain their end and get possession of wreckage, for which these Admiralty Courts allowed them one-third of its value for salvage, although we are pleased to see by the foregoing Regulations, that such wreckers were treated as felons if detected in the act.

The following will show how eager the inhabitants of this neighbourhood were for wreckage. In January, 1750, a Dutch galliott belonging to Hamburg, and of about 100 tons burthen, became a wreck on Thurlestone Sands. She was laden with wine, brandy, coffee, and indigo, and bound from Zante to Hamburg. She came on shore about ten o'clock on a Wednesday night, and on Thursday and Friday a large portion of the cargo was saved, although it was with difficulty that the country people were kept from plundering it; but on the Saturday evening as many as ten thousand people congregated around this wreck, coming from all parts, and for the sole purpose of stealing what they could of the remainder of the cargo, and were only kept at bay by the arrival of a party of soldiers from Plymouth. The ringleader of this mob, however, got killed, for being in a drunken condition, he fell upon one of the soldiers' bayonets, and got fixed to it.

These Admiralty Courts no doubt prevented a great deal of plunder, for if those who picked up wrecked goods did not take them to Lord Devon's steward, if detected, they would be summoned before this Court and receive its sentence. The Court also decided the amount of salvage that should be given. The following is a copy of the presentments at one of these Courts held at Hope, on the 21st of April, 1737 :—

"We present George Hamblin of Orford Jefford (Aveton Gifford) for taking up of a graper about fifty weight at the place the *Dagger* was cast away at Bantham (1736) harbour.

We present a tierce of wine taken up in Salcombe by Roger Jarvis, Thomas Goss, and Joseph Fairweather, now in the possession of the Lord of the Royalty to agree the salvage.

We present a mast of forty foot long taken up by Joseph Whiting of S. Milton at Thurlestone.

We present a copper teapot and one pewter dish taken up by James Jarvis.

We present John Piles, of Kingsbridge, for taking up a small cannon gun where the *Dagger* was lost."

At one time the Earl of Devon's ancestors kept boats, anchors, and cables, for the assistance of any ships in distress. It often happened that vessels, after having been saved by these means from dashing on the rocks, the crews would take advantage of a change of wind to withdraw the ship, without making satisfaction for the risk of lives, labour, and service in giving them assistance. To prevent this behaviour, a cable, anchor, or some necessary material was detained by way of deposit, until satisfaction was made. The lords of the manors are still entitled to all wreckage within the before-mentioned limits that is not claimed within twelve months; but Admiralty Courts are rarely, if ever, held now.

THE TOWN.

SALCOMBE is situated in the extreme South of Devon, built on the margin of an inlet of the sea, midway between the tract of land that juts out into the English Channel from Start Point on the east to Bolt Tail on the west. This inlet of the sea is some five miles in length, and terminates at Kingsbridge, there being several creeks that branch off from it. There are only two other towns in England that have a more southern situation, and they cannot boast of the even and salubrious climate of Salcombe.

It is in the Southern Parliamentary Division of the County, hundred of Coleridge, union of Kingsbridge, rural deanery of Woodleigh, archdeaconry of Totnes, and diocese of Exeter. It is five miles from Kingsbridge, where there is a branch station of the Great Western Railway, and to and from which an omnibus runs twice a day.

The town is built on the margin of and facing the harbour, just at the point where all the radiating creeks of the Estuary meet to join the sea, and it is snugly ensconced under the lee of a hill. Its appearance at the commencement of the nineteenth century must have been somewhat different from what it is now. The houses then were comparatively few in number, and the foreshore occupied much of the space that is now built upon.

Approaching the town by the main road from Kingsbridge, a road branches off to the left, and although somewhat steep and winding, it is much the shorter route and therefore largely used, called Bonfire Hill (a name derived from the bonfire that used to be lit here annually on the 5th of November). However, by proceeding a little further along the main road there is a new approach to the town, called the Onslow Road, giving a much easier gradient. Although the main road into the town is the longest; yet it is by far the best and most pleasant. It takes a circuitous route, but soon after passing the land mark on the right a magnificent

NORTH SANDS AND BOLT HEAD.

view is obtained of North Sands vale, the Moult Point, Bolt Head, and the approaches to the harbour. Then for some little distance the road is beautifully wooded on either side, the splendid grounds of Woodville sloping away toward the shore. Emerging from the wooded portion of the road, some prettily-situated recently built detached villas are passed. with the harbour below.

The first house on the left is the Vicarage, a Gothic structure, standing in its own grounds by the side of the hill, commanding very extensive views, and erected shortly after 1864 when Salcombe was formed into an ecclesiastical parish. Immediately below, and extending towards the town, is the Marine Hotel, standing in its own grounds, many years the private residence of the Lords Kingsale, and then known as Ringrone House. The title of Baron Kingsale having descended to the family of the late Captain de Courcy, whose widow resided at Salcombe, it came to his son, John Stapleton, twenty-eighth Lord Kingsale, who about six years after coming to the title had Ringrone house built, naming it after one of the estates in Ireland. This was about the year 1839. Formerly a rather small and incommodious building occupied the same site, and the view given on page 12 gives a good representation of the place previous to the alterations. His Lordship also had constructed, at great expense, the beautiful esplanade, several hundred feet in length, in front of the house, and that extends along the water's edge, which is tastefully laid out. This Baron died in 1847, and was buried at Malborough, where also are buried two of his sons, one of them, Michæl Conrad de Courcy, thirtieth Lord Kingsale, died on April 15th, 1874, and not being married was succeeded by his cousin, John Fitzroy de Courcy, thirty-first Baron, but Ringrone did not come into his possession. This historic and very ancient family was founded in Ireland by the famous soldier, Sir John de Courcy, created Earl of Ulster in 1181.

We copy the following from Mr Edgar Sheppard's book, "Memorials of St James' Palace," in reference to the right of the Lords Kingsale to remain covered in the presence of the Sovereign :—

"A Lord Kingsale enjoys what has been called an 'hereditary right' to remain covered when in the presence of his Sovereign. It would seem that this privilege dates as far back as the reign of King John, and is generally, if not always, asserted by the possessor of the title for the time being. The privilege is said to have had its origin in the following way. Sir John de Courcy, afterwards Earl of Ulster, was so conspicuous for his undaunted courage in the Irish wars of 1181, that he grew into high favour with his Sovereign, King Henry II This aroused the jealousy of a certain Hugh de Lacie, Governor of Ireland, who, when King John ascended the throne, plotted the destruction of Sir John de Courcy. The consequence was that Sir John was seized in the churchyard of Downpatrick, whither he had gone to do penance; his lands and estates were confiscated, and he himself was sent over to England, where he was finally sentenced by King John to imprisonment for life in the Tower. About a year after his incarceration, a dispute arose respecting the Duchy of Normandy between King John of England and the French King. The Earl, being a renowned swordsman, was called upon at his own request to represent the English King. 'The decision was referred to single combat.' The day for the dual was fixed, all preparations were made, and the combatants met face to face. But just as the encounter was about to commence, Lord Ulster's opponent, who had heard of his adversary's bravery, became suddenly panic-stricken, and withdrew at once from the contest. Thus the matter in dispute was decided, but the French King, having also heard of the valour and strength of the Irish noble, expressed a wish to see some display of his skill, and King John commanded his lordship to put his power in evidence. Thereupon Lord Ulster 'cleft a massive helmet in twain at a single blow,' a feat which the English Sovereign rewarded by reinstating the Earl in all his former honours, adding that he would do for him, or give to him, whatever he might desire. Lord Ulster replied that he neither courted estates nor required titles, but that he did desire one thing for himself and his successors, the Lords Kingsale, in reigns and generations to come, viz., the privilege of appearing covered in the presence of his Sovereign.

It appears that this claim is from time to time asserted by the Lords Kingsale. For instance, Almericus, who was the twenty-third Baron of Kingsale, presented himself covered in the presence of King William III. When his Majesty expressed his surprise at this act, Lord Kingsale is said to have replied, 'Sire, my name is Courcy. I am Lord of Kingsale in your Majesty's Kingdom of Ireland; and the reason of my appearing covered in your Majesty's presence is to maintain the ancient privilege of my family, granted to Sir John de Courcy, Earl of Ulster, and his heirs, by John, King of England.' His Majesty thereupon immediately acknowledged the claim, and moreover gave his hand to Lord Kingsale to kiss. Lord Kingsale, we are told, made his bow and continued with his head covered. On another occasion, a Lord Kingsale, in the time of George III, was exercising his ancient privilege, when the King, who knew of its existence and previous assertion, called out in an angry tone: 'Lord Kingsale, I do not dispute your right of standing covered in my presence; but my lord (pointing with his hand) there is the Queen!' This was a dignified and justifiable reproval of an unnecessary and ungracious act, the reply to which on his lordship's part is not recorded.

Once again, in the present reign, at a levee held in St. James's Palace, on June 25th, in the year 1859, the thirtieth Lord Kingsale essayed to pass before the Queen with covered head, and so assert his hereditary right. The moment that Lord Kingsale entered the Throne Room, attention was called to his presence by an exclamation from the Queen. Lord Sydney, who on that day was acting for the first time as Lord Chamberlain, was immediately informed that the gentleman was Lord Kingsale, and he at once told the Queen. Colonel Master, the Gentleman Usher in Waiting, had failed to notice the cause of the disturbance till his lordship reached her Majesty's immediate presence. The offending hat would at once have been seized by the Colonel, if the Hon. Spencer Ponsonby, now the Hon. Sir S. Ponsonby Fane, K.C B , who was standing by him, had not averted what might have led to 'a scene' in her Majesty's presence. Lord Kingsale, standing in front of the Queen, uncovered, made a low bow, replaced his hat, and passed on. His lordship wore on this occasion an old-fashioned deputy-lieutenant's hat, cocked and feathered. A few days after this occurrence the Lord Chamberlain wrote to Lord Kingsale, calling his attention to what had taken place at the levee, and informing him that his appearance with covered head in the Queen's presence had occasioned some surprise to her Majesty. The Lord Chamberlain was commanded to state to his lordship that the Queen did not dispute the privilege which Lord Kingsale claimed, and which his predecessors appeared to have exercised on former occasions, and that her Majesty had no objection to the assertion of that privilege under certain conditions. But it was desirable, whenever Lord Kingsale considered it important, in the maintenance of his right, to adopt so unusual a course, that some previous notice should be sent to the Lord Chamberlain, in order that he might submit it to her Majesty, and thus prevent any disagreeable misunderstanding which might possibly arise on the part of the officers of the Court on duty. In justice to Lord Kingsale, it should be added that, as soon as the possible consequences of his action were pointed out to him, he expressed much regret at having unintentionally given offence in his mode of exercising a privilege conferred upon his ancestor (a privilege which had been usually recognised and permitted once in every reign), and he promised that notice should be given on any future occasion."

A CORNER OF LOWER TERRACE, MARINE HOTEL, GROUNDS.

THE MARINE HOTEL.—Few hotels can boast of a more delightful situation than that of the Marine Hotel. It is

THE TOWN. 33

surrounded by its own grounds, with charmingly terraced gardens going down to the water, and can therefore be approached from the sea with as much ease as from the land. From the house and gardens can be seen the far-famed Bolt Head, with a peep of the English

ALOE IN FLOWER (1896) MARINE HOTEL GROUNDS.

Channel. Yachtsmen will probably not be slow in discovering the hotel, for no finer anchorage could be desired than may be had from Blackstone to Ilbertstow Point—a range of something like two miles—while for winter quarters no better situation can be obtained. The Hotel in particular enjoys perfect shelter from the cold and searching winds of winter, which should make its charming verandah and terraces much sought by those who desire a pleasant winter residence, with a climate in which the aloe and other exotic plants flourish. An aloe flowered on the lower terrace during the summer of 1896, of which we give an illustration on the previous page. In the transformation of Ringrone House into the Marine Hotel it was necessary to enlarge the mansion in different directions. On the ground floor or basement, is the coffee room, which is a handsomely proportioned room, having three French windows opening out on a colonnade and terrace grounds overlooking and sloping down to the sea. We question very much whether there is in the county such a handsome, and at the same time comfortable dining room, or one from which such lovely scenery can be viewed. The drawing room occupies the other half of the ground floor (the principal entrance being in the front centre of the building), and has also three French windows opening out on the colonnade and terrace grounds. One end of this room is curtained off by a heavy hanging of repp hooked back by girdles, and forms a writing room for ladies. The smoking room faces south, and is floored with wood blocks stained oak and varnished. On the first floor are sitting and bedrooms *en-suite*, and the billiard room and Hotel Bar, having an entrance from Cliff Road, which is a higher level than the ground floor. The billiard room measures 30 feet by 20 feet, lighted by three side windows and lantern light, and is heated by hot water pipes and fire place. The room is supplied with a very fine billiard table, made by Messrs Burroughs and Watts. The Visitors' rooms on the first floor are so arranged that families wishing to be private from the hotel can take suites of rooms, consisting of dining room, two bedrooms, and dressing rooms. Hot and cold water is supplied to all parts of the house, and lifts, &c.,

render communications expeditious and convenient. The hotel has its own water supply, and the sanitary and other arrangements are of the most approved character. The cost of the freehold of the premises, and enlarging and furnishing, was about £12,000, and the Hotel is owned by a limited liability company.

Leaving the Marine Hotel, five or six houses are passed, and the place is called Baker's Well. On the left hand side of the road is the site of Cliff House, for sometime the residence of the late Mrs. Prideaux, and then of her daughter, Mrs. Dowglass, who was lady of the manor of South Milton. At her death the property was sold, and purchased by Mr. R. Heriot, of London, who has recently demolished and rebuilt the mansion. The house is surrounded by productive gardens and ornamental grounds. Below the house, on the opposite side of the road, and in a line with the esplanade of the Marine Hotel, Mrs. Prideaux constructed one of about the same length, the two forming a great ornament to the harbour. At the back of the esplanade, a wall was erected, along which were planted orange, citron, and lemon trees. The garden in front of the house is the spot where the first aloe that flowered in Great Britain stood, and which attracted so much attention to it. The house at that time belonged to the representatives of Mr Barrable, the principal custom-house officer, who had recently died This was in 1774. In the middle of June of that year the aloe was first observed to have shot forth a flower stem in nearly a horizontal direction. Soon it elevated its head to an angle of forty-five degrees, and in less than a fortnight became perpendicular, making a progress almost visible to the by-stander, and increasing in extent about nine inches a day. By the month of August it had reached the height of twenty feet, when a handbill was printed and circulated, of which the following is a copy:—

"Now to be seen at Salcombe, near Kingsbridge, in full blow, a remarkable Alloe; supposed to be the largest that ever was seen

36 SALCOMBE AND NEIGHBOURHOOD.

in this Kingdom; and altho' continually exposed to the Weather, it hath grown to the following dimentions: in height 20 feet, length of the leaf 9 feet, thickness of ditto 6 inches. As the Proprietor hath been at great Expenditure to keep it for the Curious, the Terms of Admittance are, for Ladies and Gentlemen 2s. 6d. each; all others at One Shilling each Person, and to be paid at the Door."

The words "2s. 6d. each; all others" were struck out with a pen in a short time, as even one shilling was found more than people in general were disposed to give.

MARINE HOTEL, CLIFF HOUSE, &C.

As it was shown for emolument, a covering was erected on the east side, next to the road, to conceal it from view; but this was only partially effectual. By the end of September it had reached the height of twenty-eight feet, and it bore innumerable flowers on forty-two branches. The plant perished at the close of autumn. In 1842, another flowered in the same grounds. At one

THE TOWN. 37

end of the house was a small recessed wall, containing several thriving orange, lemon, and citron trees. Behind the house there is a plantation of firs, at the top of which is a small castellated building, about thirty feet in height, and used as a summer house. Closely adjoining Cliff House is the Grange, for many years the residence of the Incumbents of Salcombe, previous to the district being formed into an ecclesiastical parish. The house is constructed in the shape of three bows, in front of which is a colonnade. It is pleasantly situated and commands a fine view, but there are no plants or trees on the ground of any particular value.

After leaving the Grange, the town begins, which consists of a long, and for the most part narrow street, with other streets and courts jutting out from it. The two extreme ends were formerly called North and South Orestone, or as the spelling then was, Hoar or Old Stone. Now North Orestone has been re-named The Island, whilst the southern entrance still retains simply the name of Orestone. The Coastguard Station is situated here, near the end of the esplanade erected by Mrs. Prideaux. A flight of steps from the street leads direct to what is called the Pier, but really a substitute for one. Better accommodation being needed for landing at low tides, and this being the best available place, after much talk, it was decided in 1871 to erect this structure. The original design was for a pier fifteen feet longer than the present, but fears were expressed that it would interfere with the navigation of the harbour, and there not being a unanimity of opinion, funds did not come to hand sufficient to warrant the carrying out of the whole design, and so the unpretentious structure now known as "The Pier" was erected. Whilst their were many private subscriptions, the Harbour Commissioners and the shareholders of the Kingsbridge and Salcombe passenger steamer were the chief contributors. There are good landing steps of Cornish granite on both sides, and it is fenced around with iron railings. The pier, incomplete as it is, affords great facilities for landing and embarking passengers from excursion steamers, also for the ferry to Portlemouth, which plies to and from this place, and for the steamer to Kingsbridge. Its cost was about £100, and it no doubt greatly improved that part of the foreshore. Considerable cost has since been incurred upon its improvement by the Local Authority, to whom it now belongs.

The Post Office is situated in Fore Street near Orestone, with which is connected a Money Order Office and Post Office Savings' Bank, both established in 1861, and a Telegraph Office was added in 1870. Annuity and Insurance business is also transacted. There are three deliveries of letters a day, commencing about 8 o'clock a.m., a second delivery at 1.10 p.m., and a third at 8 p.m. Letters are despatched at 9.35 a.m., 12.50 p.m., and 4.45 p.m., with the exception of Sundays, when they are despatched at 11.30 a.m. All branches of business are transacted on week days from 8 a.m. to 8 p.m. Telegrams can be sent and received from 8 a.m. to 8 p.m., except Sundays, when the Office is closed at 10 a.m.

The rates of postage from Salcombe in 1830 were,—to London 1s., Liverpool 1s. 2d., Manchester 1s. 1d., Plymouth 8d., Dartmouth 8d., and Totnes 5d. The average number of letters posted daily in 1841 was about 25, but no record was kept of the number of letters received until 1843, when the daily average was about 35 and 40 posted. Ten years after in 1853, the average number received daily was 60 and 50 posted; in 1863, 110 received and 100 posted; in 1873, 200 received and 130 posted. At the present time the daily average received is 700, and about 30 to 40 parcels.

Leaving Orestone, we soon pass on our right the sites of the various yards, which until recently carried on such a good trade in shipbuilding, and which for many years were the main support of the place. There can be no question that the past success of Salcombe has been entirely owing to its shipping. This began in a very small way in the first instance by Mr. John Ball, who commenced shipbuilding in the yard now occupied by Mr. Patey. He turned out some good sized vessels, especially the "Lady Hobart Packet." After him came Mr. Thomas Hatch, using the same yard, with the adjoining one. With him worked the late Messrs. J. Vivian and W. Bunker, as journeymen. Mr. Bunker was a good workman, especially at boat-building, and it is said that he could, by himself, build a boat in a week. The late Mr John Evans had also established his yard by this time, and built the Amelia, a brigantine of about 100 tons burthen, which was then considered a first-class clipper, a regular foreign goer. She was afterwards altered into a schooner, and her fore-top ornamented Mr. Evans' yard for a number of years afterwards. Mr. Hatch, failing in business, Messrs. Vivian and Bunker started as partners. A great quantity of repairing work was then done for the vessels calling here, especially the Isle of Wight pilot boats which used to make this their port of call, waiting for vessels coming up Channel; and it was no uncommon sight to see a whole string of these pilot-boats at anchor in the harbour, reaching from Ilbertstowe Point to Baker's Well.

Mr. Bunker and Mr. Vivian not agreeing, the latter separated, and got a lease from Mr. Holdsworth, who then held the right to the foreshore from North Orestone to South Orestone. Having obtained the lease, Mr. Vivian filled out his yard, and began to build, and continued to succeed until he built some of the finest clippers turned out of Salcombe. To enter into details of the shipping industry would take more space than we can afford,—suffice it to say so great was its success that many of the inhabitants of Salcombe and neighbourhood became joint owners of ships, reaping thereby large profits.

Several vessels were built every year of a size ranging from 100 to 500 tons burthen, and were especially noticeable for their speed and beauty. Ships of over 25,000 tons register, employing nearly 1000 seamen, did belong to this port, and the increase of tonnage registered was upwards of 1000 tons a year. In recent years, through the depression of the shipping interest, there has been a complete stoppage to this trade, and the vessels now belonging to the port are very few. Some blame is

CONDUIT LAKE, FORE STREET.

attached to those who in the height of their success had not judgment and forethought enough to see that the trade of sailing ships could not last for ever. A short while ago shipping was a monopoly, confined chiefly to

English craft, which could obtain good freights, and vessels then left good dividends. Competition began to set in, and freights went down. Steam also came in, and iron-built ships, damaging seriously the wooden-built sailing vessels. The shipowners of this neighbourhood ought some years ago to have foreseen that this would be the case, and instead of investing their capital exclusively in sailing vessels, laid out some in steam and some in other ways. Salcombe is a sub-port of Dartmouth, but having its own registration of shipping.

A Mutual Marine Assurance Association was established in 1831, to insure the vessels belonging to the port, and was very successful up to a recent period, insuring at one time property to the value of £250,000, but met with such severe and unparalleled reverses, as to break it up.

The street above the ship-building yards is called Fore Street, extending from Orestone to Union Street. The Victoria Inn in Fore Street some 80 or 90 years ago went by the name of the Turk's Head, and was kept at that time by Mr. William Watkins, whilst the King's Arms in the same street was kept by Mr James Dawe. Adjoining the Victoria Inn in Fore Street is Conduit Lake, a name derived from the fact that up to about 1835 the principal water supply of the inhabitants was derived from a spring that had its outlet at an open shoot at this place. The first attempt to give the inhabitants a proper supply was made in 1835, when a reservoir was constructed in what is now known as the Park, and water mains laid throughout the town, standpipes being placed at convenient distances, from which the public had to draw their water. On the opposite page we give a view of Conduit Lake as it was before the standpipe was cut off, on the completion of the water works of 1895, when the water was taken into the whole of the houses in the town. Union Street is a continuation of Fore Street, and leads on to the Custom-house Quay. Officers of Customs have been stationed at Salcombe for two or three centuries, and the duties collected at one time were considerable. What the value of the imports and exports at the present time might be we cannot tell, but a minute investigation made in the year 1841, showed that it amounted then to half a million annually.

At the junction of Fore and Union Streets branches off Market Street, or what was formerly known as Chapel Street, the old Chapel-of-Ease that stood here giving it its name. The Public Rooms now occupy the site of the Chapel-of-Ease, which were erected in 1847 by shares of £5 each. There is a large hall capable of seating 250 persons, with an ante-room attached. Underneath, or on the ground floor, are large rooms, originally intended to have been used as a public Market, but the inhabitants having been accustomed to have their goods brought to their doors, they could not be prevailed upon to adopt this new system, and consequently it proved a failure, and the place has now been turned to another use, most of the space being occupied by the Salcombe detachment of Artillery Volunteers. The Salcombe Fire Engine, purchased some years since by public subscription, and now belonging to the Local Authority, is kept here. Shortly after these rooms were erected, a Mechanics' Institute or Literary Society was established in connection with them, but was of short duration, in consequence of lack of public support.

Some years ago, leading out of Market Street, was a narrow lane with a few delapidated houses, and called the Channel, but it has now given place to Courtenay Street, consisting of some neatly built houses. Here is situated the Infant School, established by private effort in 1854, and since maintained by Government grants and voluntary contributions. The present building was erected in 1861, and a class room added in 1873. This school was placed under Government in 1869. Church Hill is a continuation of Market Street, at the top of which is the Church and the Girls' School, the latter being a new building erected in 1875. Leaving the Church and proceeding down Church Hill, Buckley turns to the left and extends to Church Street and the Island. The latter is so called from a rock that formerly occupied the position that is now taken up by the quay, in front of the Wesleyan Chapel, and which at high tide was entirely surrounded with water. Some years since most of the land known as the Island was filled in for building purposes, and now a large number of houses are erected there. The foreshore between high and low water marks belongs to the Duchy of Cornwall.

The newly erected villas, forming a semi-circle above the town, have various names attached to them, but the new road along which they are built is called Devon Road, whilst the open space in front delights in the name of Courtenay Park, with the reservoirs that supply the lower parts of the town with water in its centre. The houses about here command good views of the harbour and surrounding country, many of them being let as lodging-houses. Magdala Cottages, with the Baptist Chapel, are immediately below Devon Road. This road extends to the main road into Salcombe, along which are some of the best building sites in the locality. At the back of the villas in Devon Road, is Allenhays Road, along which several new villa residences have been erected. Here also, is the Boys' National School, which was built in 1847 by grant and public subscriptions. When erected it was capable of containing all the children in the town, the girls meeting on the ground floor, and the boys on the floor above, and was so used until 1875, when the accommodation being insufficient, a new Girls' School was erected.

At the upper end of Market Street is the Central Hall Institute, occupying premises erected and furnished in 1893 at a cost of over £750. On the basement floor of the New Hall there is a capacious and well lighted Reading Room, supplied with all the leading Daily and Weekly Newspapers and Periodicals. A Recreation Room is supplied with a Bagatelle Board, Draughts,

Dominoes, and other popular games. Necessary offices are also on the basement floor. There is a stair-case leading from the basement to the ante-room and large hall above. On the main floor is the Assembly Hall, with an ante-room adjoining, separated by folding doors, so that it can be added to the large hall, and when both

CENTRAL HALL, MARKET STREET.

rooms are thrown into one, seating accommodation is provided for about 250 people. The Institute is open every day of the week from Ten a.m. to Ten p.m., and is free to all Fishermen, Sailors, and Yachtsmen visiting the port, it being the only place of the kind in Salcombe where this privilege is accorded them, and it is largely taken advantage of. The Institute is also open to the public by the payment of a small Quarterly Subscription, as well as to Visitors, an increasing number of whom now annually come to Salcombe. The Institute, therefore, is a valuable acquisition to the neighbourhood.

In anticipation of the inevitable expansion of Salcombe beyond its old bounds, the South Devon Land Company, Limited, was formed shortly after the disposal by sale of the Earl of Devon's estate, and acquired with the object of developing some 88 acres of valuable building land in the immediate vicinity of the town. This land occupies the whole crown of the hill, upon the north-eastern slopes of which the existing town is built. It is bounded by a portion of the Devon Road, the main road to Kingsbridge, and the old road to Malborough above the Knowle, having, therefore, frontages to all these roads, affording aspects to all points of the compass, commanding sea and land views of great magnificence. The property has been laid out with wide new roads, about two miles in extent, providing new walks for residents and visitors. The St. Dunstan's Road forms a junction with the Main and Devon Roads, and runs across the estate in a northerly direction, the Herbert Road, branching off from it, forming a junction with the Devon Road; the Bonaventure Road starts from the Herbert Road and terminates at the Onslow Road, whilst the Raleigh Road connects Bonaventure Road with the St. Dunstan's Road, and the Loring Road connects the Herbert Road with the Raleigh Road. The Fortescue, Kingsale, and Camperdown are also important roads. The building land has been divided into some 500 or 600 building plots, and sold, and on some of the sites villa residences have been erected. The vendors promise that particular care will be taken to ensure that no unsuitable buildings shall be erected, and the general development shall be so managed as not to prejudice in any way the great natural beauties of the locality.

The Knowle is situated above the Church, and the road to the right is called Shadycombe Road, and leads to the Cemetery, which is very pleasantly situated in a well sheltered vale at Shadycombe. A Burial Board was formed in the year 1877 of 7 members, but has now been amalgamated with the Urban District Council. The Churchyard having become insufficient for the requirements of the town, a public meeting was held in the Town Hall to consider the question of providing additional burial ground, when a Committee was appointed to select a site, and make the preliminary arrangements. This having been done, a Burial Board for the District was formed on August 9th, 1877. The Cemetery is nicely laid out and well kept, and the borders are beautifully planted with ornamental trees and shrubs. It is provided with a waiting room and public mortuary. James Anthony Froude, the historian, is interred at the north-west corner of the burial ground. The centre path divides the consecrated from the unconsecrated portions, the latter occupying the eastern and the former the western parts of the Cemetery.

Salcombe was formed into a Local Government District in 1880, and a Local Board, consisting of nine members, elected in August of the same year, but this body gave place to the Urban District Council, the first election under the Local Government Act, 1894, taking place in December of that year, the Council consisting also of nine members.

The town was formed into an ecclesiastical district in 1864, and into an independent civil parish on the 31st December, 1894, under the new Local Government Act; gas works were erected in 1866. and the population in 1891 was 1,593, exclusive of seamen afloat. The population is now estimated at 2,000.

From Shadycombe a road branches off to the right leading to some path fields, called the Crofts, and extends to the hamlet of Lower Batson. This walk of about a mile is an extremely pleasant one when the tide is in, for the fields through which the path runs abut on the foreshore of Batson Creek. The hamlet is situated in a very picturesque vale, and has been noted for a long period for its productive orchards. A peculiar custom was practised here in days gone by, as well as in other parts of Devonshire. On the eve of Epiphany the farmer, attended by his labourers, was wont to go to the orchard with a large pitcher of cider, and there, encircling one of the most fruitful trees, to drink a toast "to thee, old apple tree." It was believed that the failure of the apple crop would ensue upon neglect of this custom.

About the middle of the seventeenth century there came to reside at Batson the Rev. James Burdwood, one of the ejected clergy under the Act of Uniformity. He was of an ancient family, and had an estate at Preston, in West Alvington parish. He was for awhile Minister at Plympton St. Mary, and from thence he removed to St. Petrox, Dartmouth, where he continued until the Act of Uniformity ejected him. He then removed to Batson, where he rented an estate, remaining for five years, and during his residence here he held preaching services in his own house. Large numbers of people flocked to hear him, in fact so many came at times, that he had to hold the services in his orchard. The district had four Justices of the Peace, two of them being of a very mild and peaceable turn of mind, and would take no action to disturb the meetings of these ejected clergy, viz., Matthew Hele, of Halwell, and William Bastard, of Gerston. But the other two, George Reynell, of Malston, Sherford, and John Beare, of Bearscombe, were of a contrary disposition, and did all they could to annoy and punish these humble worshippers. Beare had been for some time previously at the head of the informers, and for good service rendered by him in disturbing what were then called conventicles, was advanced to the position of a Justice of the Peace. This Beare, with Reynell, and a crew of informers, who were at their beck, occasioned Mr. Burdwood much trouble and vexation; unhung his

LOWER BATSON.

doors, rifled his house, seized and carried away his goods, ripped off the locks on his barn doors and put others on, and obliged his wife and children to seek shelter among the neighbours. Besides this, he was also heavily fined, and finally he went to Dartmouth, where he died August 21st, 1693, aged 67 years.

HOLY TRINITY CHURCH.

PLACES OF WORSHIP.

CHURCH OF ENGLAND.—The old chapel that stood in Market Street, had well nigh an unknown history from its foundation to the middle of the eighteenth century. Then it was in a very delapidated condition; the walls were entire, but it was without any roof, or remains of pews, seats, or interior decorations. Towards the end of that century, the walls had partly fallen down, the west end alone remaining entire; at the top of the gable there was an oblong aperture of about three feet high, evidently the place where the bell had hung, said to have been taken to Malborough Church.

In the year 1800, Mr. James Yates, of Woodville, Salcombe, started a subscription for rebuilding the edifice; and through his exertions and the liberality of himself and other residents, the thing was accomplished, the whole management of the affair being left to him. The work was begun in October, 1800, a part of the old wall towards the west being permitted to remain. The work was finished, and the chapel opened by divine service on Sunday, the 23rd day of January, 1803, a sermon having been preached by the Rev. Roope Ilbert, M.A. The total cost of the rebuilding was about £500.

A deed was prepared and executed by the resident subscribers, dated the 23rd day of January, 1801, by which trustees were appointed for the chapel, who were to allot and let the sittings to rent, and apply the funds raised in such manner as they might judge best for the maintenance of a clergyman, and the support and amelioration of the building.

The trustees, on applying for a license, caused it to be intimated that there was no other source for supporting the service than the rents of the seats, and that this would not afford more than twenty-six guineas a year. On this footing the license was granted.

With this stipend of twenty-six guineas, the Bishop of Exeter, on the 14th day of October, 1803, licensed the Rev. Robert Lane, B.A., to the chapel, who was nominated by the Vicar of the parish. The living at that time was a perpetual curacy, service being held in the chapel once every Sunday. There is a tradition that the minister of Malborough formerly officiated here once a month, but of this no record is found. As it was thought advisable to represent the circumstances attending this chapel to the Commissioners of Queen Anne's Bounty, a report, signed by three clergymen and three private gentlemen, was sent accordingly in the latter part of the year 1803, and in consequence of the Bishop's influence a sum of £1,000 was alloted thereto, but for which only £2 per cent. was allowed until invested in land or tithes.

PLACES OF WORSHIP. 51

This however was at length effected by the purchase of a freehold tenement called Farmston, in the parish of Halwell, about midway between Totnes and Kingsbridge. The estate was conveyed according to the direction of the Commissioners, and the deed, accompanied by a map of the premises, deposited in their hands. The clear annual rent at first was £38, but this was considerably lessened after the peace of 1815, in consequence of the extraordinary fall in the value of freehold property. At the present time it brings in about £25 per annum.

In consequence of the increase of inhabitants, it was found necessary in 1841 to build a new church, which was accomplished through the indefatigable exertions of the Rev. Thomas Young, the then Incumbent, assisted by the principal inhabitants and landowners of the neighbourhood. It was consecrated in 1844. The cost of erecting the church was over £2600, and it is dedicated to the Holy Trinity.

It is a handsome edifice, built in the Lancet style of the 13th century, and consists of nave and aisles, and there were added to the church in 1889 a chancel, north transept, vestries, and organ gallery, at a cost of £1500. There is a square tower with one bell, and clock with two dials, one face being conspicuous from the main street and harbour, the other looking towards the entrance to the town. The church contains a fine carved pulpit, and is capable of seating about five hundred persons. The chancel window is of stained glass, a memorial of the late Earl of Devon, whilst in the north transept are stained glass windows to the memory of members of the De Courcy family. The churchyard is very tastefully laid out, and contains the American aloe, yuccas, myrtles, and the thick-leaved Chinese veronica. The register dates from the year 1843. The living is a vicarage, in the gift of the Trustees of Keble College, Oxford, and has been endowed by the late Earl of Devon. Services:—Sundays, 11 a.m, 2 45 and 6.30 p.m; Wednesdays, 10 a.m. and 8 p.m; Fridays, 10 a.m. and

7.30 p.m.; other days, 5 p.m.; Holy Communion, third Sunday in the month at 10 a.m.; other Sundays at 8 a.m; and on Wednesdays, Fridays, and Saints' days, 7.45 a.m. The living is held by the Rev. W. L. Herford. The sittings in the church are free and unappropriated.

THE CHURCH FROM SHADYCOMBE CREEK.

WESLEYAN - METHODISTS.—Nonconformity made its first appearance in Salcombe in the form of Wesleyan-Methodism, in the early part of the nineteenth century. Salcombe was included in the Kingsbridge Circuit, and the first appointment of ministers was made in 1807, when the Revs. John Jordan and Richard Moody were stationed to the Circuit. Preaching services were first held at Salcombe in a cottage in Buckley, and afterwards in a school-room in Elliot's Court. This place becoming too limited for the congregation that was gathered, two

PLACES OF WORSHIP. 53

cottages were purchased at the Island, the site of the present chapel, and converted into a place of worship, it being opened for divine service on the 6th October, 1824, the opening sermons being preached by the Rev. J. Akerman, of Plymouth, who was assisted by Mr. Wm Sherwill, of Ivybridge, and the Rev. Thomas Bersey, the resident minister at Kingsbridge. This chapel was replaced by the present building in 1849, the re-erection costing £561, leaving a debt of £243.

WESLEYAN CHAPEL, THE ISLAND.

An effort was made in 1857 to reduce this debt by holding a Bazaar in June, and by special subscriptions, also by having a Christmas Tree in the same year. By this means £143 was paid off, leaving the debt at £100. This amount was borrowed from the General Chapel Committee at Manchester in 1859, free of interest, and paid off by ten yearly instalments of £10, the chapel by this means being freed from debt at the end of 1868.

Side galleries were added to the chapel in 1861, which cost together with other work £115, the amount being raised by a Bazaar and a Lecture by the Rev. E. A. Telfer. A new school and vestries, and an orchestra behind the rostrum were added in 1883, at a cost of over £600, and recently the edifice has been re-seated and decorated, and a hot-water heating apparatus added at a cost of nearly £300. The chapel has accommodation for about 500, and is licensed for the solemnization of marriages. The first resident minister appointed to Salcombe was the Rev. J. Hartle, in August, 1853. A minister's residence was built in 1860, in Church Street, at a cost of £270. Services:—Sundays, 11 a.m. and 6 30 p.m.; Tuesdays and Fridays, 7.30 p.m.

PLYMOUTH BRETHREN.—The Brethren principles of meeting were first adopted at Plymouth about the year 1830, and were introduced into Salcombe in 1832, by the late Mr. Dowglass, of Cliff House. At that time there were only two meetings of a similar character, viz., Plymouth and Bath. For some time services were held at the residence of Mr. Dowglass, help being rendered from Plymouth to carry them on successfully. Since then they have met in various rooms, including the Town Hall, but now they have a very commodious place of worship in Folly Lane, Fore Street, erected in 1862, and will seat 200 persons. Services:—Sunday, 10.30 a.m. and 6.15 p.m.

BAPTISTS.—The Baptist denomination is of but recent introduction into Salcombe. Religious services were first commenced to be held in the Town Hall in August, 1866, under the ministrations of the Rev. F. Pugh. Their success was such that in 1868 they applied to the Earl of Devon for a grant of land on which to erect a chapel, which was acceded to. The chapel was built in the Gothic style, and opened for divine service on the 22nd day of June, 1871. The cost was over £1,000, and this was entirely paid off shortly after the opening, the whole scheme being brought to a successful completion, mainly through the exertions of the Rev. F. Pugh, who after being the pastor for eleven years, removed in 1877 to Swindon. Salcombe has since been joined to Malborough under one pastorate. A new building to accommodate the Sunday School was erected in 1896. The chapel affords accommodation for 300 persons. Services:—Sundays, 11 a.m. and 6.30 p.m.; Wednesday. 7.30 p.m.

CATHOLIC APOSTOLIC CHURCH.—The church is situated in Fore Street and consists of a large room over a store, arranged as a nave and chancel; it has been re-decorated and handsomely refitted, and has 150 sittings. Services:—Sundays, 10.15 a.m. and 5.30 p.m.; Wednesdays. 7.30 p.m.; Fridays, 10.15 a.m., and on every fourth Tuesday, 10.15 a.m.

AS A WATERING PLACE.

SALCOMBE possesses many features that make it well adapted for a watering place. There are not many, if any, sea-side resorts that can rival it in its many peculiar characteristics, such as its mild and equable climate; its beautiful and varied scenery, including the wild and romantic; the well sheltered and pleasant harbour, and the many delightful walks it possesses, make it an admirable place for those in search of recreation, rest or pleasure. Salcombe is free from the noise and commotion that is to be found at most watering places, and Visitors can enjoy themselves thoroughly in boating, fishing, riding, or walking, and now that it has been brought within measurable distance of a railway station, it is becoming deservedly well known, and increasingly patronized from year to year.

SALCOMBE AND NEIGHBOURHOOD.

It has long been the practice of persons of weak and delicate constitutions to seek relief from the cold and rigorous winters experienced in the Midlands and North of England, by migrating to warmer climes, and usually those have been sought in the South of France and in Italy. But persons are just awakening to the fact, that there are spots in their own country, possessing all, or nearly all, the advantages of foreign places for a winter

THE HARBOUR FROM NEWTON ROAD.

abode, and these English resorts possess the additional and very important advantage, that they are more easily come-at-able, and far less expensive. It is satisfactory to learn that medical men are making themselves better acquainted with the spots situated in the south of their own country that are in every way suited as health resorts, and are recommending them to their patients in preference to places in other countries.

Now of all the places on the south-west coast of England that have laid their claims before the public, there is not one of them that can show the special advantages of Salcombe. Penzance and Falmouth alone possess a more southern situation, and that only to a very slight degree; but those places lie more open to the sea, and consequently more exposed, whereas Salcombe is situated on an arm of the sea, snugly ensconced under the lee of a hill, and nicely protected on almost all points, which gives it a more equable climate than can be found elsewhere in the British Isles, and rivalling in this matter most of the places in the South of France.

For about one hundred years Salcombe has been the resort of invalids, in consequence of its mild and salubrious air, and for those suffering from chest or throat complaints, the climate offers great advantages. A writer on the climate of the south-west of England says, "The seasons appear to mingle like the interlacing of the warm and cold waters on the edge of the Gulf Stream; and along our coast-line in January, night and day have hardly a distinctive temperature, the mean difference being scarcely four degrees. There is no country in the world with a climate so mild and equable as the south-west of England, if we except the south-west of Ireland, where this peculiarity is intensified. The cause is now well understood. The Atlantic Ocean on the west is an immense reservoir of warm water, fed and heated by the Gulf Stream, so that around the land in the depth of winter the temperature of the surface water is seldom lower than 46°, and out at sea beyond the influence of the land the water is much warmer." Dr. John Huxham, a celebrated physician who practised at Plymouth in the reign of George II, recognised the climatic advantages of Salcombe in his day, and described it as the Montpellier of England. The winter of Salcombe is about the mildest in England, and being well-nigh surrounded by hills, and near the sea, its temperature is very even. There are no intensely hot summers and piercingly cold winters, and the temperature of the night does not vary much from that of the day. Westerly and south-westerly winds are very prevalent during the winter months, which cause a constant current of warm air to be swept over the neighbourhood, and it is not often the thermometer stands lower than 46° in the day. The following table shows the temperature of Salcombe for an average year, also as compared with some other places :—

MONTH.	Temperature of Salcombe.			As compared with mean temperature of			
	Lowest Regist'ed	Highest Regist'ed	Mean Temperature.	Nottingham.	Torquay.	Falmouth.	Montpellier.
January	28.0	50.0	43.26	38.4	38.9	44.1	42.1
February	30.0	51.0	43.7	39.8	43.4	45.1	44.8
March	32.0	56.0	46.16	41.3	45.5	44.7	48.9
April	33.0	57.0	49.10	46.9	47.5	47.6	57.4
May	40.0	68.0	62.8	50.8	53.5	51.9	64.4
June	45.0	70.0	62.20	57.8	56.1	57.1	72.5
July	47.0	70.0	63.21	61.8	60.5	60.0	78.4
August	45.0	68.0	62.12	60.3	60.3	60.3	77.0
September	43.0	65.0	60.6	55.4	56.6	57.2	70.3
October	39.0	60.0	53.5	48.2	49.5	52.2	61.9
November	38.0	55.0	51.27	40.9	47.5	47.8	50.7
December	33.0	54.0	47.21	37.3	44.5	44.3	45.7

A study of this table will at once show the advantages of the climate of Salcombe, and more particularly its mildness during the months of October, November, and December. The temperature of the summer months, whilst being higher than that of Falmouth, is not sultry, and the nights are wonderfully cool.

Dr. Thomas Shafter in his book "The Climate of the South of Devon," says,—

"Salcombe though situated on an arm of the sea is much sheltered, being land-locked by high and steep hills. It is open to the south only, and probably offers the mildest and most genial climate in the country, especially that portion of it which stretches southward from the town to the Bolt Head. The character of its vegetation is almost Italian. It is a situation well adapted for those of tender chest, especially in the winter and spring seasons."

Snow is a very rare occurrence at Salcombe, and when there is a fall it is usually very slight, and remains on the ground but a very short time, beginning to disappear as soon as the same ceases to fall. Skating is rendered impossible, because ice never forms of sufficient thickness to bear even the weight of a child. In confirmation of this we reprint the following from a letter by " A Visitor" that appeared in the *Western Daily Mercury*, on February 5th, 1895, when the country was experiencing the severest winter known for 40 years :—

"Last Tuesday I was standing on the departure platform at Paddington Station waiting for the 9 a.m train for Plymouth. It was a beastly cold day ; snow hung about, and the appearance was far from exhilirating. Having lately returned from India, I was anxious to get anywhere away from the snow and ice. These are my mortal enemies, so I decided to run down to Plymouth for a few days to try and get nearer a warmer climate. As we steamed out of London, the country all round was covered with snow. What a dreary and desolate sight, after the heat of a tropical climate! I shivered. No great coat or the greatest luxuries can make up for the beautiful climate I had not long departed from. Time passed on : the engine was doing exceedingly well. Up to time, for a wonder. When we got to Exeter I inquired for a Plymouth paper. Looking it over, I discovered the country was covered with snow in and around Plymouth. Wherever could I go to be out of it? A gentleman sat by my side. I inquired of him. 'At Salcombe,' he went on 'Up to when I left some weeks since, we have had no snow for the season.' I thought this must surely be the spot I was seeking, and although I had taken a ticket to Plymouth I decided to go on to Salcombe. We arrived at Brent. Snow had covered the ground, and as I learnt Kingsbridge was only some twelve miles off, I had doubts in my mind. But at last here was Kingsbridge. There was a little snow here. Where was Salcombe ?—that place without any snow. I quickly obtained a vehicle, and in about three-quarters of an hour arrived at my destination, the Marine Hotel, Salcombe. It was now dark, so I could not see much that evening. I felt quite a change in the atmosphere. Mild and calm it was. In the morning I was up early. Not a particle of snow. Hurrah! I shouted, as I looked out of my bedroom window. What a lovely view. The sun shone out beautifully. It was more like a summer's day at Torquay. The Marine Hotel stands on the banks of the estuary. This little harbour is one of the best and most charming I know of in

England. It is practically land-locked, and affords splendid shelter for yachts. During the morning I had a stroll. I was much struck with the scenery in the direction of the Bolt Head. Here I picked several primroses, and they are growing in a northerly aspect. Oranges and citrons I discovered growing against a wall at a charming residence called 'The Moult.' I

THE PLANTATION WALK.

went on walking along a narrow rugged path : I came to a corner. Here I looked out to sea. There were quite a score of ships passing up and down Channel. I stood here enchanted. This point of vantage is quite 250 feet above the sea at one's feet, and the rocks stand bolt upstraight for another 250 feet above you. It is one of the grandest peeps you can look upon. All around you there are views not to be surpassed in any part of England or the British Isles. I am spending a week here. Its suits my constitution well. I understand the climate is much warmer than the queen of watering places, Torquay, and in my opinion, this will be the future watering place in England. Invalids and those seeking warmer climates than can be obtained in any other part in

MAIN ROAD ABOVE WOODVILLE.

England should try this for the winter months. Now that the railway runs as far as Kingsbridge, Salcombe lies within easy distance of the great metropolis. I hope soon to see a line to Salcombe, and I am quite sure then it would soon become an extremely popular health resort, which I am sure will prove itself to be th Riviera of England."

Then again the air retains a dryness most unusual to the majority of watering places. Being situated about the centre of the promontory that stretches from the Start to Bigbury Bay, and the Dartmoor hills forming a background, the rain clouds are drawn inland before they get sufficiently cool to let fall their contents, consequently the rain-fall of Salcombe is much below the average. The total amount for a recent year was only 32½ inches, which is about the average, whereas if the other watering places on the south coast of England are taken, their average rain fall will be found to amount to 45 inches.

Salcombe is also remarkably free from thunderstorms, the immunity which it enjoys in this respect being doubtless owing to its peculiar advantageous position, the storm clouds either passing inland or going out to sea before bursting, and when one does occur, it is not usually very violent. The neighbourhood is sometimes visited by fogs, yet they do not remain for long, for early in the morning they will generally rise and disappear.

The beauty and variety of the walks around Salcombe are of the most charming description. There is one walk that can easily be taken by the aged and infirm, along which seats have been placed by the Local Authority. It proceeds above the town along the Devon Road, until a full view of Salcombe bay and the clear blue water at the entrance of the harbour is obtained. On the opposite shore are white sandy bays, and clinging to the opposite hillside is the little village of Portlemouth, the square tower just capping the summit of the hill. The hillside below is covered with a bountiful foliage Leaving the Devon Road by a wicket gate on the left, a narrow path leads to the Plantation Walk, from which there are pretty sea peeps between the fir trees, and at one open place a public seat has been placed for the convenience of visitors. The walk emerges on to the main road leading into Salcombe.

On emerging on to the main road, the walk can be continued by crossing over and entering another wicket gate, which leads to a spot known at one time as the "Cheesering," and from which magnificent land and sea views are obtained The path descends through another plantation of fir trees, and from its winding nature is known as the Zig-Zag, and from which there are pretty peeps of the harbour. This path terminates at the top of North Sands Hill, and the return to Salcombe can be made by the Cliff Road.

At the end of Devon Road, where it forms a junction with the main road, is a very pleasant walk, beautifully wooded in some places and well sheltered, descending to North Sands. Seats have been placed along this walk, and from the one at its entrance there are lovely views across North Sands Vale to the wooded hillsides above the Moult, and away to the Bolt Head and the harbour-mouth.

From the mildness of the climate of Salcombe, the flora is of a sub-tropical character, the slopes on the western side of the harbour being bedecked with a rich foliage of trees and shrubs, whilst many tender exotics bloom in the open air, and oranges, lemons, and citrons reach a fair state of perfection in the gardens of Woodville, the Moult, and Cliff House. In the gardens of the villa residents, the fuschia, hydrangea, and myrtle flourish throughout the winter without protection, and the clyanthus grows in a marvellous manner, it being no unusual occurrence to see it in full bloom in the early part of February. Crocuses and snowdrops appear early, and the latter occasionally are in flower as early as Christmas. The banks and shaded roads of the locality are also lined with many rare plants and ferns, and the neighbourhood of the Bolt is particularly rich in lichen and fauna. No better test could possibly be given of the mild climate of Salcombe, than the manner in which tender and half hardy plants flourish out of doors It will, therefore, be at once apparent, that the climate which can produce these results must be extremely mild, and especially suitable for invalids and for those seeking a winter residence.

The attention of the Local Authority has been given to perfecting the water supply and sanitary arrangements of the town. The water is as good and pure as can be possibly obtained. Extensive water works were carried out in 1895, at a cost of over £4000. The water is obtained from springs at Hanger Vale, and pumped to a height of 300 feet, to a high level reservoir, from which

THE HARBOUR FROM THE ZIG-ZAG.

it can be distributed to houses erected in any part of the district. An exhaustive analysis of the water was made by Dr. Wynter Blyth, and certified to be a first-class water for drinking purposes. The water works were opened on July 4th, 1895. The town is sewered throughout, and the medical officer has repeatedly reported Salcombe to be in a "good sanitary condition." The healthiness of the district may be gathered from the fact

AS A WATERING PLACE. 65

that the average death rate does not exceed 12 per 1000 per annum, and a death from any of the zymotic diseases is very rare. The death rate occasionally falls as low as 9 per 1000, and is as low as any place in the kingdom, the deaths being mostly amongst the very young or the very old. Salcombe has been remarkably free also from epidemics, and on the various occasions that cholera

OPENING THE WATER-WORKS, JULY, 1895.

visited England, the place was exempt from the scourge, although it prevailed extensively all around.

Salcombe also possesses unique attractions not only in its walks but also in its coast scenery, the rocks, cliffs, and sands being of great variety and magnificence, of which we shall speak more particularly when describing the coast scenery.

Salcombe harbour is over one mile in length from its entrance, but various winding creeks, some of them of great loveliness, branch off from it, as does also the Kingsbridge Estuary, continuing its course for over four miles up to the town of Kingsbridge. The harbour is beautifully sheltered by the lofty hills on either side, and as a consequence the water is generally placid, and boating becomes a favourite and pleasant pastime; whilst those who are not afraid of the open sea, can take a cruise outside the harbour and along the coast, either to the east or west, for sailing along these ever-changing cliffs, with bold promontories and majestic rocks, interspersed here and there with little bays and gullies, and varied with good fishing, is especially enjoyable. Good sport is obtained in sea-fishing, there being plenty of whiting, pollock, bass, and conger, and excellent sport is afforded in the season for mackerel fishing. The River Avon, well-stocked with trout and salmon, and the far-famed Slapton Ley, with its abundance of perch and other fish, are within easy distance of Salcombe. There are also plenty of prawns and shell fish to be obtained along the shores of the harbour.

Many sandy bays on each side of the harbour afford thoroughly good bathing places, with firm sand bottom, nicely sheltered, and amongst the rocks will be found many natural baths. Bathing tents are provided at some of the bathing places at a small charge, yet at most of them all the seclusion needed will be found.

In addition to the accommodation provided for Visitors at the Marine Hotel already referred to, there are many highly-respectable lodging houses, beautifully situated, and where the charges are moderate.

Devonshire Cream is everywhere well known, and in no part of the county can it be obtained to better perfection than at Salcombe. Of this delicacy the following interesting account appeared in the *Daily Telegraph*:—

"If there are any persons so plunged in darksome ignorance as never to have tasted Devonshire cream, the error should be corrected on the very earliest opportunity. A journey down to Exeter would, in fact, be amply repaid by the delights that await the person who is introduced for the first time to the genuine Devonian cream and junket. You may use the cream as butter, and spread it on bread; you may make it the substratum for jams or marmalade; you can mingle it with every description of tart and pudding; you may even drop it gently into your tea and coffee; or, when strawberries and other outdoor fruits are in season you may commingle them with the deftly-clotted product of the Devonian dairy; and it is safe to say that in every shape and form it will well repay consumption. Devonshire cream is twice blessed; it blesseth him that makes and him that takes: it gives a fortune, or a handsome competence, to the native farmer and dairyman, and it raises the most gratifying feelings in the breast of the individual fortunate enough to enjoy its exquisite flavour."

WHAT OTHERS HAVE SAID ABOUT SALCOMBE.

VERY many appreciative articles have been published from time to time about Salcombe in various newspapers and periodicals, and we here republish extracts from some of them.

OFF THE RAILWAY.—Miss Marianne Farningham wrote as follows to the *Christian World* after a visit to Salcombe:—

"It makes one very happy to have a '*find*' of any sort; but to find a spot of extreme loveliness, and known to only a few, is a delightful experience Such a place is Salcombe, situate in the extreme South of Devon, and surrounded by blendings of the best scenery of Cornwall and Devonshire. The people are hoping that soon a branch railway may connect it with the rest of the world; but I do not hope it (excepting for the sake of the Salcombe trade), for it is much better as it is. The railway ride from Paddington to Kingswear is swift and pleasant, but there is surely enough of it to satisfy anybody; and after that, to get to Salcombe, there is a real old-fashioned coach-drive through exquisite scenery of sea and shore, rock and river, lake and moor, to quaint Kingsbridge, from whence the journey is completed by steamer The old houses are near the water, but the new ones are on the hills, prettily

BOLT HEAD FROM LIMEBURY POINT.

surrounded by gardens. Some land, finely situated has been bought for building purposes, and the Salcombe people hope that their little town may develop—as it certainly deserves to do—into one of the favourite health resorts of those who are obliged to seek shelter from cold winds and sharp frosts, and prefer to find it in their own country. For Salcombe enjoys a very equable climate. Just now (February) some fields are white with snowdrops, the blue periwinkle is in blossom, and primroses will soon be plentiful. There are walls which every February are covered with a beautiful mass of the scarlet blooms of the clyanthus. Yuccas, myrtles, and the American aloe, and the Chinese veronica, the fuschia, the hydrangea, and even the orange, lemon, and citron trees flourish in the open air, and the Maiden-hair and Osmunda ferns are to be found in the woods.

The great fishing industry of Salcombe and the adjacent villages is that of crabs and lobsters, for the sea around Bolt Head and Bolt Tail furnishes an especially abundant harvest of these. During the winter the men work on the land, if the farmers can employ them, and they then make crab-pots for further use. In the summer they go out in a boat and drop the osier basket, in which has been placed some stones to sink it, and some bait to attract the lobsters and crabs. To each 'pot' is attached a cork with the owner's name upon it. After a while the pots are drawn in, their contents are counted, and sent to Southampton, and thence to all parts. There are loses in this, as in other industries. Sometimes the storms break up the lobster-cages, and carry them off into the rough sea with their contents, and the bait which is used is always expensive, for it has to be fetched from a distance. 'Still,' said a man, ' the supply is inexhaustible, and the market is sure, so we have much for which to be thankful.'

The walks around Salcombe are exceedingly attractive. That to Bolt Head, the finest and boldest headland on the south coast, is through two miles of beautiful scenery."

DOWN WEST.—A DRAUGHT OF OZONE. The following appeared in the *Barnet Times*:—

"Eh mon ! but this is real fine," exclaimed a raw-boned inhabitant of the Land o'Cakes. "Ess, I reckon 'tis," agreed the Devonian to whom the observation was addressed. We were on a voyage up channel from Plymouth, and the rugged foreland of the Bolt Head and Bolt Tail had caused the brawny Scot to break forth into his exclamation of admiration. It was a magnificent day. There was but the merest agitation of the waves, the breeze was light and old Sol was atoning for his long retirement by smiling upon us very beneficently. In the summer sun the fretted cliffs, rising precipitately from the sea, looked very charming in their russet brown dress. It is when "the stormy winds do blow" that they look formidable. This piece of sterile headland is one of the finest stretches on the South Coast of Devon, although from the Start to the Mewstone at the entrance to Plymouth Harbour the coast line is very grand and impressive. South Devon is indeed, a favoured spot; the tourist's happy hunting ground. D'ye want a real good holiday, plenty of everything—sea. moorland, upland and dale? Then go West. Too long a journey! Nonsense. Six hours from Waterloo and the fatigued Londoner can be in the land of dumplings and pasties, breathing the pure ozone of the ocean or the bracing air of extensive moorland. The great charm of Devonshire as a visiting county is the really wonderful variety of its landscape beauties. Other counties have special characteristics by which they are generally known; but not so with Devon. It is a sort of England in miniature; it may, and can, be beaten in detail, but as a whole it is unsurpassable in natural beauties. There are hills and dells, luxuriant foliage, cascades, orchards, lovely drives, Devonshire lanes—yes, Devonshire is unrivalled. On rounding the Bolt Head we entered the delightful harbour of Salcombe. The harbour is without exaggeration, sublime. The high cliffs of the east side of Bolt Head frown down on the tiny crafts below, the waters are as placid as a lake, and the surrounding country is the best to be seen on the coast. Salcombe nestles—every well-conducted village, the same as a rural cottage, nestles in something—in the hollow of several great hills, the slopes of which are rich in verdure and gay with colour. Salcombe is pretty and well repays a visit. It was too hot to stay in-doors, even for the usual after dinner weed, and we found the country so enticing that we were soon toiling up the steep hill—a Devonshire hill, with hedges full of wild flowers on either side. In a broiling sun it required some exercise of will to force the muscles into operation. After various stoppages, however, we reached the top, and there, after a vigorous mopping of foreheads, we stood awhile to view the panorama. Such splendid scenery as lay before us can only be seen in Devonshire. We were high above the summit of the Bolt Head; the harbour, with its white-sailed yachts, lay below; the sea stretched beyond; in the hollow was the village almost hidden by trees; and on every side was wooded country. "Weel," said the Scot, "this is grand." "Yes," said my companion, "it's about as good as you'll get, I think." "I think so," slowly replied the other, with the peculiar inflection of the Scotch, "it beats the country side of Inverness." "Thanks," I rejoined, "that is a recommendation indeed." Then we journeyed on, and reached the village anon. We had heard, in fact we knew, that Salcombe and Kingsbridge were celebrated for their white ales. White ale, said the natives, is good ; therefore we wanted to sample it. The manufacture of white ale is a secret, said to have descended from monkish times ; its composition we were told, was enshrouded in mystery ; still we meant to try it What mattered to us thirsty mortals its ingredients and secret blending. Not a bigger mystery, we thought, than the ordinary " bitter" or " mild." Well, we visited most of the inns, but had no white ale ; of course, we could not come out without having something ; people get dry in hot weather. At one place we were told that white ale is a winter drink, and our spirits out of sympathy fell to zero. The old salt in the old-fashioned country " tap " averred that with the addition of a little rum and a small medium of nutmeg all " mulled " together, it was delicious. I am thinking of going South on purpose to try that mixture "

SALCOMBE, BY A VISITOR. The London Correspondent of the *Rochdale Observer* gives the following account of his visit to the Salcombe district :—

"Since the rising of Parliament I have opened up a new country, which has very much absorbed my personal interest and cut me off from the life of London town, for the most part almost as effectually as if oceans and continents lay between. Yet I have not for a moment departed from the highways, the pathways, and the bye-ways of this island. Indeed, I have gone no further than the county of Devonshire. Nevertheless there is not one man nor woman in ten thousand who has the slightest knowledge of this region with which I have made acquaintance, even though it is a region of surpassing beauty, abounding in almost every attraction to delight the heart of the wayfarer, rich in variety, set in perhaps the very best climate to be found in the British Isles, so favoured in the matter of weather that, but for the newspapers, and for the fitful associations with what is going on in the everyday world beyond, I should hardly have known that, since July ended, this has not been considered to be a good summer, and that August has been set down in the book of the harvests as a bad month. So long has Devonshire, north, south, east, and west, been a show county, the haunt of tourists, praised more or less by all comers and goers, that the reader might well be sceptical as to there being any quarter of the county supremely beautiful and almost unknown. But the Salcombe peninsula is just so unknown and just so enchanting. It is off the railways and off the highways. It does not come within range on the way to anywhere. You can not possibly stumble upon it by accident. Nobody ever goes there unless he has somehow discovered the secret. Well, i's seclusion is another of its charms. There is a gentle, quaint spirit of simplicity pervading this kindly bit of territory. It takes its geographical character from the peculiar and exceptional relations between sea and land at this particular point on the coast. The almost exclusively rock-bound shore which extends from Torbay right away to Land's End is broken at Salcombe by a bold inlet of

ILBERTSTOW, BATSON CREEK.

sea which runs some five or six miles into the heart of the peninsula, spreading out right and left into broad and deep indentations in the fertile and well-wooded land, making some six or eight expansive sea lakes where you may row or sail for hours with nothing around you on every side but fair hills, vales, game covers, corn-fields, pastures, hamlets, set off by many a salt-water creek. Here you may defy the rough weather, if rough it be, in the English Channel outside the harbour, and enjoy all that makes life pleasant to the Englishman on a succession of lakes which are all the better for being sea lakes. At Salcombe we live on the ledges of the hills which rise from the lip of the sea, and look down as soon as we are out of bed in the morning, and in the intervals of breakfast, and so long as we care to remain indoors, upon the merry life of the dancing waters, the yachting, the fishing, the harvesting on the slopes beyond the waters, the sea gulls, the cormorants, and all the sea life mixed up with land life in a manner not often to be met with in any part of England. And the walks are magnificent. The coastguard tracks round the cliff headlands open up the most ravishing coast scenery. A ferry-boat takes you to the headlands on the east side of the harbour, and hence you may explore as far as Dartmouth, or take the regular coach running two or three times a day from Kingsbridge, and on that charming coast you stumble upon an unique phenomena called Slapton Lea—a curious fresh water lake separated from the sea only by a ridge of sand—a lake of water-grasses and water-lilies, abounding in fancy wild fowl, which the proprietor cherishes continually, allowing no man to disturb the great colony of feathered creatures. But if I attempt to run into details there will be no end to it. In its way, I know no place to match Salcombe."

FAR FROM THE MADDING CROWD.—The following article appeared in the *Inquirer* from the pen of Mr Frank Taylor :—

"Salcombe is a typical Devonian town of narrow, steep and winding streets, containing some 2,000 inhabitants. It is most picturesquely situated on the sloping bank of the Estuary about one mile from the sea. The Estuary, whose entrance is guarded by the lofty Bolt Head, runs some six or seven miles inland. With its clear green water, its sloping banks, here of cornfield and there of wooded slope, with its little bays and steep rocks and cliffs and bold headland, it is beautiful at every turn.

Salcombe is worthy of a visit for several reasons. Chief, the beauty of its position and surroundings. There you have hill and dale, the ever fresh sea and the bold headland, wooded slope and rich cornfield ; sea cliff walks made by the sturdy coastguardsmen, which they have to tread every night the year through in search of supposed smugglers : and true Devonian lanes with steep banks teeming with vegetation, winding over hill and through romantic valley. Almost at every turn of the road or break in the hedge some fresh glimpse of beauty is presented to your gaze. You cannot but halt to admire, and find yourself involuntarily exclaiming how like a beautiful picture it all is. Of drives in the neighbourhood there are several—to Start Point with its famous lighthouse, to Hope, to Thurlestone, with its fantastic rocks and beautiful sands, to Bantham, and others Of walks the number is almost legion. Crossing the Estuary by the ferry-boat you climb to Portlemouth, a mountain village with a fine old church, from which you have most extensive views. Thence over a wild and elevated district to Prawle Point, the most southerly of Devonshire, with its signal station, returning along the coastguard path which follows the sea cliffs. Then there are several winding valleys full of wild and sylvan beauty, with their farmhouses perched in apparently almost inaccessible places. And if you give yourselves up to the narrow Devonian lanes, and let them lead you where they will, they will bring you to unexpected places, and disclose to you unexpected beauties. But the finest ramble of all is to Bolt Head, which guards the entrance to the Estuary like an ever watchful sentinel. Skirting the Estuary for some distance you pass in succession the beautiful little bays of North and South Sands, then through a fine wood, whose ground was covered with ivy of varying size, form, and colour, primroses and wild violets everywhere; afterwards along a path cut on the hedge of the cliffs, with the sea dashing beneath you, and only the solitary cry of the gulls around, the rocks above you worn into all manner of fantastic shapes by the fury of the elements for untold ages ; and at last a stiff climb up the steep side of the headland, and you have a view of surpassing beauty seawards and inland.

Then, again, the climate of Salcombe is so wonderful. It is considered most equable, the range of temperature being less than in most places, never so extremely cold in winter or hot in summer. It is balmy, yet bracing, and health giving. True, the east wind blows there, and, as in other places, it is piercing and searching. But an old native humourously assured me it was not so bad as in other places. Of the sixteen days I was there we had a sea fog one day. On the remaining, the sky was cloudless and rich in colour, and the sun shone brilliantly from early morning until evening. On Sunday, March 26th, when there was snow and sleet in the North, it was bright and sunny, and sufficiently warm for me to sit outside and read without overcoat. Another day, when I heard of nine degrees of frost in Bolton, it was sufficiently mild to allow us to sit outside and partake of that weakness of modern society, afternoon tea But one great charm of the place is the luxuriance of its vegetation. I left home with my garden almost covered with snow. I arrived in Salcombe to see—what? The hedges teeming with vegetation ; ivy of the most beautiful form, marking and colour ; ferns of great variety, especially scolopendiums, and polypodiums, and blechnum spicant as fresh and green as if they knew not such a season as winter ; primroses by the thousands, some of them with flowers as large as a florin; speedwell, wild violets, daffodils, wallflowers, periwinkle, all growing wild; and in the gardens sweet violets, blue, and white, scenting the air, daffodils and narcissus of the choicest kinds, barberry, laurustinus, peach trees in full bloom, myrtles as forest trees with us.

To those who want a busy, fashionable resort, with wide streets, attractive shops, gaily dressed ladies, crowded places of amusement, I would say, avoid Salcombe; but if you desire beautiful scenery of a varied character, a balmy yet bracing atmosphere, bright sun and cloudless skies; if you wish to mix amongst a simple, honest, kindly hospitable people, who have always a cheery word for you: if you want to silence the hum of loom and spindle and hammer, and the chatter of buyer and seller; if you want to forget there is such a thing as a tall chimney which occasionally sends forth black smoke, or the whistle of a railway engine, then you cannot do better than visit Salcombe."

Mr. Taylor writing to the same paper after a second visit to Salcombe, concludes his descriptive account as follows:—

"Beautiful and restful Salcombe! I rejoice in your lovely surroundings in your bold headlands, in your winding estuary, in your flowery lanes, rich fields and fertile glens, in your sweet-singing birds, in your clear sky and balmy air, in your quiet, calm peaceful life. There are a few places like you, too few peaceful havens in our seagirt land where busy and weary man can rush away from the crowded streets of our large towns, forget the markets, and noisy contentions of buyer and seller; where he can escape from fret and worry of life, and breathe in new inspiration and strength and hope; and from reverent thought and study of wonders, beauties, and mysteries of nature, be touched with a deeper and loftier purity, and be brought to a keener consciousness of the Infinite One who holds all things in His embrace, and will not let the least of His children ramble beyond the reach of His power and love."

TO SALCOMBE FOR SUN.—The following appeared in *The Queen* newspaper:—

"Sunny as any one of the much vaunted foreign resorts to which society rushes off to recoup its jaded energies after the fatigues of a busy season; mild enough to suit the weakly folk who hurry away from our shores to avoid the rigours of an English winter; with a climate wherein sub-tropical plants flourish in the open air, a veritable paradise to the tired seeker after rest and seclusion—such is sunny Salcombe. Close to the sea, yet charmingly sylvan, it is far enough from the great centres of civilisation to be fairly free from the incursions of the ubiquitous tripper, the nearest railway station being at Kingsbridge, several miles up the estuary. It requires the pen of a veritable word painter to do justice to the many charms of this little township. The following extract of a letter from the pen of the late James Anthony Froude, and dated as late in the year as November 10, will perhaps give some idea of the place, or rather its climatic advantages:—"The summer here has been beautiful, and has hardly yet left us. The orange trees are in blossom, begonias brilliant; geranium, heliotrope, and

NORTH SANDS VALLEY.

fuschias bright as they were two months ago. The winter at Salcombe is winter only in name, and we are hardly conscious of it except in the short days. Only the sea is wild." It was on a fine breezy spring day that I first saw Salcombe from the deck of the little steamer which plies between that town and Kingsbridge. The little port was looking radiant in the bright sunshine, and the houses and pretty villas, built on hills and rocky eminences, tier above tier, rendered the place delightfully foreign-looking and picturesque. The water reflected an ideal west-country sky—

deeply, gloriously blue, and flecked here and there by fleecy white clouds; whilst on the other side of the harbour stretched bay beyond bay of yellow sand, sheltered and sunny, with the fine hills of Portlemouth rising far above them. Looking seaward, right in front rose the splendidly bold and rugged outline of the Bolt Head; and thither we made our way, the road, after leaving the narrow street of the town, running parallel with the water, rising gradually to higher ground, and showing beautiful views over the adjacent country of the South Hams. From Salcombe to the Bolt Head is truly a delightful ramble, the way thereto winding between luxuriant woods, with here and there a gap, showing the estuary and the grand headland itself, with the sea (and such a sea!) surging madly round its jagged base, its foam-flecked jets being tossed up from far below; the stupendous cliff looking down the while as though in grim derision at the attempt of the tides in their ebb and flow, ebb and flow, to undermine their solid foundations. On this road, beautifully situated on the slope of a hill overlooking Salcombe Bay and its harbour bar, is Woodville, formerly the residence of James Anthony Froude, the great historian.

A little below the North Sands may be seen at some states of the tide the fossil remains of a hazel wood. The rock pools here, too, will repay one for a little time spent in investigating them, abounding as they do in sea anemones of the most delicate shades and vividly beautiful colouring. Given a fine day and a receding tide, there are few more pleasant occupations for the lover of nature than an hour spent in the proximity of the rock pools near this bold headland. There he may see the dun coloured patches lying about the rocks unfold and put forth their tentacles, blossoming out into sea-flowers of scarlet, orange, or rose colour, as the case may be. As we journeyed on, glorying in the bright sunshine, the song of innumerable birds, and all the familiar sights and sounds of spring, we came upon a lovely bit of woodland literally carpeted with bluebells, and looking like a delicate azure mist rising from the ground Leaving this, we emerged again into the open and followed the cliff path, where we obtained a superb view of the Bolt Head itself, immediately facing us. On reaching the Head, a glorious spectacle presented itself. Looking seaward, ships of varying build and tonnage were seen passing up and down Channel, whilst small craft hailing from Salcombe town or Kingsbridge were straining their white wings in the fresh breeze. On the way back we found quantities of wild flowers and ferns, late primroses, early marguerites, a wealth of bluebells and ragged robin, with here and there a clump of forget-me-nots, blue as the sky above us, and the sea which lay in all its immensity around us."

THE HARBOUR.

THE entrance to Salcombe harbour is between Prawle Point and Bolt Head, these two projections forming the most southern extremity of the county of Devonshire. The land on the east side is gradually sloping, whilst that on the west is high and rugged, rising to a height of nearly 500 feet. What is generally termed the harbour, is over one mile in length from its entrance, but various winding creeks branch off from it, as does also Kingsbridge Estuary, continuing its course for over four miles up to the town of Kingsbridge. On the west side of the entrance, off Bolt Head, is a small islet called the Great or Salcombe Mewstone, outside of which, about half a cable's length, is a ledge of rocks, one of which is called the Little Mewstone, over which the sea usually breaks. To these rocks vessels should give a good berth, passing always to seaward of them. The next point north-eastward of the Mewstone is distinguished by a peculiar shaped rock known as the Eelstone.

The Range is the place of anchorage outside the harbour, but it is open to the south. There is a small sunken rock of eleven feet, called the Rickham, lying a quarter of a mile off the eastern shore of the Range. During the Anglo-French war at the beginning of the nineteenth century, a French brig got out of her reckoning, and early one morning was reported off the harbour. Some of the inhabitants determined to capture her, and having armed themselves with cutlasses, they went off in the Customhouse boat to effect their purpose. Not much resistance was offered, and soon the brig was taken as a prize of war, the crew made prisoners and taken to Salcombe, where they were detained for some time. Several of those who took part in the capture were enriched by the act, receiving a good sum as prize money.

At the entrance to the harbour, which is rather narrow, being but little more than a quarter of a mile across, is a bar of sand. It is said that this bar has been known to uncover at some very low ebb tides, and that even persons have walked some way across it, and that on one occasion a cup was picked up on the bar, and preserved for some years in the town as a memento of the event. However that may be, there is now generally from four to six feet on it at low water spring tides, and inside from two and a half to three and a half fathoms. Ships of 22 feet draught can cross the bar at high water springs, and 16 feet at high water neaps. To cross the bar in the deepest water, keep well over on the western shore, and from there to the anchorage off the town the navigation is plain and easy, with a broad and deep channel well buoyed and beaconed. About one hundred years since a very curious custom was prevalent here, and afforded a sight that must at times have been exceedingly interesting, for from this bar sand used to be dredged up, and carried away in barges for the purposes of manure, and in the year 1776-7 as many as thirty-two barges were known to be there at one time. This practice has long since ceased, farmers finding other classes of manures more productive and cheaper. Although some few casualties have occurred on this bar, yet it is not by any means a dangerous one. There is scarcely ever any broken water on it, unless produced by a strong south or south-west gale, and yachts and vessels of almost any tonnage, at proper times of tide, may safely venture over it.

In June, 1869, during a dense fog, H.M.S. Cadmus, of 1,466 tons, whilst going from Portsmouth to Devonport, was seen by one of the Salcombe pilots close to the shore at the eastern entrance, the vessel going eight knots an hour at the time. The pilot hailed them, but not in time for the ship's way to be stopped, and she struck the rocks near the Bolt Head, knocking a hole in her bow. For the vessel's safety, she was got off under the direction of the same pilot, and grounded on the bar. Assistance having been obtained from Devonport, temporary repairs were made as she lay on the bar, the ship was then lightened and floated off, and afterwards towed to Devonport.

Lord Tennyson's poem "Crossing the Bar," is supposed to have been suggested by a visit to Salcombe by his lordship. During the early part of 1889 Lord Tennyson had been prostrated by a long and severe illness, and in his convalescent state took a short cruise along the south coast in the far-famed yacht *Sunbeam*, belonging to Lord Brassey, and kindly placed at the disposal of the poet During his tour, which proved of great benefit to his

SUNNY COVE.

health, he put in at Salcombe in the month of May, on a visit to his friend, Mr. J. A. Froude, then residing at the Moult. The *Sunbeam* remained in the harbour for nearly a week, and in the evening of her departure, the Poet Laureate, with his son the Hon. Hallam Tennyson, and two nurses, remained on deck as the yacht proceeded out of the harbour on her way to Dartmouth. At the time of her departure the church bell was ringing for evensong. Lord Tennyson was not wearing the slouch hat as usual, but had donned a thick fur cap, which came down close over his ears, and was wrapped in a warm shawl, and seated thus in an arm chair, with his attendants, he admired the grand scenery stretching away to the noble promontory of Bolt Head. It was glorious weather, the

SPLAT COVE.

sun now westering threw across the evening sky golden and ruddy rays, and when the fine and stately yacht reached the sandy bar, lying just inside of Bolt Head, the sea grew angrier, and the waves gave forth a surfy, slow, deep, mellow voice, and with a hollow moan crossed the bar on their way to the picturesque harbour. All the impressions of that thrilling scene, and the voices of the sea, are translated into that beautiful poem, "Crossing the Bar." It was written in the month of October in the poet's eighty-first year, at Farringford.—

> Sunset and evening star,
>   And one clear call for me!
> And may there be no moaning of the Bar,
>   When I put out to sea.
>
> But such a tide as moving seems asleep,
>   Too full for sound and foam,
> When that which drew from out the boundless deep,
>   Turns again home.
>
> Twilight and evening bell,
>   And after that the dark!
> And may there be no sadness of farewell
>   When I embark;
>
> For tho' from out our bourne of Time and Place,
>   The flood may bear me far,
> I hope to see my Pilot face to face,
>   When I have crost the Bar.

When that noble death-song of the truly Christian poet was published, its expressions so perfectly harmonised with the eventful evening above described, that the Rev. G. F. Owen, Baptist minister then residing at Salcombe, who was on board the *Sunbeam* when she proceeded out of the harbour for Dartmouth, wrote a letter to the *Western Morning News* stating that doubtless the poet's departure from Salcombe across the bar suggested the beautiful and immortal poem. A local artist of considerable repute forwarded a copy of the letter to the Hon. Hallam Tennyson desiring to know if the suggestion as to the origin of the poem was correct, and it was very gratifying to learn from the poet's son that it was perfectly correct. The artist immediately commenced to depict the scene upon canvas, with the famous yacht crossing the bar, and was so successful in the undertaking that the beautiful painting was soon after purchased by friends of the late Poet Laureate.

A little inside the bar is a red floating beacon, marking a sunken rock, called the Wolf, which is only uncovered at the lowest tides; just inside the latter is a long ledge of rocks called Blackstone, barely covered at high water spring tides, and with a beacon at the western end. The Poundstone and Old Harry, also beaconed, are smaller rocks on the western shore. All these rocks being properly beaconed, make the harbour easily accessible to strangers. Those desiring assistance will always find local pilots near the mouth of the harbour. The red buoy over the Wolf Rock and the beacon marking the Blackstone should be left on the starboard, and the other beacons on the port hand, and then keep in mid-channel

The flood tide sets round the Mewstone, directly over the bar, towards the Poundstone Rock, whence it crosses the harbour abreast of Salcombe Castle, and sets for the eastern shore as far as Millbay, whence it follows the trend of the shores. The ebb tide sets out fairly, running nearly in the centre of the channel, until abreast of Splat Cove, when it sets more to the southward. When on the bar, it sets directly out through the Range to seawards. It is high water, full and change of moon, at 5h. 54m; ordinary spring tides rise $19\frac{1}{2}$ feet, neaps $11\frac{1}{2}$ feet.

The harbour is completely landlocked, and is one of the greatest beauty, and amongst the safest in the English Channel, with ample room for a large number of vessels to ride securely, in from four to seven fathoms, good holding ground. Yacht owners could not find a better place for winter quarters for their yachts.

There are several sandy bays along the shores of the harbour suitable for bathing, but the place most resorted to for this purpose is Sunny Cove, under Rickham Common, on the Portlemouth side of the harbour. Splat Cove also is a good bathing place, with firm sandy bottom. Batson Creek branches off from the harbour, and it is a pleasant trip, when the tide is favourable, to the hamlet at the head of the creek, passing on the right on the way up the prettily-situated farmstead of Ilberstow.

LOWER PART OF THE HARBOUR AND THE MOULT.

SALCOMBE CASTLE.

ABOUT one mile down the harbour, on the point forming the northern boundary to the entrance of North Sands, and on a rock nearly level with the water at high tide, stand the ruins of an ancient castle, now commonly known as the "Old Castle." At one time it defended the entrance to the harbour, and although but little remains at present of this old fort, yet it has had an honourable career, having been the last to hold out against the Parliamentary forces in Devon, and even in Cornwall, with the exception of Pendennis Castle at the entrance of Falmouth harbour, during the civil wars in the reign of Charles I. There is no record as to when this castle was first constructed, but Hawkins says it was attributed to the Saxons. But we do not think it can lay claim to such a venerable age. Another authority describes it as "a round fort built in the time of Queen Elizabeth, a little before the Spanish Invasion." Mr. Paul G. Karkeek, in a paper read at the Devonshire Association Meeting at Kingsbridge in 1877, says it "was more likely to have been built in the reign of Henry VIII. That monarch was much disgusted with the liberties taken in his waters by French and Spanish rovers, and by his order a survey of the south coast was made; and forts or block-houses were erected, or designed to be erected, on certain vulnerable points. Pendennis and St. Mawes Castles, which guard the mouth of the Fal, owe their origin to this king; and as Salcombe Fort occupies a very similar position, it is not unlikely that a block-house or bulwark of some sort was built there at the same time. This, however, like all the other national defences, had been neglected under the rule of the Stuarts; and when Sir Edmund Fortescue undertook to put it in order, it was only known by the suggestive name of 'the old Bullworke.'"

The fort was of an irregular form; circular on the south-west, and partly so towards the north-west; but the end to the north-east, nearest Salcombe, was narrowed almost to a point. Here the circular form terminated; while a straight wall, extending half the length of the fort, faced the high land behind it. The north-west section, which is principally in the direction of the land, is still standing nearly entire. It is built of hewn stone, about forty feet in height, and seven feet in thickness. On the inside are to be seen the holes in which the beams of the upper floor were placed. In the walls of this chamber are two port-holes and seven loop-holes for musketry, which, as the land in the rear has an abrupt elevation, seem to be all that could be of any service in that quarter.

At the time of the Civil Wars, this "Old Bullworke" had got into a state of utter ruin and decay, although occupying a position of great strength and considerable importance. Sir Edmund Fortescue, of Fallapit, near Kingsbridge, the Royalist High Sheriff of Devon in 1642, and for many months a prisoner at Winchester House and Windsor Castle, on his release doubtless saw that the castle would be of some service to the King, he undertook to refortify and man the ancient walls, and made overtures to that effect. Prince Maurice, the King's nephew, then stationed at Whitley, near Plymouth, with the Royalist forces, commissioned Sir Edmund on the 9th day of December, 1643, to refortify and man the fort. Having received this warrant, he must at once have set about the work, for in about two years he had the place thoroughly restored and fortified, as well as victualled and manned ready to stand a siege.

The following is Sir Edmund's account of the cost of this undertaking:—

"Payments and disbursements on Fort Charles, both for the building, victuallynge, and fortifying it with great guns and musquets. Perfected January ye 15th, anno. dom. 1640 (1645).

	£	s.	d.
In the building	1355	18	9
And for timber, ordnance, powder, shot, muskets, swords, and various warlike articles	1031	19	9

SALCOMBE CASTLE.

"A true and just particular of all the provisions in Fort Charles, January 15th, 1645, at which time it was surrounded and besieged by Sir Thomas Fayrefaxe the Parliament General:—

	£	s.	d
1 butt Sacke	20	0	0
10 hogsheads of punch, nine at £5 per hogshead	50	0	0
1 tun of March Beer	17	0	0
10 tuns of cider at £3 10s.	35	0	0
22 hogsheads of beef and pork at £7 10s. per hogshead	165	0	0
1 butt of oyle	20	0	0
3 hogsheads of vinegar	4	0	0
48 bushels of pease at 7d. per bushel	16	15	0
2 hogsheads of meat	2	16	0
4 hogsheads of grits	8	0	0
2000 of poor Jacks	15	0	0
6000 of dried whitings at 8d. per cent.	24	0	0
300 of ox tongues	6	0	0
500 of candles	12	10	0
Of bisquet, 8000 weight, at £9 per thousand	72	0	0
1200 weight of butter at 5s. per hundred	30	0	0
6 pecks of fruit	6	0	0
100 weight of almonds	5	0	0
15 quarters of coales at £3	45	0	0
100 bushels of charkole	5	0	0
2 cases of bottles, full with rare and good strong waters	6	0	0
20 pots with sweetmeats, and a great box of all sorts of especially good dry preserves	6	0	0
Then Churgion's chest	16	0	0
100 weight of raw milk cheese	1	13	4
30 barrels of powder, at £6 per barrel	180	0	0
1000 weight of musquet ball, at 22s. per cent.	11	0	0
10 rolls of tobacco, being 600 weight at 12d. per pound	30	0	0
for 3 sides of bacon	4	0	0
for 3 dozen of poultry	2	5	6
for 5 sheeps	3	15	0
for 35 tunne of caskes for beer, cider, beef, pork, fish, grits, meat, pease, and water, at 16s. per tunne	28	0	0
for 200 of lemons	0	16	8
The total sum is	£848	11	6
More for great shotte	32	17	6
In all it makes the full sum of	£3269	5	6

Long live King Charles. Amen.

In these accounts the amount of wages paid to those employed in re-building the fort is not stated. Hawkins, who saw the original documents, says, "that the masons, quarrymen, and carpenters, had a shilling a day each; the plasterers one shilling and two-pence; the joiners

SIR EDMUND FORTESCUE.

one shilling and eight-pence; the attendants (which it is supposed means labourers), ten-pence; and lime was at six shillings a hogshead." If wages were low in those days, provisions were cheap.

"Memorandum. That in these accounts of £3269 5s. 6d. not one
  penny is put down for beds, bedsteads, cerecloths, sheets,

blankets, bolsters, pillowes, curtinges, vallances, curtain-rods, pewter, table-boards, cupboards, spoons, buckets, tubbs, potes, glasses, bedroods, mats, all the beams and timber, chayres, stools, chests, firepanns, shovels, tongs, and irons, bellowes, and all other sorts of household stuff with which tis fully furnished.

"Attested by me, E. FORTESCUE."

	£	s.	d.
more for forty halberds at 6s. 8d. each halberd	15	6	8
for 86 great basketes to stand full with earth, on the upper decks, and on the tops of the walls, at 5s. 6d. each baskettes	23	2	0
for 46 less baskettes for the same purpose at 10d. each baskett	1	18	4
This summe is	£40	7	0

This summe of £40 7s. being added to the former summe of £3269 5s. 6d., make both together the full summe of £3309 12s. 6d.

"Ita est., E. FORTESCUE."

To obtain the money for this outlay, Sir Edmund was assigned, by an order from the Commissioners of the County of Devon, dated at Exeter, August 12th, 1644, the weekly contributions of the Parishes of Malborough and Portlemouth, amounting to £17 15s 0d.—the former being £11 15s 0d. and the latter £6 weekly,—which payments were continued until November 1st in the same year, when they were superseded by the same Commissioners ordering Mr. George Potter to pay weekly the sum of £14, this gentleman, no doubt, being the receiver-general for the County. In addition to these sums the Parish of West Alvington contributed for some time weekly £7 1s. 8d., paying in all £245 16s. 10d.

Sir Edmund, however, displayed a large amount of self-sacrificing enthusiasm in the Royalist cause, for he says that in carrying out the whole of this arduous undertaking, he did not receive a penny for himself. From the statement of the amount of provisions taken into the Fort, he appeared, also, to be very mindful of the natural wants of those under his charge, and from the quantity of punch, beer, and cider, it would seem as if he was determined that the spirits of the men should not flag for want of stimulants.

The following is Sir Edmund's list of the names of those who garrisoned the Fort at this siege:—

"Here followes the names of the officers and soldiers in Fort Charles, the 15th day of January, 1645, at which tyme twas besieged by Sir Thos. Fayrefaxe commande, the Parliament Generall:—

Sir E. Fortescue, *Governor*
Sir Christopher Luckner
Mr. Thomas Fortescue
Captain Peter Fortescue
Major Syms
Major Stephenson
Captain Roch
Captain Kingston
Captain Powett
Captain Peterfield
Captain Doues
Mr Snell, *Chaplain*
Hugh Harris
James Cownes
Thomas Lightfoot
Patrick Blacket
John Harris
Samuel Stodard; *shot thro' the head, 31st March, 1646*
Robert Nugent
Hugh Haedway
Lieut. John Ford, ran away 27th March, 1646
Matthew Bordfedd, *Surgeon*
Peter Davye, *Sergeant*
Andrew Morgan, *Sergeant*
James Dackum, *Sergeant*
Briant Browne, *Master-gunner*
Richard Lamble, *his mate*
Henry Browne, *another mate*
George Lindon, *Armorer*
Arthur Scoble, *Corporal*
John Powell, *Corporal*
Alex. Weymouth, *Corporal*
Richard Wolver, *Corporal*
Robert Terrye, *Corporal*
Christopher Wise
John Frost
John Hodge, *Corporal; shot and lame, went by leave 10th April, 1646*
William Cookworthy, ran away 8th March, 1645-6
John Gould
John Stone
Michael Small
Thos Phillips, shot thro' the left arm and side, March 12th, 1645-6
Robert Prittiejohn
Peter Cross
Walter Merrifield
Stephen Goss, ran away, 11th April, 1646
James Frost
Edwd Yeabsly
Thomas Cause
Geo. Kingston, the younger
John Evans
Hercules Giles the younger
Peter Joynter
Thomas Quarme, being sick, went by leave, 19th January, 1645-6
Hugh Perradey
Richard Winter
Arthur Lidston
Thomas Wakeham
Nathaniel Port
Peter Michellmore
Thomas Hupkins
Lawrence Mayle
James Cookworthy
Richard Martin
Briant Browne the younger
Zachary Hupkins

Total, 66 men besides two laundresses, viz.:—
Mary Browne and Elizabeth Terrye."

The dates in these documents are rather confusing, the old and new style being mixed up together. Where 1645 appears, it should read 1646 of the new style. From an entry in the book where Sir Edmund kept his accounts, we should infer that the Fort had been twice previously invested, for it says, "Item, for great shot and musket shot when Fort Charles was formerly twice besieged, £15 17s. od." But these are the only particulars he gives of it. In a letter describing the capture of Dartmouth, it concludes thus, "a party was sent to fall upon a fort near Salcombe, a harbour that lies between Dartmouth and Plimouth, and which hath frigots in it that much infests the seas." We conclude from this that the harbour was being used by the Royalist privateers as a place of safety, and that Fort Charles, commanding the entrance to the harbour, would prevent chase being given. These two previous sieges therefore, doubtless, refer to attacks being made on the Fort by the Parliament fleet under the command of Admiral Batten, but which were unsuccessful.

Sir Edmund's papers lead us to suppose that the last siege commenced on January 15th, 1646, but this date is evidently in the old style, so if we add eleven days, it will give January 26th, for the siege was not commenced until after the capture of Dartmouth and Plymouth. The former place made a very feeble attempt at resistance, and was taken on January 16th by the troops in charge of Sir Thomas Fairfax. Immediately afterwards a regiment was sent under the command of Col. Inglesby to attack Fort Charles, which was fortified with eight guns.

It is curious to note what some of the publications of that time say in regard to this Fort. The *True Informer* of January 25th, says,—

"An attempt will suddenly be made on Charles his Fort, which is now commanded by Sir Edmund Fortescue; but we hope it will shortly find another Governor. The place is verie strong, and therefore there are Ordnance designed to batter it, and a great strength of assaylants there are yet before it, and these the country are sending in to be under the command of Colonell Inglesby in the managing of the work."

92 SALCOMBE AND NEIGHBOURHOOD.

The *Moderate Intelligencer* of January 26th, says,—

"We go on to attempt upon *Charles* Fort near *Salcombe* It's commanded by Sir *Edw Fortescue*. There must be Ordnance to batter it, which are comming, likewise some additions of forces to Col. *Ingelbie's* Regiment now before it, are to be raised out of the country, which they do willingly."

On January 31st *Perfect Occurrences* has the following :—

"The country people nere Salcomb are risen, and offer to keepe in the Fort Charles at Salcomb. Kit Lukener, the great trencher man, being therein, is afraid he shall be starved."

THE CASTLE ROCKS

The Ordnance necessary to batter the Fort could only be obtained from Plymouth, and as that place was taken on January 18th, Col. Weldon, the Governor, would shortly afterwards march on Salcombe with the necessary siege guns and troops to assist Col. Inglesby, whilst there would be also some troops recruited in the neighbourhood.

SALCOMBE CASTLE. 93

On March 25, Col. Weldon made overtures to Sir Edmund to surrender the Fort, on what was termed "very faire" conditions. It was supposed by the besiegers that he intended to yield, and they sent word to that effect to Plymouth and to Parliament. But such evidently was not the intention of Sir Edmund.

How the siege was conducted is not known, but according to tradition the Parliamentarian artillery took up their

THE CASTLE AND BOLT HEAD.

positions at Rickham Common, where yet can be traced the remains of earthworks, from which place they would have a good command of the Fort. But it is probable they had other positions also.

It does not appear there was much loss of life on either side. Sir Edmund's account gives one death and two wounded, whilst the burial register of Malborough only records one interment in connection with this siege, viz., "April 24, Roger, the sonne of Phillipp Hingston, slaine against the fort of Sale." This name, however, is not found among those that were in the Fort, and it is probable he belonged to the Parliamentary Forces.

During the time the siege was on, the retired inlet of Salcombe was a scene of incessant uproar, the batteries thundering from each side of the harbour. There is a story that Sir Edmund's slumbers were disturbed one night by the leg of his bedstead being carried away by a shot, which caused his sudden appearance among his men in his shirt. However, after a spirited resistance of four months, a capitulation took place. A letter to Parliament states:—

"Charles Fort, sometimes called Salcombe, is surrendered to us, to the obedience and use of the Parliament, which is the only considerable place that the enemy has lately held in all the west parts, except the strong garrison of Pendennis Castle."

The articles of surrender were ten in number, agreed to between Sir Edmund Fortescue, of the one part, and Major Pearce and Capt. Halle of the other part, for the surrender of the Fort into the hands of Col. Weldon, of Plymouth, for the use of King and Parliament, to which articles Col. Weldon fully agreed by signing the same on the 7th day of May, 1646. The following is a copy of the articles:—

"Imprimis. That sir Edmond Fortescue Gouernor, and sir Chr. Lu kner, with there servants and all & every of the souldiers now in ye said fort Charles, shall have and anjoye in there and every of thare severall and respective places, capacities, and degrees, full liberty in thire profession of the true protestant religion professed and vowed by both houses of this present parlement, in their first grand protestation, and shall not act any time hereafter by letter or censure in theire or any of theire placess or aboads for perseuinge in ye practice and exercise of popery: Soe itt is agreed yt if any papist there be hee will forfeit ye benifitt of ye articles.

"II. That the gouernor and Mr. John Snell his chaplinge, and all officers and souldiers belonginge to the said fort, shall have free libertie to go to there owne homes, in any place or country within this Kingdom, or places bee yund seays, and they not to bee molested for ye future, they submittinge themselfes to all orders and ordenances of parlement.

"III. That the said fort may not bee knowne by aney other name than fort Charles as now itt is, or any coate of armes in ye dininge rume defaced: or any thinge beelonginge to the said fort.

"IV. That sir Edmond Fortescue, ye gouernor, sir Chr. Luckner, capt. Geor. Kingston, with there servants, bee permitted to goe to there owne homes, sir Chr. Luckner to Fallapit, thare to remaine, or elsewhare within this Kingdom under the power of ye parlement, for the space of three months' time unmolested. And if they cannot make theire peace with the parlement, then to have free liberty to pass from any port within this Kingdom bee younde ye seayes.

"V. That the gouernor sir Edmund Fortescue, his servants, and all officers and soldiers, bee quietly permitted to carry any cloathes, monneys, or other goods which they can justly clayme as there owne to thare houses, and to injoye them without molestation.

"VI. That tenn horses bee permitted for the gouernor's use from hence to Fallapit, and that any officer & soldiers have free libertey to transport his or any off theare goods by boat or other wayes to Kingsbridge, and then to dispose of them att there pleasures.

"VII. That on Saturday the ninth off this present May, by tenne of ye clock in ye morninge, ye gouernor and all his officers and soldiers of fort Charles shall then march out, and surrender ye same into the hands of Corronell Welldon, or whome hee shall appoynte, With all the ordnance, armes, amonition, victualls, and every other thing there unto pertayninge not mentioned in these articles, without spoyling, breaking, demiskinge, or consuminge of the same.

"VIII That the gouernor, sir Chr. Luckner, thire servts, and all officers and souldiers in the fort, have free liberty to march from hence to Fallowpit with there usuall armes, drumes beatinge and collers flyinge, with bondelars full of powder, and muskets apertinable, and after three vallues to yield up theire armes to those whome Corronall Welldon shall appoint to receive them, the gouernor, sir Chr. Luckner, with both theire seruants, likewayse ye officers in common excepted.

"IX. That noe officer or soldier, or any other under ye command of Corronell Ralph Welldon gouernor of Plymouth, shall any way reproach, spoyle, philfer, or mollest any of the officers or soldiers of the same fort in their march from thence to Fallowpit, or elsewhere att the same distance from hence, or in theire or any theire respective places aforesaid. Untill ye time of surrender of ye said fort their be none pass in or out, or transport anythinge by seay or land from thence, without ye knowledge of both parties.

"That sufficient hostage bee delivered on both sides for the faithfull performance of these articles.

"RALPH WELLDON, RICHARD PEARCE, EDMOND HALLE."

WOODVILLE, SALCOMBE.

The sturdy Royalist commander stipulated that he should be allowed to march to his own house with the pomp of war, and so the villages all the way to Fallapit, ten miles off, were startled by the apparition of a defeated garrison tramping along with drums beating and colours flying, and singing in the face of these pestilent Roundheads, "the sweetness, mercy, majesty, and glory of their king." Arrived at Fallapit, the garrison would then be dispersed, the men taking to their homes the recollections of the distresses or enjoyments of the siege, and the officers to make terms with the victors for their lands.

It is evident the Fort was not much damaged in the siege, and as one of the articles states that no coat of arms in the dining room or nothing belonging to the Fort be defaced, it is surprising that after the lapse of about two hundred and fifty years so little of it remains. We should have thought the inhabitants, with the honours attached to it, would have preserved it from crumbling to ruins. This Castle was the last place in Devonshire that carried the flag of Charles I, or to surrender to the arms of Fairfax. After nearly four months' siege it capitulated with all the honours of war, and its giving in arose probably from a scarcity of powder. This Fort deserved a better fate than it has met with. It is possible the articles were broken, and a Fort that had made such a stout resistance was deemed dangerous to be let remain intact, and was, therefore, demolished by Col. Weldon. The ruins have been allowed gradually to crumble to pieces, and we fear unless something is speedily done, in a few years they will have disappeared altogether. It is generally supposed the ruins belong to the Crown.

Sir Edmund Fortescue afterwards went to Holland, where he died in 1647, aged 38 years, his body being buried at Delft, where a monument is erected to his memory. A large key, said to belong to the Fort, used to be kept at Fallapit, measuring 1 foot 4 inches long, and 2 inches wide at the part that enters the lock. This key, we believe, is still in the Fortescue family.

SALCOMBE TO BOLT HEAD.

BOLT Head is the finest and boldest headland on the south coast, being distant from Salcombe about three miles, and is approached by one of the finest marine walks to be found anywhere. Leaving the town the road skirts the winding shore, the blue waters of the harbour and the open sea of the English Channel being constantly seen through a trellis of greenery. Passing the Marine Hotel on the left and the Vicarage on the right, Woodville is soon reached.

WOODVILLE is a most delightful residence, and was built in 1797, by Mr. James Yates; the foundation being laid by himself, and the whole arrangement of the grounds and plantations was executed under his own direction. A verandah or colonnade encompasses the building on three sides, while the windows to the south and south-west command a fine view of the Bolt Head and English Channel. The grounds are very tastefully laid out with various evergreens and flowering shrubs, both exotic and indigenous. In the gardens may be seen lemon, citron, and orange trees, an olive tree (entirely unprotected), and some splendid masses of the New Zealand flax, which grows most luxuriantly, and flourishes as vigorously as in its native country, whilst many fine aloes have also flowered here. One of the gardens close to the shore, which is approached from the other grounds by a bridge thrown over the public road, has a wall clothed with a number of orange and lemon trees, and where the fruit arrives at a fair state of perfection. In a deep gully immediately below the gardens, reached by a winding path through the bushy cliff, is a summer house, fixed on a perpendicular rock, in which there was formerly a good camera obscura, whilst beneath it is a boat and bath house combined. Below, immediately on the rocks, is a sort of quay, upon which is built a mock parapet with small swivels, which Hawkins says was for the purpose of firing a royal salute. He also says, "in another part is a sinuous enclosure for retaining and preserving fish in their natural element," but of this nothing remains at present. The name of these rocks is Limpyer, and a melancholy tragedy occurred here many years ago, whilst Woodville was in possession of a Mr. Henshaw. Dislike had been taken to one of the servants, and things had been missed from the house, when a search was made, and some of the missing articles found in this servant's box. She was accused of the theft, and mention was made of it at prayers the same evening, with the threat that she would be given into custody the next morning. The girl protested she was innocent, but not being able to stand the disgrace, she, the same night, went to the rocks below, and committed suicide by drowning. Her body was not recovered for two or three weeks, and at first it was not known what had become of her, although she had been seen on her way to the rocks, and a towel was found on them wrung to pieces, which she had carried with her. The whole neighbourhood was searched, with the idea that she might be hiding herself away, but all uncertainty as to her fate was set at rest by the finding of her body at Hope, where it had been washed on shore. The Henshaws became so unpopular from this sad event, that they were hissed at by the populace whenever they appeared in public, and in consequence they soon after left the place.

Woodville has had many changes of ownership since the time of Mr. Yates, a recent tenant being the famous historian, James Anthony Froude, who occupied it for three or four years, and died here in October, 1894, his body being interred in Salcombe Cemetery. Its most recent owner and occupier being Major Bennett.

About a quarter of a mile on the road from Woodville, can be seen on the rocks beneath, the ruins of Salcombe Castle, whilst in the field above is the Battery of the Salcombe Artillery Volunteers. This Battery is mounted with two guns, and when firing takes place the target is moored off the mouth of the harbour. The field in which this Battery is situated is called Gutter Field, and there is an old tradition that it derived its name from a great battle that took place there, when human blood ran rather freely over its slopes. There is not an atom of authentic information to substantiate this tradition. The larger portion of this field was planted with fir and other

ENTRANCE TO THE MOULT.

trees a few years ago. The house adjoining, standing in its own grounds, is Sandhills.

NORTH SANDS. Descending the hill North Sands is reached. The English end of the French-Atlantic cable is landed here. This cable, connecting Brest with

London, was first landed at Starehole Bottom on the 28th May, 1870, and a house was erected there to receive it. This landing not being considered satisfactory, on the 15th October, 1871, it was removed to the North Sands, where an instrument house had been erected in the meadow to receive the end, and since that time the cable has worked satisfactorily. North Sands valley is exceedingly pretty, with an uninterrupted sea view in front,

HIGHER MOULT LODGE.

the beautifully wooded grounds of the Moult on one side, and the rising ground towards Salcombe on the other, with the valley extending more than a mile, pass Hanger Mill, toward the hamlet of Collaton, make altogether as charming a piece of scenery as is to be found in the whole neighbourhood. It is proposed by the present owner to cut a road through the valley, and it will open up some splendid building sites, as good, if not better than any in the locality, and near to the town's high level reservoir. Doubtless Salcombe of the future will be in this direction. The spectacle presented by the sea-view during a strong southerly gale from here, is majestic in the highest degree, the breakers rolling in and dashing over the roadway with terrific fury. The poles near the Moult side of the Sands, were placed there to break the force of the waves, previous to the erection of the sea wall and breakwater, but were of very little good.

Evidence is not wanting to shew that at one time a forest occupied the site of North Sands bay, which in some very remote period must have been submerged by the sea, for at low water spring tides may be seen imbedded in the sand, a large quantity of trunks of trees, and on digging a foot or two below the surface, a mass of decomposed vegetable matter is met with, amongst which have been found the small sprays of trees, nuts, acorns, and leaves. Several years since some persons took out the trunk of a large oak, which they had found four feet below the surface. It was three feet in diameter and six in length, and it required the help of several men and horses to take it up. The heart was found to be as black as ebony, and intensely hard, and capable of taking a fine polish, the outer part being in a soft pulpy state to a depth of about six inches. A large piece of this wood we believe is to be found in the grounds of the Moult. Quantities of the Pholas Dactylas or Prickly Piercer are to be found in this wood near low water mark, and some exceeding four inches in length have been taken from it. From this Sand, as well as from the shores generally, large quantities of the marine plants Fucus, Salsola, and Salicornia, or what is commonly known as ore weed, is cast up by the sea and taken away for manure, the inhabitants seemingly having acquired by immemorial custom a right to it. About the sands at the entrance of the harbour, and in the crevices of the cliffs around this part of the coast, are to be found sea-kale and sea or rock samphire.

THE MOULT occupies the whole of the small promontory that separates the North from the South Sands. The grounds are beautifully wooded, and the gardens are tastefully laid out. The residence is a neat commodious edifice, in a style mainly partaking of the Gothic, and was begun in 1764 by Mr. John Hawkins, of Norton, near Kingsbridge, who intended it to be a mere "pleasure box," where he could retire for a short time for relaxation and comfort, but he did not live to finish it, for he died on the 16th September in the same year, aged 56, and was buried at Churchstow. He left the uncompleted structure to his widow, who sold it to Mr. H. Whorwood, of Holton Park, Oxford, in 1770. It would appear that this charming spot owes its celebrity chiefly to this gentleman, who exercised a large amount of taste and judgment in laying out the grounds and planting the trees. He had the house fitted up as a decorated cottage. The property remained in his hands only a few years, for in 1785 it was sold to Mr. Samuel Strode, of Peamore, near Exeter, who carried out and completed the design of his predecessor. He used to spend the summer months here, and retire to Peamore or London for the winter. He died in 1795, leaving the Moult to his widow for life, who is described by Hawkins as "the once beautiful and elegant Miss Grace Caulfield," a cousin of the Earl of Charlemont. Whilst she continued to spend the winter months at London, the Moult was her favourite spot during the summer. She died in 1805, and an elegy written to her memory in a bower on the grounds, which probably no longer exists, shews she was no ordinary lady, but one highly esteemed for her unassuming manners and benevolence.

On her death the property passed into the hands of her husband's niece, Miss Grace Strode, who at once let it to Mr. Benjamin Bousfield, who continued to occupy it till 1808, when Miss Strode disposed of the property to Mr. William Jackson, excise officer, who enlarged the house, and added other buildings on the grounds. After him it

SOUTH SANDS.

came into the possession of the late Right Hon. Reginald Earl of Devon, who as Lord Courtenay, resided there for some time, and even in his after years spent some portion of each year there. It also became the residence of the late Lord Justice Sir George Turner, of the Chancery Court, who yearly spent his vacations here, and who was so well known and beloved for his large-hearted generosity to the poor, and the interest he took in all that concerned

SOUTH SANDS AND BOLT HEAD HOTEL

this neighbourhood. He died in 1867, but Lady Turner, his widow, continued in residence until her death in 1872. Mr. J. A. Froude resided here previous to his removal to Woodville. Its present owner and occupier is Miss Foster.

SOUTH SANDS. From North Sands the road to the Bolt ascends the hill at the back of the Moult grounds. Before reaching the summit of the hill Higher Moult Lodge is passed on the right, standing near the entrance of a road leading to Malborough. The beautifully-wooded grounds from here to the road at the summit of the hill is the site, about four acres in extent, for a large hotel, which it is proposed to erect immediately, with every modern convenience and accommodation for visitors. The hotel will stand well back on the site, and will have an uninterrupted view of the Channel and the harbour. The hotel will have a frontage of 152 feet, and be five stories high, whilst the upper portion of the roof will be flat, so as to give a promenade 119 feet in length and 20 feet in width. There will also be a verandah and balcony to the ground and first floors, running the entire length of the building. To the left of the entrance hall will be a spacious coffee room, with an ante dining room adjoining, connected with the coffee room by folding doors. The drawing room will be at the extreme right of the building, and the billiard room will also be on the ground floor, as well as private, writing, and smoke rooms, together with the manager's office, and other necessary apartments. The upper parts of the building will be fitted up entirely for bedrooms, of which there will be 75. There will be a lift from the ground floor to every storey and to the promenade at the top of the building, whilst in the basement arrangements will be made for salt water baths, and all parts of the hotel will be fitted with the electric light. On the grounds will be two lawn tennis courts and a bowling green.

The whole of the land near here has been laid out for building purposes, several roads made, numerous sites sold, and several handsome villas erected.

Descending the hill South Sands is reached. This is the favourite resort for picnic parties, as it affords a good landing place for boats, and is within easy distance of the Bolt Head. The steamer running between Kingsbridge and Salcombe also makes constant excursions to this place. A small embankment has been made, and a tea house erected upon it, for the convenience of visitors. A good supply of water is procurable near by.

The Salcombe Lifeboat Station is situated here, the first boat being the gift of the late Mr. Richard Durant, of Sharpham, near Totnes, which cost over £700, whilst the house was built by public subscriptions. The boat was presented in 1869, and named the "Rescue" by Miss Durant. There being some doubt about the self-righting properties of this boat, it was replaced in 1888 by a boat constructed on improved principles, the cost being defrayed out of a bequest made by the late Mrs. Lesty, and the boat named the "Lesty."

A scramble for a short distance over the rocks forming the southern boundary of this bay, and we reach a cavern or an old disused mine, the entrance to which is none of the cleanest, but the sight afforded a few yards in from the entrance will well repay for the trouble in getting to it. Proceeding in until the light is well-nigh lost, there is seen hanging from the roof and sides a quantity of luminous moss, which at once strikes the visitor with surprise and admiration. The moss is most brilliant and of a light green colour.

Southern Mill, the hamlet of Coombe, and the farmstead of Rew are situated inland up the vale, but nothing of interest lies in that direction. The road to the Bolt from South Sands takes a sudden turn to the left, and after a short walk we come to the entrance of Courtenay Walk, that leads directly to the Bolt. This path is cut about half way down the cliff, and was made about fifty years ago by the late Lord Devon for the purpose of giving visitors the pleasure of seeing this magnificent headland, and also the glorious sea view obtained from this walk. The Bolt Head Temperance Hotel and Boarding House is situated close to the entrance of Courtenay Walk, it being a new erection, standing in its own grounds, and commands beautiful views of South Sands and the harbour, and from some parts of the house peeps of the English Channel are also obtained. A verandah and balcony, each eighty feet long form pleasant resorts, commanding sea and inland views of

ENTRANCE TO COURTENAY WALK.

great variety and beauty. There is a spacious and well-lighted billiard room, and also every accommodation for catering for picnic and excursion parties.

SPLAT COVE. The land just here and extending to the water's edge is called Splat Cove. In 1812, Sir Thomas Tyrwhitt, the Gentleman Usher of the Black Rod, was commissioned by George IV., who was at that time Regent, to select a spot on the south coast for the purpose of erecting a marine pavillion Sir Thomas, amongst other places, visited Salcombe, staying for the time at the King's Arms Inn, and selected this spot at Splat Cove as the best for the erection. The property at that time belonged to Mr. Edmund Pollexfen Bastard, M.P. for Devonshire. The project, however, was after some years relinquished as it was considered too far from London.

An interesting legend exists in relation to this place. The Bastard family, who formerly resided at Garston, near Kingsbridge, but now of Kitley, Yealmpton, at one time possessed a large amount of property in this neighbourhood, but about 50 years ago disposed of the whole, with the exception of the field immediately above this Cove. It is said the reason why they did not sell this field was in deference to an old tradition relating to an ancestor of theirs. It is supposed that this ancestor had charge of one of the ships that brought over the army of the Conqueror from Normandy. A gale arose and the fleet were scattered, and the ship of which this Bastard was commander made the shore at the entrance of Salcombe harbour, and he and his men landed on the little grass plat just above the rocks, where picnic parties during the summer months spread their cloths on their excursion trips to this place. This spot, with the field adjoining, is still retained in the Bastard family. However, in the list of those who took part in the battle of Hastings, the name of a Bastard does not occur, but in the Domesday Book, which was published about twenty years after battle, by order of William the Conqueror, one Robert the Bastard is made mention of as holding from the King (among many others) the manor of Bachestane. Would this be the same as Batson, in which manor this land is situated, and thus in any way substantiate this legend, by shewing that the Bastards held property in this locality at the time of the Conqueror?

In Splat Cove there is a cavern called Bull Hole, and it is stated that it extends about three miles, having its outlet at Sewer Mill Cove, where there is a cavern having a similar name, but whether these two cavities be really the same continuous aperture has never been proved, none of those who have entered the respective openings having had courage sufficient to proceed far enough to ascertain the fact. The tradition as to the name of these holes is, that a bull entered it at one end and came out at the other, it having completely changed its colour in the passage from black to white.

Leaving Splat Cove, Courtenay Walk descends a little through a lovely wood and avenue, where the soft resinous scent of the pines mingles with the salt sea air. The walk continues through a wilderness of honeysuckle and wild rose, whilst also there is a plentiful display of ferns, yellow broom, and foxgloves. Suddenly the sea opens beyond and below, and the view of the harbour mouth, with perhaps a vessel passing in or out, is an exceedingly bold and stimulating one.

The hill is just on a line with the Bar. The opposite shore of the bay is sheltered by smooth rounded headlands, intersected with little sandy bays, with their white fringe of foam contrasting with the blue waters. The hill slopes are varied with green sward and bracken of dull brown hue. Inland the little harbour stretches beauteous in its colour, the jutting heads lulling the rolling seas, ere they reach the moored shipping. As the hill is climbed the strange formation of the coast is more clearly seen: one great cliff jutts out sharply as the bowsprit of a mighty vessel, and as one goes round to the southward the heights above are capped with serrated and jagged peaks, on which stands the flagstaff of the coastguard. The highest of these rocks is a huge mass called Argon rock. This noble pile of rocks, viewed from either side, is very grand, and there is a peculiar hole passing through them. The pathway becomes exceedingly narrow between the sharp strange-shaped rocks, some of them rising 200 feet above. The valley of Starehole separates Sharp Tors from Bolt Head. Most persons think when they have passed this headland they have been upon Bolt Head, but such is not the case, for they have taken Sharp Tors, as this headland is called, for the Bolt. Turning the corner we are in face of another promontory, and this is the veritable Bolt Head.

STAREHOLE BOTTOM. This is the place which local tradition connects with a Danish encampment. On the 9th November, 1799, Messrs. John Cranch and James Willcocks, of Kingsbridge, explored this interesting spot. They took with them from Lower Sewer farm Michael Damerel, a servant in the employ of Mr. John Fairweather, of Horsecombe. The following is Mr. Cranch's report:—

"Just within the Warren gate, from Lower Sewer farm house, a few yards south of the ruins of a small shepherd's cot, and of a pinfold adjoining thereto, we observed a very large and lofty mound or rampart of earth and stones, which, unless it were thrown up in order to shelter the house and pinfolds, is probably a tumulus. Whether being originally a tumulus, the founder of the cottage and pinfolds took advantage of it as a sheltered situation when he built the place; or whether it was worth his while to form so enormous a bank for that purpose. I cannot confidently judge; but much incline to the former opinion, and that it may now well merit to be opened as a barrow.

"The first subject of observation in the upper part of Starehole Bottom, was a straight rampart or barrow, in perfect preservation, 56 paces in length. It is vulgarly called the Giant's Grave, though the popular tradition is equally strong, that the whole Bottom is the site of a Danish settlement or encampment, and that there was a town in it which contained sixty dwellings, or, to use the language of the tradition itself, as cited by our guide, 'By the records of England it was a Danish town and had sixty dwellers,'— which he had heard from several ancient men, particularly the late Mr. Nicholas Adams, of Batson Hall; and he had understood likewise, that brass coins had been found by Mr. Fairweather's labourers very lately, in digging and ploughing the land, the vestiges having been but recently destroyed.

"The summit, or top ridge, of this rampart or tumulus (which seems to have been for defence rather than sepulture) preserves its original sharpness; and being composed I believe entirely of stones, is not likely to be deranged. One reason for supposing it a rampart for defence seems conclusive; it has a spacious ditch behind it and commands the valley. It runs south-east and north-west, and there is reason to conclude that it was once a square, but that the sides facing the south-east, north-west, and north-east, have been destroyed by agricultural operations.

COURTENAY WALK.

"In the field next below that in which the before-described appearances remain, was lately, our guide told us, a quadrangular tumulus exactly similar to that already described in Bury-park. It was like that too called the Church, and the field then called Church-park; but this last mentioned structure is now completely deranged by the agricultural operations of its owner, Mr. Fairweather, who is lessee of the premises under Viscount Courtenay.

"With respect to a town anciently standing in Starehole Bottom, whatever a deeper historical disquisition might make of it, certainly at present it exists in a general tradition of the neighbourhood as a town or harbour and habitation of our ancient foes the Danes, as above observed, and its situation and character so precisely suit the idea of a nest of pirates and predatory invaders, that I should think it difficult to support any other hypothesis concerning it If the expression may be allowed, it is nothing but a vast cavern above ground, faced by the sea and flanked by hideous, steep, impending rocks, that can neither be ascended or descended: the military economy of the Saxon is quite foreign to such a

VIEW FROM THE COURTENAY WALK.

situation. The grand gusto and more bold and decisive genius of the Roman would have disdained a hole fit only for plunder and the operations of banditti; and it must have been equally and totally impracticable as a trading port to the Phœnician, the Roman, and the Gaul "

Under the cliffs in Starehole Bay is a cavern, and the tradition in connection with it is, that it proceeds under the earth until it reaches near to Malborough church, which is nearly three miles distant in a north-west direction. None as yet have had daring or courage sufficient to penetrate far enough to ascertain to what length it extends. Hawkins says,—

"The dripping of water, by extinguishing the torches, added to the fear of otters which resort thither, has hitherto compelled the curious to abandon every design of penetrating to the end, few having advanced above a hundred yards. The path is narrow and winding, gradually lessening from the entrance, which is above seven feet in height, and four in breadth. On the left of the bay, and near the mouth of the cave, is an excavated rock, eight or nine feet high, and about five feet broad, forming a natural arch, opening towards the sea. It is not improbable that Bull hole and the interior of Starehole cavern form a junction."

THE BOLT HEAD. At the little ruined cottage in the declivity the road ceases. A tiring climb of twenty minutes through the pathless furze-bushes, brings the more enterprising traveller to the summit of the real cape, and the extended view that lies before him, with the fine insulated rock of Mewstone in the foreground, soon convinces him that he has reached his destination. The public right of way, however, after passing the ruined cottage, follows the beaten track up the vale for a short distance, and then suddenly turns to the left, and leads to the top of the headland, and so continues along the coast. If the pedestrian on reaching the headland has time to rest quietly and survey the scene, its loveliness will soon become peopled with active life. The crags will be lined with gulls, skuas, and cormorants; the gannet will throw its heavy white body, with a pounce, on to an unlucky fish, and the graceful terns dart hither and thither with their ear-piercing cry. As he lies basking in the sun, drinking in health and quiet of spirit with all the warm odours of the herbage, he will rejoice to realize that there are still nooks in this overworn country of ours where the birds and beasts live their own lives undisturbed.

In very clear weather the Eddystone lighthouse can be indistinctly seen away to the south-west, whilst inland the bold outlines of some of the highest peaks of Dartmoor cast their dark shadows against the distant horizon.

A very conspicuous variety of porpoise was observed off Bolt Head a few years since by a gentleman when sailing in his yacht. It was in company with a number of the normally black colour, which rendered it more conspicuous. It was white on the back, with the fins greyish, the rest of the body the same colour as the rest of the herds. It is exceedingly rare to meet with these specimens in these seas; but they are not uncommon off Newfoundland and the mouth of the river St Laurence.

The Bolt is rich in wild flowers and lichens, some of the latter being very rare and beautiful. The Burnet Rose, with its fragrant cream-coloured blooms and delicious scent; the yellow horned poppy, the climbing corydalis, the bird's-nest orchis, the vernal and autumnal squill, are among the rarer of the wild flowers. But Devonshire is the land, too, of ferns, and perhaps no place produces greater variety than just this immediate neighbourhood. There is, of course, abundance of falix-mas and filix-fœmina, dilatata, polystichum, polypody, adiantum-nigrum, marinum (at Sewer Mill Cove, a mile and a half along the cliff); what a pretty fern this is when growing at home by the sea. Nothing could be more charming than the contrast of its stiff glossy, dark green fronds and the rich amber of the rocks. Also, lanceolatum, and osmunda (on Bolberry Down).

Many rare specimens of butterflies are also to be found here. There are only two localities in Devonshire, as far as known, where that fine species, the large blue butterfly, can be found, and that is the coast between Bolt Head and Bolt Tail, on the mica-schist formation, and near Ashburton. The Hoary Footman, a very rare species, has been captured here in July, and the larvæ have been found feeding on lichens on the rocks; and that very rare and beautiful species, the Marbled Coronet, which appears on the wing in June, the Grass Egger Moth, and the Thrift Clearwing are also found at the Bolt.

SHARP TORS.

BOLT HEAD TO BOLT TAIL.

THE meaning of the word Bolt seems unexplained. Perhaps it is connected with the Icelandic bol *(boli)*, a bull; at all events, the t seems to be merely a euphonic termination, for the whole manor between Bolt Head and Bolt Tail is named Bolberry. It is a desolate country, sparsely peopled, open to the storms from the south and west, and possessing none of the sweet attractiveness of South Devon scenery. To walk from Bolt Head to Bolt Tail, a distance of nearly five miles, when the wind sets at all hard from the west, is a feat to be performed only with circumspection and patience. The wind blows through the thickest garments; to take one's bearings or glance at one's map it is needful to pull up behind some crag, and secure a footing, even under such protection, with considerable care. A large portion of the walk skirts land that it has been impossible to use, and which has been given over to twisted thorn-bushes and stunted furze; in places a little more protected corn and grass are cultivated. Seawards the view is majestic; the immense arc of waters, troubled in the wind, and flashing with multitudinous "white horses," is broken, in very clear weather, by the outline of the Eddystone Lighthouse, or the form of some passing ship. The iron-bound coast below standing deep in the snowy surf that boils and surges, rising and falling in rhymic motion, now half disappears in a shower of glistening spray, now lays its blackness naked to the air; and all the time the wind rings and shrieks around, playing upon the stalks of the harsh grass as on some shrill stringed instrument.

Along the whole distance almost every rock and inlet has its name, and some characteristic incident attached to it. Of wrecks there have been a large number along this coast, and much loss of life. After passing the Mewstone, there comes Off Cove, Long Cove, and Steeple Cove (so named from a steeple-like rock), Roberdean Point (probably deriving its name from some shipwreck),

Raven Rocks (which are exceedingly romantic), Water Cove, and Stanning's Cove. Roden Point forms the eastern entrance to Sewer Mill Cove, and here a foreign ship was wrecked in 1765, laden with marble statues, some of which were recovered and were supposed to have been taken to Powderham Castle. This spot has been the scene of many a sad shipwreck, and a few years since there was lost here the screw steamer *Ruperra*, laden with cotton-seed, and the Italian barque *Volere*, laden with walnut wood and marble. In connection with this latter wreck, five persons were drowned, including the captain and his wife. A more recent wreck still was that of the *Hallowe'en*, a full-rigged ship laden with tea from China, and some remains of this wreck are still to be seen at Sewer Mill Cove.

SEWER MILL COVE. This is an inlet of the sea, having a short strip of sand, and the scenery about here is magnificent and picturesque. At the eastern entrance is a grand cluster of rocks, called Neptune's Crown, and a little way up the valley, near South Down, is Hazel Tor, a rock peculiarly grand and sublime, and viewed from a point twenty to thirty feet below, and somewhat to the west of it, presents a magnificent appearance. The rocks at the entrance to this Cove are called Priest and Clerks, being one large and several small ones.

Hamstone, a barren islet or insulated rock, lies some little distance off this Cove, to which the wags of the vicinity consign those Benedicts of the neighbourhood, whose conjugal unions prove unfruitful; ideally peopling it with the parson, the doctor, the lawyer, &c.

Professor Adeney, of New Hamstead Congregational College, London, a short time since camped out with his family at Sewer Mill Cove. He sent the following account of his camping experience to the *Christian World*:—

"We are once more in camp. This is for the seventh time. We venture to think that we are no longer novices in the art of the patriarchs who "dwelt in tents," although we may not yet be experts. There are always some useful lessons to be learnt in the school of experience, and our experience has given us many a hint to smooth the course of the nomadic life. We have the most perfect camping ground I ever saw. We are at the extreme south of the county of Devon, four miles west of Salcombe, in a most glorious cove, half way between Bolt Head and Bolt Tail, with high, wild, rocky cliffs, clad with gorse and heather, rising on either side of us; broken hills behind, crowned with fantastic crags like Dartmoor tors, and the bluest of seas in front of us, with a small island called Hamstone Rock, guarding the entrance of our cove. Our camp is pitched on a little knoll about 15 feet above the sands One stream runs down the valley to our right, and another down the valley to our left, and we are just at the point where they almost meet. There is a spring in the hillside where the sweetest, coolest water trickles out from mosses and spleenworts, and joins the larger right-hand stream among the water cresses. This is our drinking water. "There's iron in that water," said the farmer who pointed it out to me, "and it will cure anyone who has bad lungs." The air is cool and fresh, as it blows about our tents, but the sun is shining in his splendour, and the scene is one of exceeding beauty. When we bathe there are caves to explore which can only be reached while the tide is low, and after rounding a promontory of rock. A wreck lies out in the bay, for, three years ago, a large vessel came on the rocks in the fog. This coast is literally iron-bound, and the iron in the cliffs deflects the compass. They say that when the ship broke up, the shore was strewn with tea, tons upon tons of it forming a great bank right across the cove.

I think the greatest charm of this life of ours, in the midst of one of the wildest scenes of Nature, is to be found in the night sights and sounds that surround our encampment. Then we are utterly alone with Nature—three miles from a village, the nearest farmhouse out of sight up the windings of the valley. As the darkness settles down over land and sea, various objects begin to assume new forms; on the hilltop, one great mass of rock stands out against the sky like the dark profile of an old man with a tumulous nose and a large beard, while behind him his wife displays an unlovely and bibulous countenance. I was strolling on the little terrace in front of our tents late one evening with my eldest daughter, when I saw, as I thought, a lady in white muslin, with long, black kid gloves, standing alone on the slope, gazing at our encampment. Though my daughter laughed as she detected in my visitant a stone that marks the coastguard's path, I never go to my tent at night, without involuntary turning my eyes towards the silent watcher. This I record without fearing the scoffs of the frivolous, because it is just a piece of that almost weird transformation of the most familiar objects that the wizard

THE BOLT HEAD.

night has the power of effecting, in a lonely retreat far from all disturbing signs of the world's common life. When the moon was at the full, she shone straight over her silver path on the sea into the entrance of my tent; a little later in the month she shed a strange shimmer over the sky from beyond the broken crags on the eastern hill; and when there was no moon, the solemn starlight lay on sea and shore, and dim and dusky objects round the camp, peopled the solitude with their ghostly presence. Then there come the night sounds, which easily penetrate to the

SEWER MILL COVE.

seclusion of the tent. You wake up again and again on the calmest of nights to hear the gentle, melancholy wash of the restless waters, while overhead and out across the waves, the sea gulls' cry rises loud and high and wild."

In a second article describing the "Camp in a Gale," Professor Adeney says,—

"We have now finished a month's camping at Sewer Mill Cove, the grandest spot in all South Devon. Rustic diet, fresh air, sunshine, and salt-water, among scenes of surpassing interest, have combined to recommend our much maligned method of holiday-making as in every way a success. If, therefore, I now proceed to chronicle some of our more anxious moments I hope they will not be read as specimens of the whole time. It was the end of a fair and sunny Sunday. The wind rose and lashed the 'wild, white horses' into madness as they raced up the sands, or tore themselves to fragments on the crags. Darkness came down early on an angry sea and a wind-swept shore. For the better part of the night I was the sentinel, perambulating the tents to tighten a cord here, to drive in a stake there. Showers of rain were alternated with the clearest sky, in which the stars shone as on a frosty night. On emerging from my tent after a little rest and refuge while the rain had been heaviest, I was positively startled to see the changed aspect of the heavens. Never before had I been so struck with the moving of the celestial panorama. Ruddy Mars was now glaring over a hill to the south; in the east there was a pale greenish gleam of light, which rapidly brightened into the ghost of a sunrise. It was a moonrise, and the sickly lines that preceded the appearance of the satellite were soon followed by the sudden emergence of her brilliant disk. Meanwhile we stood the gale, and in the morning it abated. One day, while we were bathing, we noticed a low, rumbling sound, and directly after this, we were startled to observe that the sea had retreated several yards, although the tide was flowing at the time. The next day we were over at the picturesque fisher hamlet of Hope—a favourite haunt of artists, on the further side of Bolt Tail—and there we learnt that at the time of our sea movement such a phenomenon had been seen as the oldest inhabitant had never before witnessed. Though the sea was quite calm, all of a sudden it ran up far above high water mark, floating the fishermen's boats and the baskets that were lying about on the beach; and then as suddenly it drew right back beyond low water mark. The astonished inhabitants ran out of their houses to see this startling eccentricity of behaviour on the part of their familiar sea.

We had a second and worse gale. In my previous sketch I mentioned a little rocky island, that stands out to sea about half-a-mile from our cove. We had thought we should like to have a bungalow there; but now the sea came right over it, shooting up twice its height, spreading out a vast mass of white waters, that completely hid it for a few moments, and then leaving a lacework of milky streams all over its cracked and weather-worn surface. Then a strange thing happened. In the middle of the night, suddenly there came down a deluge of rain from the north. In half a-minute the gale of wind had vanished, driven back, cowed, and crushed by this new-comer. A coastguard and an old resident both told me they had never known such rain in the neighbourhood. It flooded the farmer's kitchen in the west valley, and spoilt the stores in his wife's larder. A little moisture came through our tents, but it was only a spray, and nothing to hurt."

Dragon Bay is the next place arrived at, after leaving Sewer Mill Cove, so called because of the wreck here in 1757 of a London ship bearing the name of *Dragon*. A family called Chambers were drowned in connection with this wreck, and their bodies were recovered and interred at Malborough, where a slate headstone was erected bearing the following inscription:—

"Here lye the bodies of Rhodes, Daniel, Mary, and Joseph Chambers, sons and daughters of Edward Chambers, of Jamaica, who were shipwrecked at Cathole, within this parish, August 23rd, 1757."

Then comes Lantern Rock, supposed to be so-called from its whimsical appearance, and a little further on is Goss' Wall, supposed to be half way between Bolt Head and Bolt Tail. The land adjacent is called Cathole, supposed to have been anciently a resort for wild cats. Beyond the wall, on Bolberry Down, is an oval pit, with a bank or mound, three or four perches long, which is thought to have been a military station. Close here is a wild piece of ground, near two very large stones of equal size, called Pixy Dance. This is said to have been the principal resort of the fairies, in Devonshire called pixies, and they are reported to have been often seen here playing their endless varieties of whim and vagary.

The open down or common stretching away inland and to the west is called Bolberry Down, and here were established on the 29th May, 1768, the Kingsbridge Races, or, what were then called, in order to avoid the penalties, "The Kingsbridge Annual Diversions," where prizes for less than £50 were competed for. They were held every year in the month of June, until 1771, when they were removed to a better course on Middle Sewer farm, and continued until 1782, when they were changed to a place in East Allington parish, being discontinued the same year, and then gave origin to the Totnes Races.

THE COAST WEST OF SEWER MILL COVE.

Ralph's Hole is situated nearly on the top of the cliffs of Bolberry Down, and is a cavern about twenty feet long, six or seven feet broad, and eight feet high. It is directly facing the sea, which is between 400 and 500 feet below in almost a perpendicular direction. There is a rock at the west corner of the entrance, which projects to within two or three feet of the precipice, in such manner that a single person from within might easily defend his habitation against a host of foes, for the cavern is only approached by doubling this rock, only one being able to pass at a time, and that with considerable difficulty, so that they might successively be tumbled down the precipice. There is a tradition that at some remote period a person called Ralph made this place his abode for many years. It is supposed by some that he was a pirate or malefactor, having taken refuge here from the bailiffs or constables. With a prong for his weapon, he kept his pursuers constantly at bay. On Sundays he was accustomed to wander abroad, his wife assisting him through the remainder of the week in getting provisions. No date is specified when this notorious person lived, and if he ever did exist, it is probable he was a noted smuggler.

The coast about here abounds with iron, but not in sufficient quantities to pay for working. John Easton, of Dodbrooke, commenced a copper mine in 1770 not far from Ralph's Hole, but did not proceed long before he discovered it was only mundic, the place being afterwards known as Easton's Mine. John Cranch, who investigated this neighbourhood in 1799, says, "about twenty yards from Easton's Mine is a most admirable and abundant chalybeate spring, moderately impregnated, very pure, and grateful to the taste." The most valuable discovery, however, has recently been made, gold being found, it is said, in sufficient quantities as to warrant the formation of a syndicate for working the same. Quantities of plumbago have also been discovered in the same vicinity.

Slippery Point is just beyond Ralph's Hole, and then comes the Graystone, upon which is a coastguard look-out house. Ramillies Cove is so named because of a terribly sad event that happened here. H.M.S. *Ramillies*, of 74 guns and 734 men, was overtaken in a terriffic gale on the 15th February, 1760, near this coast. She was commanded by Captain Taylor, and mistaking Bolt Tail for Rame Head, the vessel was running in, as those on board supposed, for Plymouth Sound, but really on to the rocky shore near the Bolt Tail. The mistake was discovered too late for the safety of the vessel, for she became embayed, and when near the rocks, the anchors were let go, and all the masts were cut away. She rode, however, in safety until the evening, when the gale increased to such an extent, that the cables parted, and the vessel drove on shore, when she soon broke up. Out of the 734 persons on board, only one midshipman and twenty-five men were able to save themselves by jumping off the stern on to the rocks. It is stated that some of the guns of this ill-fated ship are still lying in from seven to eight fathoms of water off the mouth of this Cove. There is a cavern here, and it is so peculiarly situated that it can only be entered by boats at certain states of the tide in very calm weather. It cannot be seen from any part of the cliffs above.

The Bolt Tail is not a very lofty headland. but it projects far into the sea The extreme knot of rock which is Bolt Tail is partly separated from the mass of the headland by a valley running north and south. The view is entirely different from that obtained at the Bolt Head. Bolt Tail commands Bigbury Bay and the whole west coast of the county, as the Start commands Start Bay and the east coast The furthest of all the headlands in view is Rame Head in Cornwall, and the breach in the coast directly above is Cawsand Bay leading to Plymouth Sound. Wembury Point and Stoke Point come next, enclosing between them the mouth of the river Yealm; then Kingston Head, covering the estuary of the Erme. Right in front stands Burrow Island, a fine mass standing out to sea in front of the Avon River; from its crags

Turner contemplated the Bolt Tail with delight through a summer afternoon. Nearer still, the curious object a few hundred yards from the shore, like two children's bricks set on end and tilted against one another, is Thurlestone Rock, with Thurlestone Church upon the cliff behind it, and closer still, almost at our feet, is the picturesque village of Hope.

SALCOMBE TO HOPE COVE.

LEAVING Salcombe by the Malborough road, just after passing the Knowle, on the left, is a lawn tennis court, recently laid out, open to visitors by the payment of a small weekly subscription. Proceeding by way either of the Onslow Road or Bonfire Hill, the main road to Malborough is soon reached. A short distance on this road there is a turning to the right, which leads to Higher Batson. Here there is a very ancient house, but fast getting into ruins, called Batson Hall, belonging to Mr. Bastard, of Kitley. Though now covered with ivy and very much dilapidated, it still bears traces that at one time it was a house of some importance; but local tradition says that it was once a prison. In the yard in front of the house there are some interesting ruins.

ILTON CASTLE. Continuing on the main road, and, when about half way to Malborough, another lane branches off to the right leading to Ilton. Some little distance from here is the site of the ancient Ilton or Ithelstone Castle. Not a vestige of it can be seen at the present time, and it must have fallen into a ruinous state, and so have become removed at a very early date, for in the middle of the eighteenth century the place had become overgrown with brambles, so that not a stone of the building was to be seen, but in 1780, on this being cleared away, traces of the foundation were discoverable, which showed that the building must have been a square structure, and flanked with turrets. As early as King Henry II. time, it was the dwelling of a person named Bozun, whose inheritance after some time became divided between two daughters. One married Sir Hugh Ferrers, and the other Sir John Chiverston, who is supposed to have erected the castle in 1335. After him it came into possession of his son, and then of his grandson. This

VIEW FROM BONFIRE HILL.

grandson married a daughter of Hugh Courtenay, the ancestor of the future Earls of Devon, on whom he settled the house and land, as he died without issue, and it remained in the family of the Earls of Devon up to the time of the sale of the Devon estates a few years since. In the sixteenth century it must occasionally have been the residence of Sir William Courtenay, for we find that in November, 1588, eight of the officers of the *St. Peter the Great*, one of the ships belonging to the Spanish Armada, and which vessel was wrecked at Hope Cove, were lodged in his custody at Ilton Castle. This place must have been used as a kind of prison, for we find that during the siege of Salcombe Castle, the Parliamentary forces employed in the undertaking were often committing deeds of plunder and violence to the inhabitants of known Royalist proclivities, and would convey them to Ilton Castle as prisoners. On the 12th March, 1646, they attacked the house of Mr. William Randall, of Mill, Stokenham. The soldiers, after making several fruitless attempts to enter the house at night, fired through the window, wounding Mr. Randall's daughter in the breast, from which she died a few days afterwards. Mr. Randall the next day was taken prisoner and conveyed to Ilton Castle, where he was shamefully treated, and frequently threatened with death. His son took food to him daily, but the jailors cruelly told him every time that he need bring no more food, for, said they, pointing to a gallows near, "to-morrow he will be hanging there." Mr. Randall, however, remained faithful to the Royalist cause, and obtained his liberty when Cromwell became Protector.

It must be 100 years ago that the last vestige of the old castle was destroyed. When the castle was built by Sir John Chiverston in 1335, England was at war with France and Scotland, and no doubt King Edward III. was glad to have the noblemen build up places of defence in his own country. A few years since some alterations were being made to an old barn when there was found in the wall a pentagonal granite pillar, which must have come from the old castle. At the back door of the farmhouse is a beautifully turned arch in the form of a semi circle; this was very likely a tithe barn. The orchard is terraced, and the ground about here has many indications of old buildings. The stone is soft, and if the castle was built with it, it would not be any difficulty for an opposing force to demolish. It is quite possible that more about the old castle may be found out some day, and its history would be very interesting. A large meadow adjoining the existing farmhouse shews indications of its being the site of the castle.

Continuing our journey towards Malborough, Yarde is passed on the right, although the house cannot be seen from the roadway. Formerly it belonged to a family of that name, and is said to have been in their possession for twenty generations. Toward the end of the fourteenth century it changed hands, and came into the possession of the Dyers, and in 1765 Mr. Samuel Savery, became possessed of it, who died in 1790, and is buried in Malborough, in the Yarde vault, near the chancel. It has changed hands again since then.

MALBOROUGH is situated on very high land, commanding an extensive prospect, and was, doubtless, in the far away past a place of some importance, as its name would suggest—"*Mal*," meaning a meeting place. The village is divided into two parts, known respectively as Higher Town and Lower Town. A portion of the village was formerly in the parish of West Alvington, but it has now been added to the parish of Malborough to which properly it belongs. The parish up to a recent date formed part of the Vicarage of West Alvington, but, together with South Huish, was made a separate vicarage. The Church of All Saints is evidently an ancient structure, whilst the chancel, tower, and spire appear to be of greater antiquity, and formed part of a previous building. The register, however, does not date earlier than the year 1640. The Church is a very spacious one, and is built in the Perpendicular style, consisting of chancel, nave, and aisles. The chancel window of stained glass was erected in memory of Mr. Andrew Pinwill, of Salcombe; whilst the other in the south aisle was given anonymously. In 1870 the church was thoroughly restored at a cost of £2,502, it having been entirely re-seated, new roofs constructed, the windows re-filled with stone mullions and tracery, and the old gallery under the tower removed, the place there being thrown open, and the bells rung from the floor. There is a set of six bells, two of them being re-cast and the whole re-hung in 1879. The church contains a curious old font, a piscina, and a stoup. The living is in the gift of the Dean and Chapter of Sarum. Some of the monuments in the church and the graveyard speak of the sad loss of life on the sea coast of this parish. The spire has been twice struck with lightning, and on one of the occasions, which occurred in the month of August, 1829, it was accompanied by a very strange and peculiar incident. A parishioner, whose descendants still reside at Salcombe, had died a few days previously, and before death he had stated that if he was not buried before mid-day, his friends would have difficulty in burying him. The relatives were not able to get him interred before mid-day, but, strange to relate, just after the arrival of the funeral party at the church, and whilst the officiating clergyman was engaged in reading the burial service, there came on a fearful thunderstorm, and the flashes of lightning were so vivid and the thunder so appalling, one flash of lightning striking the church spire, that the utmost consternation and alarm took hold of clergyman and the funeral party, insomuch that all rushed out of church, leaving the corpse behind, and they did not return until the storm had passed away.

Previous to the erection of the church at Salcombe, all the dead were taken to Malborough for interment, and it must have been a dreary addition to the slow and painful pageantry of death, to toil, perhaps in rain or storm, more than two tedious miles up into this exposed village. The body died in the soft air, among the ripening lemons, blossoming aloes, and half tropic luxuries of the sea-side town, but could not rest among them. On sunny days a pleasanter fancy might possess the mind of the bereaved, for Malborough church is the highest point for miles, a beacon for all the parishes round; and those left behind, and scattered here and there, might rejoice that they all could see the resting-place of their dead.

The charities are of the net annual value of £130, and belong jointly to Malborough and Salcombe. The income is derived principally from rents of cottages and land bequeathed by Richard Dyer and Mrs. Alice Bayning; the former directed that £4 per annum be appropriated to paying a schoolmaster for instructing a certain number of poor boys. A portion of the proceeds of these charities are devoted to the maintenance of the fabric of the

ILTON CASTLE FARMHOUSE.

church at Malborough, the remainder being administered by a body of trustees. There is a Baptist chapel, erected in 1815 and enlarged in 1872, situated here. New National Schools were erected in 1873, the cost being largely borne by the charity funds of the parish. The school is a mixed one, taught by a master.

Passing Malborough there are two ways of getting to

Hope,—one road branching off to the left, and then to the right, proceeding as due west as possible for about two miles, passing the hamlet of Bolbury on the way. The traveller has need to use his compass, or he may never find his way through these muffled and serpentine lanes, so narrow that the ferns almost touch one another at the top, and the last shoots of the brambles do positively get entangled. It is a country full of streams, clean shoots of spring coolness starting at every turn out of little mossy caverns in the wayside, keeping the ponds and tiny golden pebbles in an eternal agitation by the precipitating of their waters. Here and there among the apple-orchards a cluster of farm buildings peeps out in all its beautiful decay, a mere cluster of ivy and cotoniaster, old thatch and immemorial house-leek. The men, women, and children will be most likely away to work, and the humanity of the place will be represented by a dog that barks with the pleasure of hearing a footstep, a group of stately geese, or a long row of pigeons presenting their delicate necks on the ridge of an ancient barn. At last the bright line of Bigbury Bay comes into view, a hasty descent, and the sea-side village of Hope is reached.

GALMPTON. Another, but longer, yet more frequented way of reaching Hope from Malborough is through the village of Galmpton, in the parish of South Huish. This parish is situated in a deep vale of romantic beauty, and extends to Bigbury Bay. The old church of St. Andrew cannot be seen from the main road, but it is in a very ruinous condition and unused. It is a small ancient edifice of cragstone, with plain square tower and four bells, and the eastern window is mantled with ivy. Some time since there were found imbedded in the east wall of the transept some very interesting alabaster carvings, but they were in a sadly mutilated state. In 1867, whilst the clergyman was conducting service, one of the windows was blown in, and then it was determined to construct a new church; but the major part of the inhabitants being at Galmpton and Outer Hope, it was decided to erect the structure at the former village. The site was given by Lord Devon, and the fabric is in the Early English style, consisting of a chancel, nave, north transept, and one bell. The windows in the chancel are all filled with rich and beautiful stained glass, placed there to the memory of the late Lord Justice Sir George Turner. The church was consecrated in July, 1869, and is dedicated to the Holy Trinity, the cost of erection being over £2,000. The register dates from the year 1565. There is also a chapel at Galmpton used by the Plymouth Brethren, a day school being held on the same premises. A National School was also erected here some years ago.

HOPE COVE. Leaving Galmpton the road gradually descends for about a mile, and the village of Outer Hope is arrived at, only separated from Inner Hope by a short road that rapidly ascends and then just as rapidly descends. These villages are situated under the shelter of the rocky and precipitous headland of the Bolt Tail. There is one small but respectable Inn, the Hope and Anchor, usually monopolised by artists, and two or three comfortable little cottages at Outer Hope where visitors may find lodgings. Stretching so far south one would naturally expect to see evidence of the genial temperature in garden produce, but, beyond a tall fuchsia or two hanging its crimson tassels by some white-walled cottage, there is little to indicate a climate where the orange and lemon might ripen without the help of glass, and every sheltered nook rejoice in the beauty of an almost tropical luxuriance But the all-absorbing nature of a fisherman's occupation seems to leave little margin for gardening; his "bread is on the waters," his garden is the sea. The fishermen of Hope Cove are a hardy and independent race, but civil and obliging Some of their honest faces are familiar, perhaps, to visitors to the Royal Academy through the inimitable pictures of Hook; his "Crabbers" and "Seaside Ducks" were painted at Hope. Although gardening in this part of Devonshire is of the most primitive description, the lanes and hedge-rows are a never failing source of interest to the botanist and fern hunter. The cliff scenery, too, is magnificent. Hewn and chiselled by the keen edge of the storm, draped and fringed and tasselled with wild flowers, ferns, and dwarf shrubs, the rocky ledges garnished with the spotted eggs of countless sea birds, every few steps reveal some fresh object of interest and delight to the naturalist and the artist. Of the many species of wild flowers which abound in the hedge-rows a large proportion possess fragrance, and the short soft grass along the cliff walks abounds with elegant little floral gems. Among them is a curious little Orchid, about six inches high, having a spiral wreath of lavender-pink flowers surrounding the stem (*Neottia spiralis*). Shakespeare's man, "He who gathers samphire—awful trade," need not have endangered his neck at Hope. The cliffs (which belong to the chlorite and mica schist system) are in many places completely covered with its dull Mesembryanthemum-like leaves, and greenish yellow blossoms.

The Shippens, the look-out of the coastguards, is a commanding and important eminence, and from here may be obtained the most extensive view of the surrounding coast and neighbourhood. Close to the flagstaff is an old cannon recovered from the wreck of the *Ramillies*.

There is a beach, which is nicely sheltered, and the place ought to become a favourite resort for visitors. During certain winds vessels put in here for shelter, but probably never so many at one time as on the 3rd day of September, 1855, when there were nearly sixty vessels anchored within a short distance of each other, and these usually quiet villages, by the influx of sailors, became a scene of great animation.

On the side of the hill which separates the two villages, a chapel-of-ease was built in 1862, at the expense of the late Earl of Devon and Sir George Turner, but since the erection of the church at Galmpton, it is only used occasionally. At Inner Hope there is a neat and commodious Wesleyan chapel.

The Coastguard Station is at Inner Hope, and also a station of the Royal National Lifeboat Institution. The lifeboat and house were given by the Grand Lodge of Freemasons of England as a thank-offering for the recovery of the Prince of Wales from a dangerous illness, in 1877, and the boat is named the Alexandria. In the old wrecking and smuggling days, the inhabitants of these villages played an important part in it.

HOPE BAY.

OUT OF THE BEATEN TRACK.—The following article appeared in the *Echo* from the pen of Luke Ellis:—

"Year by year it becomes more difficult to get away from the busy haunts of men to where Dame Nature tarries awhile alone in her glory; out of the sound of shrieking engines and rumbling wheels; away from the tumult and unrest of crowded streets. There are still, however, some quiet nooks where one may, for a

few days, breathe genial air, and refresh the jaded spirits, not only with the sight of
"Fresh woods and pastures new,"
but the ever-shifting pictures of sea and sky and cliff which engirdle sunny Devon, and the more rugged and picturesque old county further West.

It is not everyone, sound of wind and limb though he may be, that likes east wind, even when unmingled with keen, biting sleet. How delightful the change must be to those who can hurry away

THE SQUARE, INNER HOPE.

to the shores of the Mediterranean, put the eternal hills at their back, and blue seas in front of them, while the green slopes are reddening in the rosy hues of windflower, the golden narcissi or the squills and scillas that outvie in turquoise hues the heavens above them. Is it possible to discover at home, here in England, a genial air that the afflicted may breathe in the open at a time when east winds prevail? A place remote from towns—a happy valley, fragrant of spring, vocal with bird music, with firm sands, lichened boulders, a homely cottage to live in, wholesome food, and of the human kind, a hardy race of the toilers of the sea. Our destination is as far south as one can go. A hugh barrier of mica schist fends the little village from the east. The western limit is a rocky promontory called the Bolt Tail—the eastern, the Bolt Head. Under the Tail nestles the little village of Hope. As one saunters down the steep, narrow road, with its margins aglow with wild flowers and crowded with ferns, the sea stretches before us, flecked with white-sailed fishing-boats and various craft on their way down Channel, and, gradually, as evening draws in, one can distinguish, at 16 miles' distance, the Eddystone Lighthouse.

I was on a visit to a friend, and had no occasion to seek lodging. A clean little lime-washed cottage, whose windows afforded a charming land and sea scape, gave the fair, quiet and sweet rest that was needed. The measured pulsings of the tide, the splash and gurgle of the waves among the smooth boulders, the cry of sea-birds, or the "Yo, ho!" of the fishermen as they hauled up their boats on the beach, were all significant.

It occurred to me while sauntering about among the fishermen next morning that I had seen several of their faces before somewhere, and then I was informed that Mr. J. C. Hook, R.A., the inimitable sea painter, had made a stay in the village, and that his "Seaside Ducks" and some other pictures were painted here. Fish abounds, especially the crustacea round the foot of the rocky promontory. Now and again the smart little clipper ran over from Plymouth to collect the catch. While watching a hale, old man, a retired coastguardsman, I was invited to go out with him after mackerel. So we pulled to the white line that separates the rough water from the smooth. John hoists the sail, and like a white-winged bird the little craft skims over the blue waves. "Out with your line, sir," says John, and with a plated minnow armed with hooks it is dropped with a score yards of line, and gleams through the water with a phosphorescent glow. "Now you have him, sir; keep the line taut, and haul in without slacking." So it came swirling through the glittering waves like a silver flagon. The bottom of the boat was soon covered with a gorgeous mass of iridescent colour, green and purple, carmine and silver; how the brilliant yet subtle tones varied as the sunlight smote them! But the wind dropped. We took in sail and pulled back, waiting, as we approached shallower water, to try for sea bream. After taking a couple score even when almost dark, the Eddystone beamed brighter still, and the friendly light in our cottage window signalled us home.

And then what a feast we had! While waiting for the preparations, a brother of the brush tapped at the window to inquire if we would like some mushrooms. It is strange the natives don't seem to care for them. So our friend, just as the moon was rising, stalked onward to the sloping banks of the Bolt Tail, and quickly gathered a peck. Mackerel and stewed mushrooms, with a dish of snow-flaked potatoes, formed a delicious meal. I was told a somewhat singular circumstance—that fishermen—these, at least—prefer, fresh-caught fish to butcher's meat A healthy, contented, and sober life, the men seemed to enjoy; there is just enough spice of danger in the calling—going day after day, with their lives in their hands, has evidently a sobering influence, so one seldom hears the boisterous merriment and the "loud laugh that speaks the vacant mind." I have noticed this thoughtful quietness of demeanour elsewhere.

There is a magnificent view from the cliff, hundreds of feet below which the Atlantic breakers are thundering all day long. Wild life is especially abundant—rare birds, fox, badger, otter, hares, rabbits, stoats, and weasels. The cliffs are clothed with ivy, bramble, clematis, ferns, affording the botanist as well as the naturalist, a splendid field for research. Among the rarer birds frequenting this part are the osprey, sand grouse, peregrine, falcon, hoopoe, waxwing, nightjar, and Cornish chough The same anomaly is observable here with regard to gardening—with a climate capable, as one may notice, of ripening oranges in the open air, there is an utter indifference to cultivation of either fruit or flowers."

SOME SEA-VILLAGES.—Miss Marianne Farningham, writing to the *Christian World* says,—

"There are two delightful places in South Devon, beloved of artists, and known to few besides, which are called Hope Cove and Thurlestone. The map of Devon reveals several considerable spaces as yet untouched by the railway; and among them is that which forms the extreme South of the county, and includes the land that lies above Prawle Point, from Start Bay on the East to Bigbury Bay on the West. Those who wish to be "Far from the maddening crowd," and hold communion with Nature, who find their books in rocks, and can make companions of birds and flowers, may obtain here a Paradise of rest and pure pleasure. There are, indeed, plenty of villages to select from, but Hope is one of the best. Is it not a pretty name? There are seventeen or eighteen places in the British Isles that bear the same name; but surely the Hope of Devonshire is the loveliest of them all. It is only a few miles from Salcombe, and it is close to the sea. The climate is delightful, such as may be enjoyed in the South of France, on the shores of the sunny Mediterranean. It is sheltered by the rocky headland of Bolt Tail, and on all sides there is the

COAST SCENE AT HOPE.

grand beauty of hill and valley, rock and sea. The village is small, but extremely picturesque. Most of the houses are thatched, and a little artistic taste has been employed even in the thatching, so that they have a difference from that of the same class of cottages in the inland towns of the midland counties. There is a small inn, which is usually occupied by artists, for almost every year at the Academy are pictures which have been painted at Hope. Here there is quite enough to satisfy those who dislike noise the most; and the possibility of long days of uninterrupted work, such as life's busy places long for in vain. Also there are men and women of strong and striking individuality, whose faces are worth painting, and whose conversations are worth listening to. These people have lived by the sea; their bread is on the waters, the waves and the wind have spoken to them, and in their brown faces and flashing eyes there are the marks of intercourse with nature. They reverence the sea, and even fear it more than strangers do, because they better know its power. They have been robbed of their comrades in the great depths of the ocean; women have lost their husbands, and fathers, sons, and brothers, who will not be restored to them until the sea gives up its dead; and although they find it for the most part gentle, and even generous, they do not trust it overmuch, and a considerable portion of their time is spent in watching the clouds and the winds, and in speculating upon the weather.

What a mighty power this wind is the Hope people know as well as any. Even on a lovely summer's day there is a fresh breeze blowing, and the leaping waves are glorious sights to see. There is a magnificent walk over the downs to Thurlestone Sands, and the larks sing, and the wild flowers blossom, and the sea is so beautiful that such a walk will be long remembered. Thurlestone is so named from a curious "Thirled" or pierced rock which stands up in the sea, as brave and resolute as ever, though a million storms have tried to beat it down. Through its arch the waters rush with a tremendous noise when the weather is rough, and the marvel is that the rock has such powers of resistance. It has given to the people of the neighbourhood a motto, which may be passed on—

        Bear every shock
        Like Thurlestone rock.

The coast is altogether interesting. This arched rock of red conglomerate, thirty feet high and forty long, resting on Devonian clay slates, is of itself enough to make it so; but besides this there are signs of a submerged forest here, and lovely sands and lofty cliffs to explore. An ideal summer holiday might be spent either at Thurlestone, or Inner or Outer Hope."

HOPE COVE TO BANTHAM.

THE whole of the coast line, from Bolt Tail to Stoke Point, near the entrance to Plymouth Sound, forms Bigbury Bay, but it is not our intention to extend our journey westward further than Bantham on the eastern side of the river Avon, and whilst the visitor is at Hope Cove, he will be at the best point for starting on his peregrinations to view what is worth seeing on this coast. In this neighbourhood there is much that is interesting and picturesque, and some portion of the coast has many a harrowing tale of shipwreck and disaster to record.

On some part of the coast near Hope Cove, there came on shore in the November gales of 1588, one of the ships attached to the Spanish Armada. Attached to this invading fleet were two hospital ships, and one of them was named *St. Peter the Great*, and this was the vessel that came on shore. She had outlived many of the storms that had wrought much havoc and destruction to some of the larger and more important vessels of the fleet, and had apparently made the entire circuit of our Islands. She was over 500 tons burthen, a large ship for those days, and being a hospital ship, was laden with drugs and medical stores When she left Spain she was in charge of thirty mariners, having also one hundred soldiers, and fifty persons attached to the hospital on board. The adverse winds and circumstances they had met with, together with disappointed hopes and expectations, had thoroughly dispirited the crew, and in the month of November, 1588, the ship was driven on to the rocks near Hope Cove, and she soon became a total wreck. Of the 180 persons on board when she started from Spain, only 140 were saved from the wreck, the remainder having either died during the voyage or were drowned at the time of the casualty. The people of adjacent villages were soon on the spot, and so vigorously did they set to work in plundering both ship and crew, that they secured all the plate and treasure, and even the seamen's chests were not secure against the raids of these greedy wreckers. Mr George Cary, a Deputy Lieutenant of the county, heard of the wreck at Plymouth, and at once proceeded to the scene of the disaster, and on his arrival found the hull full of water, shortly after breaking to pieces, and the drugs and "potecary stuff," of 6000 ducats value, nearly all spoiled by the sea water. The ordnance, however, was saved. A few years ago several Armada coins, evidently belonging to those on board this ship, were found on the sands at Hope. The coins were about the size of a florin, and on one side was a Maltese cross, whilst on the other could be deciphered the Spanish arms surmounted with the royal crown, and in some the name of Philip could be made out. Most of the coins were very much worn by the action of the sea water.

The whole of the crew were taken prisoners, and 120 of them were located in one house, being supplied with all necessary food; whilst 20 of the officers were disposed of as follows; ten of them were sent into Kingsbridge; the apothecary and surgeon were taken charge of by Mr. Cary himself at his residence at Cockington; and eight were sent to Ilton Castle, in charge of Sir William Courtenay. The whole were guarded night and day, and Mr. Cary assigned to each prisoner one penny per day out of his private means until the pleasure of Her Majesty's Privy Council was made known. With the exception of the two with Mr. Cary, the prisoners were left in charge of Anthony Ashley, Clerk of the Council, who took up his abode at Ilton Castle with Sir William Courtenay. It would appear that orders were first given for the prisoners to be executed; but this order having been countermanded, Mr. Ashley took down the names, offices, and quality of each, and if any were able to purchase their liberty, note was taken of such. He made a report to the Council on the 12th November, and in it he writes of the prisoners:—

"X or XII of the best sorte are placed in a towne called Kingsbridge, where order is taken for the provision of their wants, and accompt kept of their expense. The rest until your Lpps. further pleasure knowen, are remaining together in one house, whither they were first committed, where they are safe kept, and provided of necessarie food."

In the same report he says:—

"By late examinations taken of the Spaniardes, I fynde that certain besar stones and other simples was purloyned out of the shippe, of which besar stones I hope to recover the most of them. I have been bould to staie this messenger hitherto, thinking I should have been able to have advertised some certaintie of them, but must now leave the same to my return, which shall be as speedilie as I maie."

THURLESTONE ROCK.

On taking the coast route for Thurlestone the path is approached by a gate immediately after leaving Outer Hope, as seen in our view on page 140, but it is only available for pedestrians. It is little more than half-a-mile to the commencement of Thurlestone Sands, the visitor being amply repaid for his exertions, by the magnificent view obtained from this cliff road. Persons riding or driving have to proceed considerably inland, taking a road near Galmpton to bring them to Thurlestone Sands. These Sands extend for nearly a mile along the coast.

Lying just off the eastern end of these Sands is an arched rock of red Triassic conglomerate, resting upon Devonian clay slates. It is the most remarkable and peculiar rock on the south coast, and stands about thirty feet high, whilst it is forty feet long. The hole is twenty feet in height by ten broad. It can be approached at low water spring tides, and in a storm a peculiar noise, heard at a great distance, is caused by the rush of water through this hole, and is generally considered as an indication of approaching rain. From its singular natural arch, as the "thirled" or pierced rock, Thurlestone parish takes its name, and not from Thor, as is sometimes supposed. The parish appears in Domesday as Torlestan, held in demesne by Judhel of Totnes, with a soldier as under tenant, and an enumerated population of thirty-five. About one mile inland is the village of South Milton. The church of All Saints in this village is in the perpendicular style, consisting of chancel, nave, aisles, south porch, and a square embattled tower with six bells. The chancel retains its sedilia and piscina, and there is also a piscina in the south transept, and a stoop in the south doorway. The font, said to be Saxon, is surmounted by a conical carved wood cover; in the church is also a carved oak screen, very old. In 1885 the church was restored and re-seated, and the south transept new roofed, the works costing close on £1,400. The living is a vicarage in the gift of the Dean and Chapter of Salisbury. The register dates from the year 1600. The Wesleyans have a chapel in the village, erected in 1882.

There are indications that some portions of Thurlestone Sands form the site of a submerged forest. It was here, about the year 1772, that the wreck of the *Chantiloupe* occurred, a vessel returning from the West Indies. Those were the days when wrecking was practised in all its worst excess, and tortured with the fear of being murdered, a wealthy lady of the name of Burke put on her richest dresses, and awaited the final shock with her necklaces about her bosom, and her hands covered with jewellery. It is supposed that she was related to the famous Edmund Burke, for as soon as the wreck of the vessel was known in London, he came down and stayed in the neighbourhood, stating that a relative of his was, he feared, on board. Most probably he never heard what her fate was. By a strange coincidence, with the exception of one man, she was the only person thrown on shore alive, but so far from being protected by her magnificence, it attracted to her all the wreckers, who fought with one another as they tore the jewels from her neck, and cut off her swollen fingers to secure the rings upon them. Her body was buried in the sand, but was dug up by a dog, when blood was discovered upon the ears and mutilated hands. A lady in the neighbourhood sent and had the body decently interred. The murderers could not be traced, but tradition says, that "all the men who were in it came to a bad end."

The village of Thurlestone is about half-a-mile from the coast, and is a long straggling village. The church is in the Perpendicular style, consisting of chancel, nave, south aisle, porch, and square embattled tower, containing five bells. The chancel, which is the earliest part of the church, was restored in 1867, and the body of the church re-seated. The curious and finely carved old pulpit is placed about half way down the nave; the font is Norman and in good preservation; the reredos is of stone, and the chancel retains its piscina. The register dates from the year 1558; the living is a rectory, with $35\frac{1}{2}$ acres of glebe and a good residence, rebuilt by the late rector, in the gift of Lord Churston. In this parish are the villages of Buckland and Bantham. The former is situated in a beautifully sheltered vale, and not far from it, but further inland, is an Elizabethan mansion, called Clannacombe.

Neither at Thurlestone, Buckland, or South Milton is there any inn, and this occasions at times some slight inconvenience to strangers, especially with vehicles, but the neighbouring farmers will generally give all the accommodation that is necessary.

Bantham is situated at the mouth of the river Avon, and here there is an inn, called the Sloop. The harbour is small, with a bar entrance, and it is narrow and winding. Only small vessels and barges can gain an entrance into it. The sands about here are firm, and consequently pleasant to walk on, but some caution is needed in bathing outside the harbour, as a dangerous surf often quickly rises, and a short time since a sad loss of life took place from this cause. The Ham is a large expanse of wild tuffy land, and is used principally for sheep grazing.

As an instance of the folk-lore of this neighbourhood, the late Mr. Pengelly, of Torquay, relates that one beautiful summer evening, whilst walking from Aveton Gifford to Bantham, he was overtaken by a farm labourer, with whom he entered into conversation by remarking,—

"'Tis a fine evening."

"Yes, 'tis; but there'll be rain before the morning."

"Rain before morning! Why, there's not a cloud to be seen and we've had no rain for some weeks, what makes you think there'll be rain?"

"Well, the frogs make me think so I've zid lots of 'em jumping across the road this evening. There goes another!" And he pointed one out. "I'm sure there'll be rain before the morning."

He proved to be right; for though the sky was still cloudless, when I went to bed at the "Sloop" at Bantham, there was rain enough before the next morning to convert the thick dust into thick mud.

A DEVONSHIRE FISHING VILLAGE. Under this title a correspondent of the *Daily Graphic* writes :—

"Our undiscovered country is in South Devon. It is reached by the Great Western Railway; but we are not by any means there when we have finished the train journey, for Bantham is our destination, and Bantham is five miles beyond Kingsbridge, at which sleepy little town the train stops. The road to the tiny little fishing village is one to make the flesh of a nervous Londoner

MOUTH OF THE RIVER AVON AT BANTHAM.

creep; it is all up and down hills like the side of a house, and we go ahead at a brisk trot, for South Devon horses seem to grow claws like cats, and think nothing of climbing precipices. In due time we arrive, safe and sound, at Avon-Town-on-the-Ham, corrupted in the lapse of centuries to Bantham.

The village consists of one short row of thatched white-washed cottages, dominated by the coastguard station, a picturesque group of low buildings clustering round 'th' big 'ous,' which is a pretty weather-board erection belonging to a London barrister. Some eighty feet below the River Avon flows placidly to or from the sea, as the changing tide dictates. It is a salmon river, and one of our favourite amusements is to watch the drawing of the pools. The seine is thrown twice daily, and great is our excitement when the net comes in, and we count from six to twenty of the shining beauties struggling in its toils. Sometimes a big bass or two come in with the salmon, and then the competition among the thrifty housewives waxes keen, for that succulent fish is sold here at twopence the pound, so that sixpence will buy dinner enough for three people. We can always buy salmon (when caught), the demand for it being limited though the price ranges as low as tenpence to a shilling the pound; but comparatively few bass are taken in the pool, and they are sold in strict order of application. Every morning, somewhere in the small hours, the salmon are taken up the river by boat to Aveton Gifford, thence to be conveyed to the Plymouth Market.

We are a frugal lot at Bantham, and we live cheaply. The farthing tough cake is as large as a London penny roll, home-cured bacon is sixpence a pound, and apples are to be had at ten a penny. Rents are proportionately low, the only drawback being that lodgers are almost non-existent. Half a dozen visitors may find accommodation by engaging their rooms from year to year in advance, but if a stranger came unexpectedly he would have to sleep on Bantham Ham unless a kindly hearted villager let him make a bed on the kitchen settle. Every cottage has its settle, high-backed and wide-seated, drawn up to the hearthstone, beneath which stone the most delicious bread is baked, after a fashion long gone out of use everywhere but in Bantham.

Down below the salmon pool the river takes a bend on its way nto the Atlantic, and here stream and sea between them have constructed what our yachtsmen call 'the most dangerous place in the world,' that is to say, a treacherous bar of shifting sand where breakers rise up suddenly, even in calm weather, for the destruction of the unwary. The sun is setting over the sea and by that setting sun we know that it is time to lay down the pen and join our friends on the wall. The wall is the 'esplanade' of Bantham. There we rendezvous morning, noon, and night; there the fishermen resort to debate whether the bar is safe for going out; there the coastguard stands to sweep the horizon with his spy-glass; and there, yes there, we dry our bathing-gowns and towels!"

BURROW ISLAND, which was formerly called St. Michael's Mount, is situated at the mouth of the river Avon, and is two-and-a-half miles from Bolt Tail. It is about a quarter of a mile long, and as much in breadth, rising with a steep ascent to the centre from every side, and contains about ten acres of sheep pasturage. A bridge of sand connects it with the main land, which is left dry at half ebb. There are some rocks on the east side of the island called the Merries, at which a boat can land safely. There is good anchorage ground of clean sand from one-and-a-half to two miles off, with 7 to 12 fathoms of water. A chapel is supposed once to have stood here, but at the present time there are only the ruins of what was once a pleasure house on the summit of the island. A large quantity of pilchards were formerly caught about this coast by the drift net. The nets were of great length, and drifted about in deep water, whither the tide would carry them, with one end attached to the boat. Passing shoals in their course were intercepted by it, and in their efforts to pass through, became entangled in the meshes. The number thus caught of a night often amounted to several thousand per boat, but this industry has now almost disappeared, very few pilchards being found in the Bay.

A short distance from Burrow Island, along the coast, is the coastguard station of Challaborough, and on the beach close by have been detected good samples of a submerged forest.

THE RIVER AVON rises on Dartmoor, and flows pass Brent, Loddiswell and Aveton Gifford, emptying itself into Bigbury Bay. It is a trout and salmon river, the fishing being under a double conservancy, viz., the Avon and Erme Fishery Board of Conservators, who grant season day and weekly trout fishing licenses, and season salmon licenses; and the Avon and Erme Fishery Association, who are lessees of certain fishing rights, and grant season day and weekly fishing tickets. Much has been done for the improvement of the Weirs, and poaching, at one time very rife, is now almost abolished.

The Avon is navigable for barges as far as Aveton Gifford, a pleasantly situated village, with a good county bridge crossing the river. The Church of St. Andrew is an ancient stone structure in the Early English and Decorated styles, situated on an eminence a short distance from the village, and consisting of chancel with chancel aisles, nave, transepts, and central tower containing eight bells. In 1869 a portion of the walls was rebuilt, and the interior thoroughly restored, at a cost of about £2,500, raised by subscriptions, including a donation of £500 from the late Miss Froude of Denbury. An organ was placed in the Church in 1875. Walter de Stapledon, a rector of this parish, was consecrated Bishop of Exeter in 1307; at the time of his election he was professor of Canon Law at Oxford and chaplain to Pope Clement V. In 1314 he founded Exeter College, Oxford. For several years he was Lord High Treasurer, and was beheaded on the 15th October, 1326, by the adherents of Queen Isabella. The living of Aveton Gifford is a rectory with 97 acres of glebe land. The Rectory House is a modern mansion in the Elizabethan style, and stands in very pretty grounds. There are Chapels for Wesleyans and Bible Christians, and a commodious National School. Mr B. J. P. Bastard, of Kitley, is lord of the manor; at one time the lords of this manor had the power of inflicting capital punishment. The late Archdeacon Froude, father of the historian, was born at Wakeham House, in this parish A market and two fairs were granted to the lord of the manor in 1287, but have long since ceased to be held. The population is 796.

We have now gone westward as far as it is our intention to go; a return to Salcombe can be made by the road from Aveton Gifford to Malborough, and thence to Salcombe.

SALCOMBE TO KINGSBRIDGE.

PROCEEDING to Kingsbridge from Salcombe by water, we go to the head of the harbour, and then take a sudden turn to the left, round Ilbertstow Point, where a road has been cut by Mr. W. R. Ilbert, with the object of opening up the land adjacent for building sites, and here also is the proposed site for the terminus of the Salcombe extension of the Kingsbridge

KINGSBRIDGE ESTUARY.

Railway. At this Point what is known as the Kingsbridge Estuary commences. The open space at its entrance is called the Bag, having a great depth of water, and vessels of any draught can lay here with perfect safety during the fiercest gales. Vessels entering the harbour with explosive articles on board, or coming from foreign ports where contagious diseases are prevalent, are compelled by the regulations of the port to anchor here. This position is much used as a mooring place for yachts, for which it is specially adapted On the eastern shore a picturesque wood will be seen to rise from the water's edge, and extending away until it is lost in the distance. This is Halwell Wood, and the steamer from Salcombe to Kingsbridge stops here when passengers have to be embarked or disembarked. A small entrance will be seen facing the Estuary, above which is a circular shed,

HALWELL BAY.

erected by a former owner, for the convenience of picnic parties, who used to resort to this charming spot during the summer months. This shed, which is open in front, commands, through the oak trees, some of the most beautiful views imaginable of land and water. A path leads through this wood, terminating in a picturesque little cove, a short distance from which is Halwell House, which cannot be seen from the water. The present owner for some unaccountable reason has closed the path through this wood, and now visitors can only proceed around under the cliffs.

A creek branches off from the Estuary here, extending for about two miles to the village of Frogmore. Some varied scenery will be noticed in passing up this creek, and will well repay a visit. It is navigable for barges, and even small vessels, which may often be seen unloading their cargoes of coal, limestone, or manure. A large flour mill formerly stood here, but it was destroyed by fire in 1845, and was not rebuilt, but the ruins have become so covered with ivy, that it is sometimes mistaken by strangers for a ruined castle or monastry.

Near the entrance of Frogmore Creek is a small islet or rock called Salstone, about one hundred feet in length, and more than fifty in breadth. It is entirely covered at high water, and then only the beacon at its southern end, and a long pole with a cross piece, can be seen, as indicating its situation. The late Colonel Montagu, F.L.S. and F.W S., the naturalist, author of the "Ornithological Dictionary," "Testacea Britannica," &c., in digging on this islet, discovered the *Amphitrite Infundibulum*, which he fully described in the ninth volume of the "Transactions of the Linnean Society." In the same volume he mentions some interesting additions he made to the British fauna. Among the crustacea, he particularises *Cancer Astacus Subterraneus*, a new and curious species, discovered in digging for *Solen Vagina*, at a depth of two feet below the surface. This gentleman resided at Kingsbridge for nearly sixteen years, and made the greatest part of his collection of valuable and rare birds and animals in this Estuary. On his death, which was caused by lockjaw, produced from stepping on a rusty nail in 1815, his collection was purchased for upwards of eleven hundred pounds, by Mr. W. E. Leach, M.D. and F.R.S., for the British Museum, where it very properly now forms part of that extensive national assemblage of curiosities.

Salstone Rock has also become famous, for that in the old days of persecution, in consequence of its being extra-parochial, it became the safest and most frequent rendezvous of the ejected clergy, and is especially associated with the name of Hicks. On one occasion the Rev. Messrs. Hicks and Brand walked from Kingsbridge to Chillington Creek, and then started for the rock in a boat. A large company had already assembled (among whom was the Rev. Mr. Burdwood, who as before stated, had taken a farm at Batson), and they were chanting "God is our refuge and strength." The Rev. Mr. Brand preached from "A remnant according to the election of grace;" the Rev. Mr. Hicks followed with a discourse, suggested by their position, upon "The Rock of Ages;" the Rev. Mr. Burdwood gave a brief address upon "Christ is all in all." Then bending before high heaven, several prayed that they might be strengthened to suffer, and that better times might be granted to the nation. Night and tide came on, but on that praying ground they lingered until the water washed their feet, telling them to arise and depart.

The land abreast of Salstone belongs to Lincombe, a farmhouse a little inland. Not far from the shore is Lincombe Hill, and next to "beloved Salstone," this hill was held dear by the ejected clergy of the district, when the old rock was inaccessible, because of its retirement and safety, and they frequently made it their place of resort for praise, prayer, and mutual fellowship.

One fine Sabbath morning, such a morning that of itself lures to worship, the Rev. Mr. Hicks was preparing to leave his home for the general tryst, when his wife exhibited unusual alarm and agitation for his personal safety. He quietly calmed her perturbation by the quotation of a Scripture text, which he said had been vividly impressed upon his mind, "My presence shall go with thee." Walking along the narrow and usually solitary road, he felt so cheerful as to compare his soul to a well tuned harp, whose cords gave answering harmony to the music of the divine Player He had not gone far before he was joined by others, who also were making their way to the place of secret worship.

The hill of Lincombe is a pretty sharp ascent from all sides; the summit gained, a magnificent prospect presents itself, parish after parish with their turreted towers; a wide expanse of rich and highly cultivated pasture and arable land, intersected by the Estuary and its numerous

SALSTONE ROCK.

creeks, spreads beneath a lovely and charming landscape. Three roads meet at its top; and from each of these had come from surrounding villages and farmhouses, many persons who did not shrink "to suffer affliction with the people of God." Tethering their horses, and putting the saddles in a half circle for seats, on which sat the aged and infirm—there gathered a brave, patient, attentive, and above all a prayerful band of earnest listeners. Mr. Hicks began the service by pouring out his soul in prayer until the hills seemed to respond to his supplications. The prayer ended, he drew from his pocket a well-worn leather-coated Bible, and read as lessons, 1 Peter i. and Psalm lxxx. The text he chose was "The sufferings of this present time are not worthy to be compared with the glory which shall be revealed." With a loosened tongue he had power given him to utter the thoughts which flowed free and fast, greatly moving and affecting the people. Finishing one division and about to begin another, an uneasy movement betokened apprehension of danger; sounds of horses feet were heard, revealing the fact that they were pursued. Hastily breaking up, and bidding each other a tender farewell, they dispersed in various directions, the hill and tall hedgerows covering their retreat. Mr. Hicks fled to the house of a very honest farmer, who was known to have sympathy with these persecuted people. The farmer, thinking he needed closer concealment than the family hearth, took him to the upper story of an out-building, where he could both see and hear what was going on below. He had just reached his hiding place, when a furious magistrate, attended by a servant, rode into the courtyard, sternly asking for "these seditious brawlers." Seeing the old decayed buildings, which were completely overrun with ivy, he declared he would have them closely searched, and if any of those "scoundrels" were found it would be better for the farmer if all his ricks and barns were in a blaze. Reinforced by several of his followers, the search began in real earnest. From the house the searching party soon turned to the out-buildings, and clattered up the ladder to the place where Mr. Hicks was hidden. One of the men seized a pitchfork, and probing it into the straw, nearly sent its prongs into his body; but he was not discovered; and so after a while, having grown weary of a search which proved fruitless, they beat a hasty retreat—the discomfited justice and his followers striking across the country in another direction. The good farmer and his son went up to the hiding place of Mr. Hicks, and summoning the rest of the family, they embraced each other and wept for very joy over the good man's preservation. Mr. Hicks remained until night closed in, and then found his way home to Kingsbridge.

Continuing the journey up the Estuary, an extensive breadth of water is soon entered, called Wide-gates. On the left is a creek which runs in for some distance, terminating at Blank's Mill, where there is a stone bridge, over which is the old road to Salcombe. Rowden Point juts out a little towards the Estuary, when another creek is formed leading to Collapit, beautifully wooded on either bank, and terminating at a picturesque bridge, forming part of the road from Kingsbridge to Salcombe. It is a very pleasant trip by boat up this creek, but it should only be attempted near high tide, as the water is very shallow. The northern entrance to Wide-gates is called Gerston Point, a short distance from which is Gerston, the ancient seat of the Bastard family. The house cannot be seen from the water. Here the highly respected family of Bastard resided from the days of William the Conqueror till the year 1773, when Lady Bridget Bastard, daughter of the Earl Poulett, who had retained possession of it during a long widowhood, died and the ancient mansion became deserted; her eldest son, Mr. William Bastard, had some time previously removed to Kitley, Yealmpton, where the descendants of the family still reside. During the eighteenth century the gardens at Gerston were famed for producing oranges and lemons trained against walls in the manner of peach trees, and sheltered only with mats of straw in winter. Some of the fruit, as large and fair as any from Portugal, was presented to the king by Lady Bridget Bastard's brother, Vere, the third Earl Poulett, about 1770.

About Widegates and other parts of the Estuary, many rare and valuable birds are frequently met with. As early as 1800 Colonel Montagu found the Cirl Bunting breeding at Tacket Wood, and sixty-five years later Mr. Edmund A. S. Elliot, M.R.C.S., of Kingsbridge, took a nest at the same place, and this bird is a fairly common resident in the neighbourhood. In the year 1808, a Buff-backed Heron was shot at South Allington, one of the only two obtained in Great Britain. Col. Montagu often saw the Osprey fishing in the Estuary, and about 1835 a White-tailed Eagle was shot at Halwell Wood. In May, 1842, thousands of Arctic Terns were caught by the easterly gales and driven into the Estuary, where scores were knocked down and killed with sticks and stones. In the severe winter of 1852-3, several Whooper Swans were shot on the Estuary, and about the same period a Bee Eater was shot near Ilton Castle. In May, 1876, an immense flock of Bar-tailed Godwits came into the Estuary, and about the same period two Bewick's Swan were shot.

On the opposite shore is a piece of land called Charleton Marshes, now used as a rifle range for the Kingsbridge Volunteers. This land was reclaimed by the Earl of Morley causing an embankment to be constructed in 1806, 165 yards long, 10 feet high, and 75 feet in base, and enclosing between thirty and forty acres of land. In the following year it began to vegetate.

CHARLETON is not far from here, divided into two parts called East and West, and is a long straggling village. It appears that Churletone was the ancient and probably the more correct way of spelling Charleton. Assuming that the name is derived from the Anglo-Saxon ceorl or churl, meaning husbandman or peasant, the name of Churletone would then simply mean the habitation or "ton" of the peasantry or villagers. Many people derive the word Charleton from "Charles," and no doubt there are many Charlestowns and Charlestons deriving their name from the Stuart Royal family, but there is nothing in this village to connect it with a "Charles" and seeing it undoubtedly bore the name of Churletone in 1344, the former derivation is certainly the most satisfactory.

COLLAPIT BRIDGE.

A good view of the church, with its peculiar embattled tower, with turret containing four bells, is obtained from the Estuary. It is dedicated to St. Mary, and built chiefly in the Decorated style. It was mostly rebuilt in 1849-50, at a cost of £1,300, obtained by public subscriptions; and consists of chancel, nave, transept, north aisle, and porch. Such portions of the original work as were fit to be retained were embodied in the new structure, the ancient sedilia, &c., on the south side of the chancel being especially worthy of notice. Bishop Stafford's Register says, on the 20th of April, 1396, the living being vacant, his lordship admitted Sir Laurence Allerthorp, chaplain, "on the presentation of that noble man Thomas de Berkeley, Lord of Berkeley, the true patron thereof," and he was instituted the same day. The parish is here called "Charleton in Southammes." A year later this Rector effected an exchange with a certain Master John Suggeston, Rector of Brawlingham in the Diocese of York, Thomas, Lord Berkeley, the patron, consenting; and the new Rector, in the person of John Grantebrigg, his proxy, was instituted on the 27th of April, 1397. In 1402 Suggeston died, and on the 3rd August in that year, the Bishop instituted Sir John Camme, chaplain, on the presentation of the same patron. He was Rector for about six years, and on his death, in 1408, the Bishop instituted Sir John Wynterburn, chaplain, on the 18th October. The register dates from the year 1560. The living is a rectory, with 30 acres of glebe and residence, in the gift of the Marchioness of Northampton. The lordship of Charleton was granted by Henry VIII. in the thirty-fifth year of his reign, to Queen Catherine for her dower. After her death it came to Edward VI. and from him it descended to Queen Mary, who by letters patent of the 22nd June, in the first year of her reign, granted it to the Earl of Huntingdon. It has frequently changed hands since, and at present the manor belongs to the Marchioness of Northampton, daughter of the late Lord Ashburton.

An inlet of the sea called Bowcombe Creek separates the parish of Charleton from that of Dodbrooke. A horizontal swing bridge was constructed over this creek in 1845. Leaving this bridge, Highhouse Point is soon reached, a place where boats can land at almost any time of tide, and it is one mile from the town of Kingsbridge. Here the steamer *Salcombe Castle*, plying two and three times daily between Salcombe and Kingsbridge, lands and embarks her passengers when there is not sufficient tide for her to proceed further up the Estuary. At Highhouse Point is the Cemetery belonging to the Kingsbridge Burial Board. Looking westwards the village and church of West Alvington will be seen on the hill, and a large portion of the foreshore on the western side is in that parish. The church of All Saints is a fine building in the Early Perpendicular style, and consists of chancel, nave, aisles, a chapel set apart for the Ilbert family, and an embattled western tower with four pinnacles, containing six bells. The following epitaph is on a tombstone in the churchyard:—

"Here Lyeth the Body of Daniel Jeffery the son of Michael Jeffery and Joan his wife he was Buried ye 2 day of September 1746 and in ye 18th year of his age.

This youth When In his sickness Lay did for the Minister send
that he would come and with him Pray
But he would not attend. But when this young man Buried was
the minister did him admit
he Should be carried into Church
that he might money geet. By this you see what man will dwo
to geet money if he can
who did refuse to come and Pray
By the Forsaid young man."

Bowringsleigh, the residence since 1696 of the Ilbert family, is an ancient mansion, portions of which date from the thirteenth century, but the principal existing features are of the Early Tudor period. In the hall is an elaborate oak screen, of the time of James I, richly embossed with ebony and mahogany; the chapel, connected with the east wing of the house, which was partially destroyed by fire in 1843, contains a rich 15th century screen, brought from South Huish church: the ceilings of the reception rooms are beautiful specimens of the plaster decoration of the time of William and Mary; and there is a collection of valuable pictures. The mansion was completely restored and considerably enlarged during the years 1868-73.

Continuing our journey up the Estuary, Messrs. Date's shipbuilding yard is passed on the right. From this yard many a smart and trim vessel has been turned out for the foreign and coasting trade. Although a branch line of railway has been opened to Kingsbridge, yet the district still depends upon ship carriage for a large portion of its supplies. Before the days of steamers, Kingsbridge was, like Salcombe, a busy port, and still does a bit of shipping with the craft which can get up to the quays. The Estuary flows to the foot of the town, where ample quay room is afforded for the import and export of merchandise of all descriptions. The export trade is corn, cider, flour, beer, and other produce, estimated at the value of from £50,000 to £60,000 per annum, and the importation of coals and timber is also very considerable. There are two small cargo steamers that run regularly two trips weekly to and from Plymouth, one carrying passengers as well as merchandise. Just opposite the quays is a small creek called Tacket Wood, over which a bridge was constructed by the county in 1768, and over it is the old road leading to Salcombe. There is an old established rope walk not far from this bridge, nearer Kingsbridge, employing several hands.

At the upper end of the Estuary, a portion of the foreshore was reclaimed, and an embankment made in 1880, now forming a pretty promenade, upon which are planted trees, and comfortable lounging seats are fixed at short distances, forming a pleasant spot (especially when the tide is up) in which to enjoy a book or other pastime.

The old road from Kingsbridge to Salcombe is a typical Devonshire road, up hill and down, with hedges so high that one cannot see over them; but at the occasional gates and gaps lovely peeps of the beautiful country are obtained. The road passes over the bridges at the head of Collapit and Blank's Mill Creeks. For nearly the whole of the way there is a wealth of vegetation, almost tropical in its profusion; in the early Spring primroses by the thousand, if not million, with blooms in some cases as large as a five shilling piece; violets from deepest purple to lightest blue; celandine, cranesbills

COLLAPIT CREEK.

sea-pink, white campion, blue-bell, wild forget-me-not, gorse aflame with bloom, harts-tongue ferns, and other plants too numerous to mention. Beautiful butterflies are seen flying hither and thither in the warm sun, and the air rings with the song of merry birds, thrushes, larks, blackbirds, sedge-warblers, yellow-hammers, chaffinches, rooks, and many another.

KINGSBRIDGE AND DODBROOKE.

OF the two towns at the head of the Estuary, so closely connected that they appear but one. Dodbrooke can claim an earlier origin than Kingsbridge The earliest allusion to the borough or vill of Kingsbridge is believed to occur in the Hundred Rolls, which record the results of enquiries instituted by Edward I, on his return from the Holy Land, for the purpose of correcting the territorial abuses which had crept in during the reign of his father, Henry III. During this turbulent period many proprietors had usurped rights of free chase, warren, and fishery, market tolls, &c. Jurors were appointed in each Hundred to assist in ascertaining these rights in the several manors. The Abbey of Buckfast then held the manor of Churchstow, and accordingly when my Lord Abbot was summoned, in the year 1276, to answer by what warrant he claimed view of frank-pledge, the regulation of the measure and price of bread and ale, and the power of hanging his convict vassals on his manor gallows, the jurors of the Hundred of Stanburg found that within this manor of Churchstow was a new borough which answered for itself by six jurors, and had a market on Fridays, with a separate assize of bread and ale. Although the jurors assign no name to this new borough, there can be little doubt that they referred to Kingsbridge; and about half a century later, by a deed of 1330. Roger Crokere, of Kyngesbrigge, made a grant of all his lands, &c., there, to be held of the head lord of the fee. The name of Kyngesbrigge also occurs in 1347 as one of the ports that were called on to provide a naval subsidy.

Of the origin of this name there is no satisfactory account, and various opinions have been expressed as to whether it means the Burg of the King, or the Bridge of the King. There is much to be said on both sides, but whilst the Saxon word "byrig" means a burg or town, yet the name is generally supposed to be derived from one of the bridges over the brooks that join the Estuary at the town's foot. This very natural inference is strengthened by the invariable use in the earliest deeds of the Anglo-Saxon termination of "brigge," "brige," &c., and these words clearly mean bridge. There are preserved in Kingsbridge Church some very ancient documents, going back to the early part of the fourteenth century, of which Mr. W. Davies, solicitor, Kingsbridge, has made a very careful examination, and we shall make occasional reference to the results of his examination. He says in these documents the name of the town is spelt in the following forms:—

Kynggesbrigge,	Kingisbrigge,	Kyngesbrige,
Kyngesbrygge,	Kynesbrugge,	Kyngysourge,
Kyngisbrygge,	Kyngesbrigge,	Kynggesbrydge,
Kyngisbrugge,	Kyngysbryghe,	Kyngysbryge,

Kyngsbrygge, and in other forms.

And goes on to add:—

"The Estuary extended much further up, and was much wider than at present. One of the principal places of the town would be what is now Mill Street. There were the mills of the great Lord Abbot and Convent of Buckfast and the Lord of the Manor; and at these mills all corn had to be ground. Across the arm of the Estuary near the junction of the Union Road with Mill Street there was probably a bridge, which Prebendary Hingeston-Randolph conjectures, and I think rightly, gave the name to the town. He says there was an important road leading to West Alvington and the south country, and considering that the richest land lies to the south, and that this road would connect not only West Alvington, but Malborough, Salcombe, Hope, Milton, and Thurlestone with Kingsbridge, there is little doubt but that it was the most important bridge on the king's highway."

The other conjecture is, that Kingsbridge has frequently been styled burgus or borough; and it could hardly have acquired a separate manorial existence after the Conquest without royal authority. Therefore, may not the original name have been Kingsburg, or the king's borough? This explanation does not harmonise with the device of a three-arched bridge under a crown on the ancient seal of the Kingsbridge Feoffees, but it must be noted, on the other hand, that this seal is only from two to three hundred years old, whereas the old town seal is of a very different character, as shewn on a document bearing date 1475. There is, also, a legend that a Saxon monarch, coming with his retinue to the marshy swamp through which the brook Dod oozed its way, stopped short at the prospect of soiling, if not engulfing, the Royal sock and buskin. Hesitating in consideration as to how he should get to the opposite side dryshod, someone stepped into the middle of the stream, and offered the king his back. The king accepted the offer, and was taken across safely; hence the name of Kingsbridge.

The omission of all mention of Kingsbridge in the Taxatio of Pope Nicholas IV, which was completed in 1291, shows that although it may at that date have had a separate, or perhaps subsidiary, manorial existence, it formed part of Churchstow for ecclesiastical purposes. It is fairly demonstrable, however, that the Church of Kingsbridge is more ancient than is usually supposed. At all events one certainly existed on the site of the present church in the early part of the 13th century, and probably long before, as appears from one of the ancient documents preserved in Kingsbridge Church, which relates to the examination of witnesses at Exeter, taken in Bishop Stapeldon's time in 1309. Mr. Davies says:—

"The evidence of numerous witnesses was taken, among whom was William of the Combe, who swore before the Court at Exeter that there had been a chapel in Kingsbridge possessing a chantry with the rights of using all divine offices and services except the right of sepulture, and that these rights had existed in his own time and also that he had heard they existed in the time of his father Richard de la Combe, and of his grandfather, Peter de la Combe, and he had also heard from William de Rake and John Politerre, centenarians, statements to the same effect, and further, that the matter was of common knowledge and report through the district. William of Syreford (Sherford) and Augustine of Syreford were also examined, and stated that they recollected these rights being exercised for sixty years or more, and Robert de la Prata gave evidence to the same effect."

Although evidence was taken in support of the claim of the inhabitants for the right of sepulture in a church-

HEAD OF THE ESTUARY AT KINGSBRIDGE.

yard at Kingsbridge at so early a date, yet little notice seems to have been taken of the matter by the authorities, and it was not till more than one hundred years after, that the requirements of the inhabitants were attended to, and that they were relieved from the serious inconvenience of being obliged to take all their dead to Churchstow for burial.

Towards the close of the fourteenth century the rector (as he was then styled) of Churchstow granted liberty " to the abbot and convent of Buckfast to build a church in honour of the blessed Edmund, King and Martyr, in their demesne in the vill which is called Kingesbrig." The inhabitants were nevertheless to acknowledge their dependence on Churchstow by annual offerings at the Feast of the Assumption. The following is a copy of the grant :—

"Know all men present and to come, that I, M. de Litlecumb, rector of the church of Chirchstowe, have granted the abbot and convent of Buckfast to build a church in honour of the blessed Edmund the king and martyr, in their demesne in the vill which is called Kingesbrig, so that they grant all the profits of the said vill belonging to the church for the maintenance of a chaplain who may celebrate divine service in the aforesaid church for ever. And that all the inhabitants of the said vill may hear divine service in the said church, and enjoy all ecclesiastical rights there, so that they visit their mother church, namely Chirchstowe, at least once a year (to wit), on the Assumption of the blessed virgin Mary, or within eight days after, with offerings, because the aforesaid vill lies within the limits of the parish, but the church of Chirchstowe hath never been accustomed to receive anything of that place, namely Kingesbrig, and therefore, as it is entirely without prejudice to the mother church, and a great work of mercy, I freely grant that divine service for all the faithful in Christ, living and dead, shall, by Christ's permission, be celebrated in that place for ever. That this my aforesaid grant may remain firm, I have put my seal to this present writing in testimony and confirmation thereof."

A chapel was accordingly erected, and dedicated to St. Edmund, King and Martyr. This served its purpose for the time, but burials had still to be performed at Churchstow; and as Kingsbridge grew, this burden became too heavy to be borne, so that on August 26th, 1414, after another petition and remonstrance Bishop Stafford, with the consent of the Dean and Chapter, the Abbot of Buckfast, and Roger Bachelor, the rector of Churchstow, issued his ordinacio for carrying into effect the petition, and he consecrated the Chapel of St. Edmund a parish church, and on the following day blessed its cemetery, subject to certain tribute to Churchstow. This ordinacio was also agreed to by Robert Hulle, junr., John Hacche, John Holdyche, John Wordell, and Walter Legh, parishioners of Churchstow, and Roger Saundere, John Veel, John Torryng, William Sormound, Andrew Blakehalle, John Redewyll, Richard Lockynton, Roger Dyer, Thomas Luere (or Lever), Robert Bold, David Ryder, Robert Blake, and Thomas Olyver, parishioners of Kingsbridge. The tribute to Churchstow must have ceased many years ago, as Kingsbridge now pays no tithes to anyone, and is a strange example of a parish entirely free from tithe or modus. Some half century later the Abbey obtained a grant for their town of Kingsbridge of a weekly market, and a three days' fair, though the market, at least, was of far older date.

Sir William Pole asserts that "Kingesbridge belonged to the Erles of Devon, and after the attainder of Henry, Marquis of Exeter, purchased by Sir William Petre, and is nowe the Lord Petre's." Evidence is wanting to support this wide statement; but it is clear that the Courtenays held some property in this town, as well as in Dodbrooke, at least as early as the year 1416. Mr. W. Davies says:—

"The name of Courtenay first appears in 1416, and a deed of that date states that Edward de Courtenay, Earl of Devon, granted a lease to John Mathen " of the burgage which John Prestecote held." This lease shows that at that time the Courtenay family still held property in Kingsbridge, and they probably did so for some time afterwards, as a Peter Courtenay was Portreeve in the year 1486, and if he was of the same family, it is tolerably clear he would not have been chosen as Portreeve, unless he was a man of substance having visible property in the town. The arms of the Courtenay family can be seen to-day in stained glass inserted in a window behind the organ at the eastern end of Kingsbridge Church. They are not in their original position, for in Hawkins'

History they are described and stated to be in the glass of the window over the Communion Table. Possibly they were removed from this centre east window and relegated to their present obscure position at the time when the somewhat gorgeously coloured affair was placed at the east end. They display the much-discussed "lion rampart, azure," which mysteriously crept into the arms of the de Redver's family, who were the first Earls of Devon, and thence came into the Courtenay shield, I believe, through Mary de Redvers, who was married to Sir Robert Courtenay in the reign of Henry II. This fragment of glass may be referable to the latter part of the fourteenth century after the Earldom was revived by Edward III, but probably it was placed with other stained glass work in the centre east window at the restoration of the church, which took place in pursuance of the Ordinacio of Bishop Stafford in 1414."

Hugh, Earl of Devon, who died in 1423, was possessed of two messuages in Kingsbridge, and two at "Dodebrok." There is, however, evidence to show that the manor of Kingsbridge pertained, as the manor of Churchstow certainly did, to the Abbey of Buckfast, down to the date of its dissolution. In 1555, Pope Paul IV. confirmed the grant which Sir William Petre had received from King Henry VIII; and with this knight's heirs the manor of Churchstow, and the manor and borough of Kingsbridge, remained until the year 1793, when Robert Edward, ninth baron Petre of Writtle, sold the latter to Mr. John Scobell, of Nancealvern, near Penzance, one of whose ancestors had, two centuries before this, married a daughter of William Webber, alias Gilbert, of Churchstow and Bowringsleigh. The manor had been so long held by the careless lessees of an absentee lord that the new possessor was driven to legal means of re-establishing some of his ancient rights against encroachments. From him the manor descended to Mr. John Usticke Scobell, who in 1874 sold it to Mr. John S. Hurrell, the present lord.

In the possession of the feoffees of the parish lands there is a curious view of the central part of the town dated 1586, and drawn, after the fashion of those days, partly as a plan and partly as a bird's-eye view, but

KINGSBRIDGE FROM TACKET WOOD.

giving a very fair idea of the appearance of Kingsbridge about the time when Leland, the librarian of Henry VIII, described it as "a praty towne." This view shows many of the appendages of manorial government. In the middle of the street, opposite the church, stood the timber-built Exchange or Market House, then called the Chepe House, leaving on either side passages barely wide enough for vehicles. In this building the manor courts were held, and it retained its old form until it was taken down in 1796. A little farther down the street was a long open linhay, used as the butter market. A penthouse shed, supported in front by pillars, and called, even in its old age, the New Works, separated the churchyard from the street. Outside the church stood the parish stocks, which can be seen now in the south porch of the church, and many an offender has passed a weary hour in them, subjected to the jibes and probably the offensive missiles of the younger inhabitants. Near one end of the Chepe House stood that dread instrument of torture, the pillory, which was shaped something like a huge capital T, the offender's hands being placed in holes at the ends of the crosspiece, and his head in a hole at the junction of the beams, and while there he suffered extreme torture, not only from his strained position, but on account of the tempting mark his face presented for the unresisted application of rotten eggs, offal, stones, or any missile that came handy. The parish pound occupied the higher corner of the road leading to Churchstow. Mr. Hawkins speaks of a Banquetting House of the Abbot of Buckfast, towards the top of Fore Street. The Church House stood on part of the site of the present King's Arms Hotel. Although the breadth of the street above the Chepe House was very ample there was but a narrow central passage, ten feet in width, reserved for horses; whilst the broader spaces on either side were occupied by raised causeways for foot passengers, who on market days had to dodge their way amongst the cattle exposed for sale. This state of things existed until the carriage-way was widened to twenty feet, about the year 1794. On the north side of the brook dividing the parishes of Churchstow and Kingsbridge, were meadows once belonging to Buckfast Abbey, but marked in the view as "Syr John Petre's lande, called Norton." Norton, was the hill that commanded the town on the north, and Nornden the dene or valley below. The Abbot's Mill in Mill Street, had also passed into the hands of Sir John Petre.

Kingsbridge is a small but important market town and parish, distant about five miles from Salcombe. It is the head of a Union and County Court District. The town consists, with the exception of one or two by-streets and passages or courts, of one long wide street, sloping from the top to the bottom of a hill. This is Fore Street, about sixty feet in breadth, the footpaths being flagged, and there is a general appearance of cleanliness and good order. Kingsbridge is and always has been the metropolis of the South Hams, and is now united with Dodbrooke in one parish, viz., the parish of Kingsbridge and Dodbrooke, governed by an Urban District Council, consisting of twelve members, successors to a Local Board formed on April 24th, 1893. The town and district is well lighted and drained, and the water-works were carried out in 1793, and are now under the control of the Urban Council, who are arranging for an enlarged supply of water.

Near the quay, in Dodbrooke, is Pindar Lodge, the birthplace of Dr. Wolcot, whose writings are familiar under the name of "Peter Pindar." He was born in 1738 and died in 1819. He was the most powerful master of forceful satire of a rough and ready type in the English tongue. He studied as a lad at the Grammar School, and the story is told of his blood-curdling adventures with the town shoemaker, against whom he had a spite. It is said that the shoemaker twitted the lad with being thrashed at school, which so irritated the future "Peter Pindar" that he planned a murderous revenge. He fired a pistol in the shoemaker's face. Blood poured down his checks, and there were all the elements of a tragedy; but it turned to comedy. Young Wolcot had filled his pistol with bullock's blood. Wolcot always had a liking for the scenes of his youthful escapades, which are referred to in several of his "Odes." Most unpleasant in character, he claims praise less for his abilities than for his sturdy independence

In a narrow turning to the left, after leaving the quays, is Mill Street, in which are situated the Town Mills, now used for the sole purpose of grinding corn, employing some five or six hands. At the beginning of the 19th century the mills were in full work for the manufacture of woollen and cotton goods, and on the Western Backway, in connection with the factory, was a large wool combing shop, the two together employing not less than sixty work-people In 1845 the mills were again turned to their original use, that of grinding corn. Somewhere at the bottom of Fore Street there formerly stood an old house which at one time was the home of the Abbot of Buckfast, who usually spent Lent here because "fish was plentiful." The house contained some fine carved wainscotting, &c. The chief shops are on either side of Fore Street, the most picturesque and oldest object in this street being the Shambles, belonging to the lord of the manor, and used by butchers and others, situate under the east end of the church, and were first erected about 1586; five of the granite pillars which support the building were in their present position at that date, and three others were added later. The rooms above are used as offices by the owner.

The Town Hall, built in 1850 by a joint-stock company, at a cost of about £1,500, will seat 500 persons; it is now the property of the parish feoffees, and is used for the benefit of the town. The clock in front of the Town Hall was presented by the late Mr. Thomas Peek, and erected in 1875. A reading room, police station, and other institutions are comprised in this building, and the County Court, whose jurisdiction is co-extensive with the

176   SALCOMBE AND NEIGHBOURHOOD.

Union, is held every alternative month, and Petty Sessions are held on the first Monday in every month.

The parish church of St. Edmund, King and Martyr, stands on the western side, at the rear of the Shambles and adjoining the Town Hall, and was built as we have before referred to, about the year 1414. It is chiefly in the Early English and Perpendicular styles, consisting of chancel, nave, aisles, transepts, north and south-west

THE SHAMBLES AND ENTRANCE TO TOWN HALL.

porches, and a central tower with spire, containing eight bells. In 1761 the old set of bells were taken down and put on board a vessel for shipment to London, there to be recast, but the vessel was captured by a French privateer, and the bells carried off as a lawful prize. A new set of bells had then to be cast in London, and sent down and hung. The aisles were added in the fifteenth century, forming chapels on either side of the chancel, and in the eastern pillars supporting the tower are hagioscopes: the chancel retains a piscina and a fine ancient stall or miserere, and there are piscinas of the ancient chapels in the south transept, referred to later on. The reredos of Caen stone was restored in 1889, and decorated in gold and colour. The large and ancient font of Polyphant stone is Early English; the screens separating the chancel from the chapels are unique, the tracery being very rich; the rood screen, the only remains of which consist of ten of the lower panels, have been worked together to form a pulpit and prayer desk; and the south-west porch are all work of the early part of the fifteenth century. Immediately inside the doorway is a water stoup constructed of a piece of ancient window tracery of very Early English date. The only old window of the church is in the south chancel aisle, and, as well as the iron work protecting it outside, belongs to the sixteenth century. The church was restored in 1860, and new bells hung in 1877. The earliest register (for baptisms) is dated 1695; the rest date from 1754, and are in good preservation. The living is a vicarage, annexed to that of Churchstow, and was formerly in the gift of the Lord Chancellor, but now of the Bishop of Exeter. By an old document in the church it is evident there were chapels attached to the first church, for Mr. Davies says,—

"In 1379, William atte Cleve granted to John Roper a tenement in Dodebrooke, and the grantee was to pay to the Wardens of the chapel of St. Saviours, Kingsbridge, the sum of threepence on the usual quarter days, and there was a power of distraint by the Wardens of the Store of St. Saviours in case of default. A point of interest is the payment of money to keep up the services in the chapel of St. Saviours. The chapel or chantry was then probably similar to those little side chapels or shrines so familiar to those who have been in Roman Catholic churches abroad, and which are dedicated to several saints. When our church at Kingsbridge was cruciform, as it was at this date, there were in the south transept two of these little chapels, and this is evidenced by the fact of there being two ancient piscinas still existing there. One of these chapels was that of St. Saviours, and was the one in the south wall of the transept, and the other in the east wall of the transept was probably that of the Virgin, while the principal altar at the east end was dedicated to St. Edmund the King and Martyr. There is a later deed in 1384, by which the grantor, Henry Mayou, gives two shillings a quarter, after the death of his fourth wife Joan, to the chapels of St. Edmund and St. Saviour, in order that prayers might be said on the anniversaries of the deaths of his four wives, Matilda, Joan, Idonea, and Joan. To say the least of it, the gift cannot be called a generous one at the rate of sixpence apiece for each soul, and as the fourth wife Joan was still alive, one would have thought she might have secured better terms for herself"

"By a deed dated 23rd February, 1528, Thomas Symon, Dorothy his wife, and Dorothy Lake, widow, conveyed to John Cokeworthie and Elizabeth his wife, the following premises, the descriptions of which are interesting, namely, 'a certain tenement which the Parish Priest holds of us as tenant at will and two cellars underneath the same, a garden called an erber (herb), and half of an apple garden (apelle gardyn) lying to the west of the churchyard, and the garden belonging to the church on the north side thereof; also two butchers' stalls on the path which leads to the middle of the King's Street, and half-an-acre of land at Knowle.' This deed shews that at that time the parish priest had no house of residence in Kingsbridge by virtue of his office, but was simply a tenant at will. The gardens called the herb and apple gardens probably occupied the ground afterwards enclosed as the lower churchyard, while the garden to the north is the land now probably built over by the houses in George Court."

The name of "Cokeworthie" is noticeable, as he was probably an ancestor of William Cookworthy, who was born in Kingsbridge in 1705, who whilst yet a lad lost his father, who was a weaver, and his mother being left in poor circumstances, the lad walked to London to enter on his duties as an apprentice with a firm of chemists. He afterwards established a successful drug business in Plymouth, and between the years 1745-50 made his great discovery of china clay, and became the founder of the Plymouth China Clay Works, where the first true porcelain made in England was produced. He died in 1780. On the half acre of land at Knowle above referred to the Vicarage house was erected some fifty years ago by the Rev. Richard Luney, who was then Vicar of Kingsbridge.

The church contains few monuments of interest save one in Carraca marble by Flaxman, and the memorial of

George Hughes, leader of the Puritan clergy of Devon, who when ejected from St. Andrew's, Plymouth, in 1662, retired to Kingsbridge to end his days. The inscription is by his famous son-in-law, John Howe. Besides Mr. Hughes, John Hicks, the ejected minister of Stoke Damerel, found an asylum at Kingsbridge, where he was subjected to much persecution at the hands of the local magistrates, as we have already stated when referring to Salstone Rock. On one occasion being charged with murder he was sent to Exeter for trial, but was acquitted. He was the historic "John Hicks," for giving shelter to whom, after the battle of Sedgmoor, Lady Alice Lisle was condemned by Judge Jefferies, and executed. Hicks was also condemned and hanged for participation in that Monmouth rebellion of 1685.

William Duncombe, by will dated 1691, founded a lectureship in connection with the parish church, of the present annual value of £120, and within the church is the following epitaph to his memory;—

> "Here lyeth the Body of Mr. William
> Duncombe, the son of John Duncombe, of
> Buckingham Sheire, Esqre., who was some
> time fellow of King's College in
> Cambridge, and the First School Master
> of the Free Schole in Kingsbridge, and
> tought thare 28 yeares, and Brought
> up many Young Gentlemen, who by
> His Industry became useful members
> both in Church and state, and dyed the
> Last day of December, 1698, and left
> All that he had to pious usus."

In Kingsbridge Church the visitor will look with some curiosity upon an oft-quoted epitaph cut on a headstone near the chancel door. It runs,—

> "Here lie I at the chancel door;
> Here lie I because I'm poor;
> The farther in the more you'll pay;
> Here lie I as warm as they."

The epitaph is claimed by a dozen other churches, but here it undoubtedly is. It is the sole memorial of Robert

Phillips, commonly called Bone Phillips, himself his own poet, who died July 27th, 1793, at the age of 65 years, and whom local tradition has been content to describe—somewhat unkindly—as a drunken old vagabond, a cooper by trade.

The marriage register of the parish of Kingsbridge for the year 1654 gives some curious instances of marriage customs that were in vogue during the Commonwealth. On the 24th August, 1653, the Parliament enacted:—

THE MARKET PLACE, FORE STREET.

"That whosoever should agree to be married within the Commonwealth of England after the 29th September, 1653, should (21 days before such intended marriage), deliver in writing unto the Register (therein appointed) for the respective parish where each party to be married lived, the names, surnames, additions [which is probably an error for conditions], and places of abode of the parties so to be married, and of their parents, guardians, or overseers, all which said Register should publish three Lord's Days then next following at the close of the morning exercise in the public meeting-place, commonly called the church or chapel, or (if the parties desired it) in the market-place next to the said church or chapel on three market-days in three several weeks next following, between the hours of 11 and 2, which done the Register should make a certificate thereof, without which the persons thereinafter authorized should not proceed in such marriage. That such person intending to be married, should come before some Justice of the Peace of the same county, city, or town, with such certificate, and if no impediment the marriage was to proceed thus:—The man to be married taking the woman to be married by the hand, shall plainly and distinctly pronounce these words:—

I, A B., do here in the presence of God, the searcher of all hearts, take thee C. D for my wedded Wife, and do also in the presence of God and before these witnesses promise to be unto thee a loving and faithful husband.

And then the woman taking the man by the hand shall plainly and distinctly pronounce these words:—

I, C. D , do here in the presence of God, the searcher of all hearts, take thee A B., for my wedded Husband, and do also in the presence of God and before these witnesses promise to be unto thee a loving, faithful, and obedient wife.

Whereupon the said Justice was to declare them man and wife, and no other marriage was to be valid within the Commonwealth."

The rest of the Act relates to the election by the inhabitants of each parish on or before 22nd September, 1653, of a register (never called in the Act Registrar), who must be sworn and approved by some Justice of the Peace, and as to the discharge of his duties, he was to keep the register book and enter all marriages, births, and deaths. We append a copy of an entry in the Kingsbridge Marriage Register, a sample of many others of a similar kind to be found in that year:—

"A Contract of Marriage between Francis Blackeller of Stockingham, of the one part, and Margaret Hooper, of East Allington, of the other part were published att Kingsbridge, in the markett place, on three markett dayes, in three severall weekes. And no exception. And the said Francis Blackeller and Margarett Hooper were married the eighth day of July, in the yeare of our Lord one thousand six hundred and fifty four."

There are also entries in the register of the publication of banns in the choir of the church. The entry of the above marriage is imperfect in not having the dates of the three publications, and especially in not having the signatures of the magistrate and witnesses. The ceremony would not be performed in the church, and the parties had to go before the Justice, not he to come to them, hence the convenience of access to such an officer would often determine the place for the ceremony, which no doubt accounts for the fact that during the year in which this entry occurs there are entries of numerous marriages; in fact, far more than there are in any one year now, although the population of the town has increased considerably since then. The magistrate probably resided at Kingsbridge, and so people from the country places round would come there to be married, the ceremony being performed in the market place, near the Shambles. The Act continued in force until the Restoration, when the parochial clergy again resumed their former place and duty.

With respect to what was the design of the original seal of the town of Kingsbridge, about which there has been some doubt, Mr. Davies says,—

"A deed exists dated the 20th day of March, 1475, which is perhaps the most interesting in the whole collection of deeds in Kingsbridge church, and for several reasons, the chief being that there is attached to the deed the only existing impression in wax of the original common seal of the town of Kingsbridge. That it was the town seal admits of no doubt, for it is expressly stated in the deed that it is such. The device is a mound or monde with an archiepiscopal or double cross issuing therefrom, and the letters J and S being placed on the dexter and sinister sides respectively, and exterior to the device. The deed is a concession from Robert Gye and Thomas May, the churchwardens of St. Edmund, to John Scoos, sen., giving the latter permission to build the south wall of his new house on the site of the churchyard on the north side. It is tolerably well known that the present footpath called Higher Church Steps, leading from Fore Street to the Workhouse, was originally comprised in and formed part of the churchyard, and in this deed we have before us what seems to be evidence of the first encroachments in this direction. The deed itself is rather dilapidated, but the seal is in first-class preservation, the impression on the wax coming out as clearly as if it was made only yesterday."

There are several Nonconformist places of worship in Kingsbridge, and nearly all of them are situated in Fore Street. The Baptists are the oldest Nonconforming body in the district, and their Society was founded in 1640, but it is not stated when the first chapel was erected, but it probably would be in Meeting Lane, not far from the present building. In the existing chapel there is a tablet commemorating the memories of Leonard Kent, Philip Weymouth, and Arthur Langworthy, who laboured and suffered for the truth's sake in the reign of Charles II in connexion with the church, and in 1689 it is stated the Rev. Samuel Hart was the pastor. Toward the close of the seventeenth century the Rev. Martyn Dunsford was appointed pastor, and in 1702, during his ministry, a new chapel was erected, and when he died in 1703, his body was interred within the sacred edifice. The Rev. Crispin Courtis succeeded to the pastorate early in the eighteenth century, and his oversight of the church lasted for fifty years. He died on December 14th, 1768, and his body was interred at Venn yard, an interesting burying place in Churchstow parish, but situated near the village of Aveton Gifford, given to the Baptists by Mr. Richard Langworthy, of Hatch, in 1673. In 1798 the congregation had evidently outgrown the capacity of the "Meeting House," the name the place of worship was known by, and it was decided to erect a larger chapel, not on the same site, but a little lower down the Lane, which was accordingly done, and the old chapel was converted into cottages. This was during the ministry of the Rev. H. Penn, who after a successful pastorate of 19 years, died on October 25th, 1802, at the age of 44 years, and his body was interred near the door of the new chapel. Mr. Penn was succeeded in the pastorate by the Rev. John Nicholson, who died on August 26th, 1832, and his body was buried in Venn yard. The chapel was enlarged in 1852, from which time it has met the requirements of the congregation. It will seat 350 persons. A school room is in the rear, built on pillars over a disused burial ground,

184   SALCOMBE AND NEIGHBOURHOOD.

It would appear that the Congregationalists are the successors of a body of Presbyterians, who had a Place of Worship in Fore Street, not far from the existing Wesleyan chapel, and afterwards removed to a new chapel, erected in 1780, on the site of the present Congregational Chapel. It remained as a Presbyterian Church until 1791, when an important change took place, and the congregation adopted the Independent or Congregational mode of worship and tenets of belief, and henceforward

THE GRAMMAR SCHOOL AND UPPER PART OF FORE STREET.

they were known by this name. The chapel for years was known as the Higher Meeting House, and the Baptist as the Lower Meeting House. The chapel was altered and enlarged several times, until in 1858 it was entirely demolished, and the present neat and commodious edifice erected on the same site. It was renovated throughout in 1891, and it will seat about 500 persons.

There is no evidence that either of the Wesleys ever visited Kingsbridge, but Whitfield visited the town, and arriving at 8 o'clock in the evening of February 8th, 1749, found a thousand people waiting for him on the quay, and at once began to preach. "In the solemn still moonlight," he says, "I hope some began to think of working out their salvation with fear and trembling." He at least on this occasion obtained one convert, a lad named Philip Gibbs, who says, "being little of stature, I got up, not into a sycamore tree, but into an elm tree," and was so wrought on by the preacher that a new life was awoke within him, and he afterwards entered the ministry, and was pastor of the Baptist Church at Plymouth for a great number of years, dying on December 5th, 1800.

It was at the commencement of the 19th century that Wesleyan-Methodism was introduced into Kingsbridge, and then not by means of any regular preacher, but through the agency of some Welsh militia men, who were stationed at the Barracks, Kingsbridge, for a time. These Welshmen were godly and evidently very strongly attached to Methodism, for instead of contenting themselves by attending the services of some one or other of the religious bodies at that time in the town, they organized services of their own, meeting together in a cottage in Dodbrooke, and conducted their devotional exercises in their own native tongue. These meetings attracted some amount of attention amongst outsiders, and some of the residents of the town became desirous of joining them in their worship. They accordingly invited the public to join them, and sent the town crier around to announce the times when their services would be held, and for the convenience of those attending, conducted them in English instead of Welsh. The services were very successful, insomuch that a school room had to be hired in Kingsbridge, and regular services held every Sunday. The society formed attracted the attention of the Conference, and in the year 1807 that portion of the County extending from Brixham to

Kingsbridge was formed into a Mission district under the name of the South Devon Mission, the Rev. John Jordan, the first minister appointed, taking up his residence at Kingsbridge as superintendent preacher. The present property in Fore Street was purchased in 1813, the chapel erected in 1814, and enlarged and improved in 1870, and will seat 400 persons.

The Brethren's chapel was erected in 1853, with a colonnade before the principal entrance; the chapel stands back from the street, from which it is separated by a lawn; there are 300 sittings.

The meeting house belonging to the Society of Friends, in Fore Street, will seat 200 person, but the Friends are now extinct in the town, and the building is used by the Salvation Army. George Fox, the first of the Quakers, visited Kingsbridge in 1655, and again in 1663 and 1668. The Friends had an ancient burying ground in Fore Street, on the site where now is erected the engine house and Feoffees' room.

The Grammar School, situated at the upper part of Fore Street, is one of the oldest pile of buildings in the town, with a house adjoining, in which is some well carved wainscotting, said to have belonged to the monks of Buckfast. The school was founded in 1670 by Thomas Crispin, who was born in Kingsbridge in 1607-8, but most of whose life was spent in Exeter, where he was in business as a fuller. A portrait of Crispin hangs on the walls of the school house. In the year 1691, Mr. William Duncombe, the first master of this school, appointed by Crispin himself, left £50 per annum to a lecturer, who was to preach once on a Sunday, as well as once a month on a week day in the parish church. He also left £10 a year to three poor scholars, who should be educated at the school, to be enjoyed by them for four years. The school is now managed under a scheme of the Endowed Schools Commissioners, by which twelve governors are appointed for six years in rotation, three by the trustees of Duncombe's Charity, three by the trustees of Crispin's

Charity, three by the magistrates of the Stanborough and Coleridge Division, and three by the ratepayers. The endowments yield an income of about £300 yearly.

The Devon and Cornwall Banking Company have an imposing new pile of buildings in Fore Street, with the Post Office adjoining. Lloyds Bank, the Wilts and Dorset Banking Company, and the Naval Bank have branches here. At the top of Duncombe Street, where it joins Fore Street, is a building erected by the Feoffees, the upper storey containing a large room used for Urban District Council, School Board, parish and other meetings, whilst the under part is used as a Fire Brigade Station, under the management of the Urban Council. In Duncombe Street is also situated the St. Edmund's Hall, which is used for the Church Sunday-school, parochial, and other meetings. The rooms are also used by the St. Edmund's Institute, which is affiliated to the Young Men's Friendly Society. Just opposite this building is a Masonic Temple, where the members of the Duncombe Lodge of Freemasons hold their meetings monthly.

Duncombe Street was formerly the northern boundary of property called Shygerland or Sygerland. The line of the present street was probably identical with the lane called Syger Lane, or the steep lane, which in course of time became changed to Sugar Lane, a name by which it went up to a few years ago. The street may owe its original name to David Sucar, who in the beginning of the 14th century had a house near St. Edmund's Church. It is now called after the first master and munificent benefactor of the Kingsbridge Grammar School.

The manor of Kingsbridge is the property of Mr. John S. Hurrell. A manorial court is held every two years, at which a portreeve and town crier are appointed. As to the origin of the title portreeve, Mr. Davies remarks, "the title of portreeve or portgrave is from the Anglo-Saxon word portgerefa, signifying the town reeve or principal lay personage of the town. The title was probably held in Kingsbridge down to the reign of Henry v, and then

KINGSBRIDGE FROM NORTON HILL.

the portreeves, with one exception, aspired to a higher dignity, for in 1414, 1415, 1422. and 1425, and probably in the intermediate years, they were designated Mayors of the Burgh of Kingsbridge, and although from 1425 downwards they dropped from their higher estate, yet we find in the reign of Henry VIII. the title seems to have been sanctioned in high places, for a receipt is in existence from a Collector of Royal dues in the West of England, shewing clearly, that whatever the portreeve himself thought about it, the Royal Collector signed this receipt as 'Received from the Mayor of Kingsbridge.'" The list of portreeves for Kingsbridge from the year 1332 to 1492, compiled by Mr. Davies, will doubtless be of interest:—

1332	John Clement	1423	John Torrynge (Mayor)
1337	John Boghewode	1424	John Jaycok (probably)
1341	William Strika	1425	Richard Bourynge (Mayor
1342	Adam Noreys	1429	John Veele (probably)
1346	Roger Deghere	1441	Hugh Ropere
1361	Richard Heryuge	1452	Wm. Boway
1370	John Toker		Wm. Blakehalle (bailiff)
	John Velda (bailiff)	1456	Wm. Boway (probably)
1371	John Lombe, jun.	1457	John Bradleghe (probably
1376	Peter Holdyche	1459	Hugh Ropere
1378	Thomas Bowy	1460	William Andrew
1384	John Radewille	1461	Thomas Gey (probably)
1391	Robert Combe	1462	John Maleburghe
1395	John Hordeuel		Wm. Davelys (bailiff)
1396	John Hacche (probably)	1463	John Maleburghe
1397	Stephen Strange (probably)		(probably)
1398	John Hacche		William Bayleghe (bailiff
1400	Richard Lokyntone	1475	William Cornysshe
1410	Thomas Duer	1479	Richard Hille
1411	Roger Saundere	1486	Peter Courteney (sic)
1414	Andrew Blakehalle (Mayor)		Nicholas Ozant (bailiff)
1415	David Ryder (Mayor)	1489	Sir John Hallewille
1416	Roger Saundere (probably)	1490	Robert Gye
1418	Roger Saundere		John Serle (bailiff)
	Robert Bolde (bailiff)	1491	Robert Gye
1422	Robert Torryng (Mayor)	1492	Stephen Wynter

"There are more gaps in the list than names, but that may be partially accounted for by the fact that a portreeve may have held his office for many years."

The Manor House is a fine building standing in its own grounds at the upper part of Fore Street, and is the residence of the lord of the manor. The house and grounds formerly belonged to Mr. Scobell, the then lord of the manor, and was known as the Manor House. Having sold the property the name of the house was altered to the Knowle. Mr. Hurrell having become the owner he gave the house its original name. The land was formerly part of property called the Knowle, designated in the ancient records La Knolle, described as a plot of land of an irregular four-sided figure, extending probably the whole length of Duncombe Street to the brook on the south side, and abutting the main road from the corner of Duncombe Street to the top of Wallingford on the west, bounded by Wallingford Lane on the north, and on the east by the brook or watercourse dividing Kingsbridge from Dodbrooke.

In 1797 Colonel Montagu, who had resigned his commission in the army, came to reside at the Knowle, now the Manor House, and devoted his whole attention to natural history, writing a score or more books on the subject. In June, 1815, the Colonel had the misfortune to tread upon a rusty nail, lockjaw supervened, and he died on the 20th of the same month. His old and attached friend, the Rev. K. Vaughan, of Aveton Gifford, who was at his bedside during his last illness, having asked him where he would wish to be buried, his characteristic reply was, "Where the tree falls, there let it lie." It is not known with certainty where he was buried, but it is asserted by some that he was buried in the parish church, but that when the latter was restored in 1860 the coffin, with all the rest in the church, was despoiled of its leaden shell, and all trace of the vault obliterated. There is no entry in the register of his interment, and no memorial stone can be traced. The family records suggest that he was buried in the grounds of Knowle.

The public property of the town is of considerable value; it is mostly vested in feoffees, and the proceeds are distributed by "the chiefest portion of the inhabitants in vestry assembled." It is estimated that the annual value of this property, when existing leases shall have expired, will amount to upwards of £500.

A Burial Board of nine members was established in December, 1865, but the Cemetery at Highhouse Point was not procured and laid out until 1874. It is an acre in extent, and contains two mortuary chapels.

A School Board of seven members was formed on the 9th August, 1887, for the united parishes of Kingsbridge and Dodbrooke.

A large cattle and pleasure fair is held on the Thursday after the 19th July in every year, and extends to the end of the week. The head-quarters of the E Company 5th Volunteer (Haytor) Battalion Devonshire Regiment are in Fore Street. There is a spacious armoury belonging to this Company, and about two miles south of the town, at Charleton Marsh, is an excellent range.

In addition to the shipbuilding yard and rope manufactory already referred to, there is an iron foundry, two breweries, a large roller flour mill, and implement works, and these are the principal industries of the district. At the early part of the 19th century Kingsbridge was a thriving industrial centre, for in addition to the woollen and combing trade there were three tanyards in full work, and it was quite a sight at that time to see on pay nights (Saturdays) the curriers and tanners crowding around Mr. Branscombe, the tanner's offices. There is now only one tanyard, and the tanning trade is practically gone. There were then three tallow melting chandlers employing many men; now all gone. With gas and oils there is not the demand for candles there was then. Malting then was largely engaged in, employing many hands, but the malt houses are now lying empty or turned to other uses.

The principal hotels are the King's Arms, established for nearly a century; the Albion, and the Anchor, from which coaches run three times a day to the sea-side hotel at Torcross, on Start Bay, and twice daily through to Dartmouth. Two newspapers, the *Kingsbridge Journal* and *Kingsbridge Gazette*, are published weekly.

It is interesting to note what the approaches to the town were like in the early part of the second quarter of the 19th century. A person coming from Plymouth would very likely be glad to get out of the waggon and walk down Norton Hill, then much steeper than now, the lower part having also been considerably improved in recent years by carrying the road over the line of railway. As he ascended the hill on the Kingsbridge side where is now the Vicar's garden, he would have found an old orchard with a very dilapidated fence. Where is now the vicarage and lawn was then a field with apple trees around it, and about that time this field was often occupied by crowds of people, a great part of whom occupied raised seats witnessing a wrestling match. Coming from Loddiswell the first habitation in view was a house known as Cat's Castle, for long untenanted, and after some years formed the material for a huge bonfire on a 5th of November. Where is now Barnfield House was then an old barn and cow sheds. The house near was the old poor house, and next door was then a tumble-down dwelling inhabited by persons who paid no rent. Bridge Street was an open sewer or brook, through which the tide flowed regularly. There was a raised footpath that led along by the side, but when the tide was up carts and even horsemen were forced to go around by Duke Street.

If ever Kingsbridge becomes a health resort, for which it is so well adapted, it would soon make its name known for the warmth of its climate, its situation, and its scenery. Excursions may be made to the adjoining seaside resorts, which are numerous, and comfortable lodgings can be obtained in most of the villages at moderate charges and to suit all classes of visitors. Within a radius of six miles the open sea may be reached at many divergent points—Bantham Sands, where the River Avon ends its course, Hope, where Bolt Tail rises to a height of some hundreds of feet out of the sea; Salcombe, to which place the *Salcombe Castle*, a new and commodious steamer, makes frequent trips daily down the Estuary. By one of these trips the visitor is certain to be delighted at the scenery presented, gradually opening and expanding as the craft glides through the water, passing first Charleton Church on the left, and West Alvington on the right. High on the hills to the westward, and very conspicuous, is the spire of Malborough Church, which can be seen from almost every point in the South Hams, and is so well known on that side of the moor as Brent Tor is on the other. Passing through what is called "Widegates," soon the harbour proper of Salcombe is entered, and in turning the corner the splendour of the scene is suddenly thrust upon one, with the noble hills of Portlemouth on the left, and straight before in rugged outline Bolt Head. Excursions can also be made to the long stretch of sands at Slapton and Torcross. Some of the fairest lanes in Devon are there, presenting at each month a new panorama to the enchanted visitors. In April the hedgerows are yellow with primroses, growing as thickly as buttercups in a field. A month later, and the wayside is blue with the flowers of bluebells and wild hyacinths. The ferns are fresh and luxuriant in October. Loddiswell mill lies a couple of miles away—as pretty a spot as can be imagined. The river Avon runs to the sea through its double arches, finding a home for fish on the way.

Kingsbridge Poor Law Union comprises the following twenty-six parishes:—

Aveton Gifford, Bigbury, Blackawton, Buckland-Tout-Saints, Charleton, Chivelstone, Churchstow, East Allington, East Portlemouth, Kingsbridge and Dodbrooke, Kingston, Loddiswell, Malborough, Modbury, Ringmore, Salcombe, Sherford, Slapton, South Huish, South Milton, South Pool, Stokefleming, Stokenham, Thurlestone, West Alvington, and Woodleigh. The Guardians meet every alternate Saturday; the population of the Union in 1891 was 17,648, and the area 71,510 acres.

The population of the united parishes of Kingsbridge and Dodbrooke in 1891 was 2885.

DODBROOKE can claim an earlier origin than Kingsbridge, and appears to have derived its name from the Saxon surname Dodda, and would imply the brook of Dodda. In Domesday it is named Dodebroch, in the possession of Godeva, widow of Brictric, the sheriff, and she paid geld for four hides of land, of which she held in demesne as much as four ploughs could cultivate; and there was a wood of small growth, eight furlongs in length, and one in breadth. Dodbrooke is believed to have been held under Godeva by a family whose members wrote themselves De Dodbrooke, and whose possessions finally devolved upon an heiress who married Alan, the son of Rowald. In the year 1276 the jurors of the Hundred of Coleridge found that Alan claimed assize of bread and ale, with a weekly market on Wednesdays, and a two days fair at the feast of St. Mary Magdalene, all which had been granted by a charter of Henry III. The weekly market has long since been discontinued, but the annual fair is held on the Wednesday before Palm Sunday. Henry Fitz-Alan died in possession of the manor in 1318. Great strife arose between this lord of Dodbrooke and his powerful neighbour Ralph Monthermer, lord of Stokenham, and afterwards Earl of Gloucester and Hereford; and we learn that Henry Fitz-Alan impleaded Matthew, the son of John, and forty others, for throwing down his pillory in Dodbrooke. The feud resulted however in the abandonment of all claim on the part of Monthermer. At last the line of these lords of Dodbrooke ended in an heiress named Elinor, who, by her marriage to Thomas Champernowne, of Modbury, carried the manor and advowson of Dodbrooke to the ancient race since settled at Dartington. There is clear evidence of the ownership of the Champernownes as early as the year 1464; and Westcote, writing in 1630, informs us that "some of them lie interred in the north aisle, with their proportions cut in stone." The north aisle of Dodbrooke Church was long since taken down, and the Champernowne monuments have disappeared.

Langewylle or Well House stands on the site of an ancient large mansion, and there are extensive remains of ancient masonry still existing on the property, and of great interest to the antiquarian. In 1374 it belonged to the Geye family, and then probably to the Champernownes. Bishop Stafford in 1403 licensed a chapel for divine service, dedicated to St. Mary atte Wylle, which was probably connected with Langwell House. In 1478 Dodbrooke boasted a hermitage. This recluse probably lived in a cell close to the church, and belonged to Sir Richard Champernowne, who by his will in that year provided a sum of eight marks a year to the priest to say mass in Dodbrooke church, and provided specially for "his anchorite who gave herself continually to prayer." A part of the chancel of Dodbrooke church was also from time immemorial attached to Well House. In 1896 the Rev. T. C. Lewis, the Rector of Dodbrooke, purchased the property, and has since converted this part of the chancel into a chapel dedicated to St. Mary atte Wylle.

The parish and town of Dodbrooke is so closely connected with Kingsbridge, that their boundaries are very indistinctly defined. A cattle market is held on the third Wednesday in every month, and is attended by a large number of butchers and agriculturists; an open square near the centre of the town, called Market Cross, is devoted to the purposes of this market.

The parish church of St. Thomas a Becket stands at the north end of the town; it is in the Perpendicular style, consisting of chancel, nave, aisles, and square tower, at one time surmounted by a spire, which was removed in 1785; the tower contains five bells. The church is of the sixteenth century, and there is an old and beautifully carved screen. The church, partially and badly restored in 1846, was again restored in 1886, when the chancel was rebuilt, a north aisle added, divided from the chancel and nave by an arcade of six arches, three of which were taken from the ruins of the now disused church of South Huish; the ceiling of the south aisle

ON THE AVON, NEAR LODDISWELL STATION.

was removed, exposing the oak roof, which is enriched with carving and bosses. The parish register dates from 1725. The Rectory House and grounds adjoin the church.

Dodbrooke is famous for being the first place where white ale was brewed, and which is still manufactured in this neighbourhood only. White ale is a beverage made of malt, hops, eggs, and flour, and fermented with an ingredient called "grout." The taste for this composition is rapidly declining, but the manufacture was at one time so large that the rector levied a tithe on it, which is chargeable to this day; tradition assigns the introduction of this peculiar beverage into the district to the surgeon of a German regiment which was at one time quartered here, but one who has made the beverage a special study, has come to the interesting conclusion that it is really the old English ale, described as being a thicker drink than beer, and that the white ale of the South Hams is a survival in some form of the ale once drunk by our forefathers all over England.

In the last quarter of the 18th century two young men residing in a village adjoining the Moor made up their minds to leave home and seek a living elsewhere. They were both carpenters by trade. When they came near Ashburton the roads diverged to what was considered the two most rising and flourishing towns in the west of England, Torquay and Kingsbridge, and the two men decided to separate. Kingsbridge was then considered pre-eminently the most important town. The two young men, one named Harvey and the other Cowling, when they came to the cross road tossed a penny which should take his choice of the two places. Mr. Cowling won the toss, and it was to the chagrin of Harvey that Cowling choosed Kingsbridge. Anyone who has read of the rise of Torquay will find that the main spring and presiding genius of that town's first great rise was the Mr. Harvey here mentioned. It is the old saying, what great events from little causes spring. What might have been the difference had the penny fallen otherwise?

THE KINGSBRIDGE RAILWAY.—Before the advent of the railway Kingsbridge was a great coaching centre, three and four coaches running daily to and from the Great Western Station at Wrangaton. Great as was the improvement from the coach to the railway, equally great was the coach upon the methods of locomotion in the earlier parts of the nineteenth century. If persons desired in those days to go or come from Plymouth they had the chance to ride in a lumbering waggon, stowed away amongst all sorts of merchandise or lumber, but with this disadvantage to the traveller, he being live lumber and not likely to break (except in his temper), was generally stowed away by the driver in an uncomfortable situation. But then as a sop to the aristocratic traveller of that day, an enterprising townsman, Mr. Thomas Haynes, put on a one-horse spring trap, which can best be described as a square box on two wheels, a cover on top, curtain around, which could be opened or drawn at pleasure. Afterwards when the late Mr. Foale started a coach to Plymouth, great and dire were the prophecies of ruin and disaster in respect to that said coach. If persons wanted to go to Exeter they had to go by waggon, the proprietor of which was the late Mr. R. Foale's father. They went as far as Totnes in those waggons, when they were transferred to others of the same firm, managed by the present Mr. Joseph Foale's father. The conveyance to Dartmouth was even worse, over fearful roads, and the waggon for a great part of the year on its return was loaded principally with salt fish, which was not particularly pleasant for the passengers.

The opening of the South Devon Railway from Plymouth to Exeter naturally led to improved methods of travelling, and the ten miles between the nearest station and Kingsbridge was constantly travelled over by a good service of coaches. These in their turn were abolished when the branch line of railway was opened from Brent Station on the main line of the Great Western Railway to Kingsbridge in 1893. The passenger station at Kingsbridge is situated on West Alvington Hill. The line makes a somewhat abrupt curve on leaving the station over a fine bridge that spans the private road leading to Bowringsleigh, and then runs along a pretty piece in a straight line to the tunnel at Sorley, which is about 600 yards in length and takes a minute to pass through, from which it emerges on to a high embankment. Turning again in a sharp curve it crosses an iron bridge on Rake Hill, from which a splendid view down the Avon Vale is obtained, the river winding its course like a silver streak until lost in the distance. Loddiswell station is situated in Woodleigh Bottom, and is about a mile from the former village, but a little nearer Woodleigh, but serves both villages. The line then proceeds on to Topsham Bridge, and follows the river, avoiding its serpentine meanderings by means of numerous bridges, on to Gara Bridge, where the line is double, with a platform on each side. This station is about mid-way between Brent and Kingsbridge, and is beautifully situated in a well-wooded vale. Very few railway depots are favoured with such a splendid situation as this. It is in the heart of a lovely vale, with wooded hills rising steep all round and the river sparkling along between. The railway crosses about forty-five bridges in the course of the twelve and a half miles. Between Gara and Avonwick it passes some of the most beautiful scenery to be seen in Devonshire. Diptford is passed on the right, with its fine church tower and then Avonwick station is reached, situated a little below Avonwick village, and meets the requirements of that place and also Diptford. The south side at Brent Station is the accommodation for passengers to and from Kingsbridge and the north side for the main line.

The branch line diverges from the main line close to Brent Station, and runs down the Avon Valley. The Avon continues its course almost due south from Brent to the English Channel, and the railway keeps it company so far as Loddiswell.

SALCOMBE TO SOUTH POOL.

IF for no other purpose, a visit to this village is worth making, in order to view the scenery along the shores of the creek leading to it. At the head of the harbour, where branches off the Kingsbridge Estuary, South Pool Creek commences, running in a north-east direction, and soon forms into two arms, the one to the right extending but for a short distance, and terminating

SOUTH POOL CREEK FROM GULLET.

at Waterhead. The creek to South Pool is navigable at high tide by barges and boats. At the entrance of this creek to the left is a farmhouse called Westercombe, and further inland but not visible from the water, is Scobell, which belonged to a family called Scobbahull in the times of Kings Henry III. and IV., and from whom it derived its name. Its present owner is Sir Henry Peek. During the proper tides boating on this creek will be found an enjoyable recreation, the scenery being of a varied description. The abundant vegetation and beautiful foliage lining the foreshore on either side, literally run down and bury themselves in the water; and, one enthusiastic traveller has described it as the Rhine in miniature. The finest moss, of downy softness, covers every bank, while the great family of ferns scatter themselves in orderly confusion until one is bewildered with their diversity and variety. The wild convolvulus also, with its snow-white and trumpet-shaped figure, hangs gracefully from many a hedge row, while the fox-glove, the mallow, and clematis ornament every inch of uncultivated ground. It is, however, in the spring of the year when vegetation is the most enchanting, when the eyes behold with delight the thickly-studded orchards decked in bloom, when the perfume of the wild honey-suckle and the innumerable flowers, cultivated and uncultivated, bring to the senses a delight that one does not soon forget.

On the right is passed Gullet, a little inlet, with a farmhouse in the foreground, and prettily-situated apple orchards in the rear. To land here and climb the hillside on the left, a charming view is obtained, the creek winding its way between well-wooded banks on either side, until its waters become merged in those of the harbour, with the town of Salcombe in the distance. Down deep in the wooded recesses of a romantic vale, and at the head of the creek, nestles the village of South Pool, beautifully sheltered from the withering east wind, and opens its lap to the gentle and life-giving breezes of the sunny south and south-west.

It appears to have derived its name from its ancient owners, the De Pola's. The manor belonged, when the first Henry was king, to Lord Nicholas de la Pola, whose son went with Richard I. into the Holy Land, and from whose family it passed to the Pomerays in the time of Henry III.

The living is a rectory, with 45 acres of glebe and residence. The Charities consist of an annuity of 21s. left by Leonard Dare; a gift of 25s. a year, left by Andrew Horseman; and £85 yearly, left by the late Mrs. Praed for the school and other purposes. There is a National School for boys and girls, with residence for the master adjoining. Capt. A. P. Halifax is lord of the manor, and principal landowner. The population in 1891 was 346.

The Church stands upon a hill above the village, its tower standing out boldly in the immediate foreground; it is dedicated to St. Nicholas and St. Cyriack, consisting of nave and chancel, with aisles, transepts, west tower, containing six bells, and south porch; it is mostly of the 15th century, with traces of an earlier date, the font being, apparently, of Norman character. There are remains of a fine screen, half of which has been carefully restored, and the edifice retains a piscina and stoups. It was partially restored, with only moderate success, some years ago; and, later, the east end of the chancel has been adorned by the insertion of a new window of rare beauty of design, the stained glass in which is intended to be a memorial of certain members of the family of Canon Cornish. There is a remarkable altar tomb in the chancel, within a canopied arched recess, of Thomas Bryant, a former Rector of this parish, adorned with a carving of the Resurrection in front, and on the tomb is the recumbent effigy of a priest vested, apparently, in cassock, surplice with large open sleeves, hanging in plaited folds, and over this a stole, quite after the modern use and aspect, and a like instance, of pre-reformation date, is not known. The tomb bears the following inscription:—

"Hic jacet Dnus Tomas Briant quondam Rector hujus Ecclesiæ et Portlemothiæ." *(Here lies Mr. Thomas Briant, late Rector of this Church and Portlemouth).*

No date is apparent on the tomb, but Mr. Bryant was a pluralist, being Rector of this parish and the adjoining parish of Portlemouth, in 1536.

Under a window in the south transept is the recumbent effigy of a lady in a long close-fitting dress and mantle, conjectured to represent Muriel, wife of Sir Thomas de Courtenay, lord of the manor of South Pool in 1340. There is a white marble monument in the east wall of the south aisle, with a narrow canopy, and a black slab for the inscription, with a verse on the under part of the monument, part of which however is so much obliterated that it cannot be made out; but on the left side are two boys behind a man kneeling, and on the right side a woman and three girls behind her kneeling. The following is the inscription:—

"This Monument is erected to the deserved memorye of Leonard Darre, Esq., and Joan his wyfe, the daughter of Sir George Bond, Knt., alderman of London and late maior of the sayde cittye in the memorable yeare 1588. Joan deceased the 10th of December, 1608 whom her husband followed on the 28th of Marche, 1615, leaving issue of their bodyes 2 sonnes and 3 daughters."

In 1690 the Patron presented to the living a clergyman that did not meet with the approval of the Bishop, who inducted instead the Rev. Gawen Hayman, and it is said the latter obtained possession of the church by having a key made from an impression of the original taken in wax. Against the north wall of the church a monument of black marble is erected to this Rector's memory, stating that the integrity of his life, the purity of his manners, his modesty, temperance, and affability soon gained the good will of both patron and parishioners, and the epitaph further states that he was the best master, the best friend, the best husband, the best father, and one of the best Christians that the age in which he lived produced. He held the living for 47 years, dying on the 8th February, 1735, aged 74 years. There is also a marble stone in the floor of the chancel to the memory of his wife, who died on March 19th, 1746, aged 76 years, and of her it is stated that she was respected by the rich and beloved by the poor, and in her temper she was remarkably cheerful, and in her behaviour very inoffensive.

In the early part of the 19th century there was an ancient monument in the graveyard, on the east side, near the chancel wall, and which by some means was destroyed, and a flat stone that covered it bore the following inscription:—

"Depositum Gulielmi Streat, quondam hujus Ecclesiæ rectoris qui obiit XI die Junii, Anno Dom. 1666." *(Here is deposited the body of William Streat, late rector of this parish, who died the 11th day of June, in the year of Our Lord 1666).*

SOUTH POOL CHURCH.

Of this Rector it is stated that previous to his death he had promised marriage to one Mistress Dorothy Ford, and that he was disinterred and a marriage ceremony gone through on the following November 27th, and that the body was not interred again until August 31st, 1668.

Of the ancient Rectors of this parish, the following notes have been taken from Bishop Stafford's Register.

On the 28th March, 1398, the Bishop being in London, the Vicar-General of the Diocese instituted Sir John Reed, priest, to the Rectory of "South-pole," which was vacant by reason of the death of Sir Edward Patryngg, on the presentation of Sir John Dynham, knight. Reed died in 1406; and on the 10th of August in that year, the Bishop, being at Clyst, instituted John Aller, chaplain, as his successor, the patrons being James Aumarle, John Pole, Robert Maynard, Thomas Hertescote, and John

SOUTH POOL VILLAGE.

Bole. He did not long enjoy his benefice; for, in the following year, June 24th, 1407, the Bishop, at Crediton, instituted Master William Langeton, on the decease of Aller, the same patrons—apparently trustees—again presenting. Langeton died early in 1414, and on the 19th of February in that year, Bishop Stafford instituted Sir

John Carvargh, chaplain, Robert Maynard and Thomas Hertescote alone acting as patrons for this turn.

In the first volume of the same Bishop's Register, there is a curious account of the Relaxation of an Interdict under which this parish was laid in the beginning of the 15th century. The Bishop, being at Crediton, writes on the 8th of October, 1410, to "the Dean of Wodelegh," and to the curate in charge of South Pole and chaplains serving in the Parish Church there, setting forth that, whereas the said church was lying under an interdict, on account of a sermon having been preached in it by a certain secular chaplain, name unknown, who had no cure of souls there, and who had been brought in by certain of the parishioners, not (as it appeared) out of contempt but through ignorance, but who had neither licence nor mission, the Bishop, in compliance with the wish of the noble Lady, Margaret Peverel (a parishioner there), tempering rigour with mercy, was pleased to relax the said interdict, requiring the said Dean to publish the fact in the church of South Pole, and in other convenient churches in the neighbourhood, and to certify the Bishop thereof under his authentic seal. The Lady Margaret was evidently an influential "parishioner." In fact she was Lady of the Manor, and lived, therefore, under the very shadow of the interdicted sanctuary, for the Manor of South Pole passed from the Pomerays to the family of de Cirencester and afterwards it was the property of Sir Thomas Courtenay, from whom it passed to the Peverels, and from them to the Hungerfords, descending to Henry Hastings, Earl of Huntington, who sold the Manor to the Heles.

The tide flows to the entrance of the village, where the creek terminates, the road being carried over it by a bridge. Near this bridge is an old elm tree, of large proportions, much venerated by the villagers, and pointed out as one of the sights of the neighbourhood, but there is no particular history attaching to the tree so far as we have been able to discover.

SALCOMBE TO THE START.

THE Start Lighthouse lies distant from Salcombe by the shortest route close upon six miles. The ferry is taken at Orestone, and having crossed over the harbour, a landing is effected on the other side. The village of Portlemouth is situated in a very elevated position, and the road leading to it from the ferry is the steepest bit of hill to be found for a long distance, but an extensive and splendid view is obtained at the top. Here, on a little table-land projecting from the hill-side, is the finest view in all the district, if only the tide be high. The harbour lies some distance below, the several creeks divided from each other by rounded grassy promontories; the town of Kingsbridge nestles in the northern distance; opposite, giving light and character to the hill-side, stands the town of Salcombe, while the harbour widens to the south and closes in the noble outline of Bolt Head.

Portlemouth Church is dedicated to St. Onolaus, a supposed Danish saint, but nothing is known of him; it has been suggested, however, that St. Olaus, or St. Olave, may have been meant. The church stands in a commanding situation, and is a cruciform building, consisting of nave and chancel, with aisles to both, and transepts, north porch and west tower, the tower being the oldest part of the church, which, with that exception, was rebuilt in the 15th century. There is an ancient stone font. The church was restored in 1881, at the cost of the late Duchess of Cleveland, and is now chiefly remarkable for what remains of a once magnificent rood-screen, richly carved, and sumptuously decorated in gold and colours, with many quaintly executed figures of saints in the panels of the lower part. It is 13th century work.

The effect of this screen is marred by the strangely mistaken re-arrangement of the levels of the chancel floor, the practical result of which is that the officiating minister's head is closely caged behind the tracery of the openings, involving a loss both of sight and sound.

GOODSHELTER, WATERHEAD CREEK.

On September 13th, 1399, the Vicar-General of the Diocese (the Bishop being absent in London), admitted Sir William Gore, priest, to the Rectory of Portlemouth, vacant by the death of Sir John Belamyslond, on the presentation of Sir Richard Champernon, knight. Gore died in 1405; and on the 22nd of May in that year, the Bishop admitted to the vacant benefice, John Thomas, a deacon, Sir Richard Champernon being the patron on this occasion also. Being only in deacon's orders at the time of his institution, the Bishop granted him a dispensation (on the 22nd of September next following), to enable him to prosecute his studies in the University of Oxford " for the space of four years," an arrangement which was common enough in those days, but is, happily, impossible now. At the northern end of the churchyard there is a lynch gate; many of the monumental stones in the yard have become much worn by age, and the inscriptions illegible. On one of the tombstones in the churchyard, placed over the grave of a farmer who had been poisoned by his servant girl, the following epitaph was inscribed:—

"Here lieth the body of Richard Jarvis, of Rickham, in this Parish, who departed this life the 25th day of May, 1782, aged 77.

> Through poisons strong he was cut off,
> And brought to death at last;
> It was by his apprentice girl,
> On whom there's sentence past.
> Oh may all people warning take,
> For she was burned to a stake"

The girl was executed at Exeter, and the body afterwards burnt; the latter punishment being thereafter abolished. The visitor will search in vain for this epitaph now, it being worn out by age. Many of the stones bear sad testimony to the great loss of life by drowning, and there is one large grave not far from the belfry door, containing six bodies, the crew of a French schooner named the *Pauline*, driven ashore at Rickham some years ago, all of them being drowned, and the bodies recovered a short time afterwards.

Portlemouth hill must be descended to get on the road to the Start, which lies for some distance along the foreshore, in a northerly and then easterly direction. The Parsonage lies, deep buried, in a secluded little nook close to the water's edge, shadowed by overhanging hills and trees of no recent growth. The old Parsonage house, taken down in 1882, and replaced by a new building through the munificence of the patron, was situated nearer the little bay than the new building. The outbuildings attached to the old Rectory comprehended an older Rectory, a most curious and interesting mediæval Parsonage, much knocked about and dilapidated, but perfect nevertheless, and of the 14th century date. The principal door, a well-proportioned archway of stone, simply chamfered, leading to a passage between the screens; and although the partition and floors had been repaired or renewed, and that in rough fashion, till little was left of their original materials, yet all remained in the original place and order, and hall and kitchen, with bed-chambers, two in number, above them, still stood, to shew what manner of "manse" the clergymen of Portlemouth, in the olden days, were content to dwell in. It is to be regretted that this rare specimen of a mediæval Parsonage could not have been suffered to remain, either as a curiosity, or for some more useful purpose.

The road for some little distance skirts the creek and is moderately level, but in some parts can scarcely be rivalled, even in this part of Devon, for sudden ascents, not inaptly compared by the unaccustomed wayfarer to "climbing the roofs of houses," and as sudden descents into the valley beneath. At one point, near Goodshelter, there is a very steep hill, descending into a deep gully or creek, traversed by a stream, and to which the tide flows at times, a road leading out of it on the other side. This marvellous highway is most picturesque and, in places, romantic in the extreme, especially at the western end, where the road winds gracefully and pleasantly along the shore, and commanding striking views of the estuary.

Goodshelter consists of a farmhouse and one or two labourers' cottages, built on the side of the hill overlooking the little bay. A little further on, at the end of the creek, is Waterhead, where there is a picturesque old flour mill, with its water wheel, abutting on to the foreshore Waterhead is less than two miles from Salcombe, and when the tide is favourable a most enjoyable row or sail can be made up this creek, the scenery on the way being of a varied description, and the banks on either side well wooded. There is a landing place near the old mill. The shortest route to the Start now is through some path fields, terminating near the entrance to a narrow lane leading to the village of Chivelstone, the dark weather-stained tower of the church being a striking object from the creek just left, and is best seen from a distance.

Chivelstone Church is dedicated to St. Sylvester, and consists of nave with aisles, chancel, south porch, and western tower. The chancel is the oldest part, being of early 14th century date, the aisles having been added (as was almost invariably the case in Devonshire churches), a century or more later. Unfortunately the east window has perished, and been replaced by a well-intended but poorly designed substitute; but the old side windows remain (one of them having been transferred, however, to a modern vestry, built against the north wall), and these are very good two-light windows, with simple but effective tracery. The church generally is in poor condition, especially the tower, which seems almost on the verge of ruin. Some portions of the adjoining arcade have also given way, the pillars having been undermined by the vaults, with which the soil under the church is honeycombed in a manner quite unprecedented in the case of a little country church like this, surrounded by a sparse agricultural population. Intramural interment must have been the order of the day for many a long year at Chivelstone, and the local workmen are not credited by tradition with any scruples as to the propriety or safety

OLD MILL, WATERHEAD.

of cutting away the very foundations of the pillars that uphold the roof. The ancient rood screen remains, in a fairly perfect condition; the original painting and gilding, still effective even in decay, testify to the olden splendours of what must once have been the glory of this church. The Chivelstone pulpit is a real curiosity. It occupies its original place, at the north-east angle of the nave, close to the screen, and is made in one piece, the trunk of a large oak tree having been hollowed out for the purpose. Externally the trunk was shaped into seemly form, and covered with cunning carvure, all richly gilded and painted like the screen. Chivelstone is joined to the vicarage of Stokenham. South Allington House, the seat of Mr. T. Harris Pitts, is at South Allington.

The road leads direct through the village, past South Allington, on for Kellaton, and after ascending a short hill, the road branches off to the right, and then to the left, descending past the hamlet of Bickerton to Hallsands.

HALLSANDS.—Though England contains many odd nooks and corners, possibly none surpass the little village or hamlet of Hallsands, the chief peculiarity of which is that it does not seem to possess a square foot of soil in the whole place. The visitor may look north and south along the curving horns of Start Bay and see plenty of green fields and fields of waving corn. And closer home, almost overhead, uprise the cliffs, which form the background of the hamlet, breaking off into gentler slopes, where the mallow and the foxglove, and the luxuriant clematis find plenty of soil into which to thrust their roots. But down in the hamlet itself there is nothing but gravel and rock. The peculiarity of Hallsands is that it lies upon bare gravel, more or less compact, or else upon platforms of bare rock, just where the mile of steeply sloping grass which sweeps round from the Start gives place to a line of cliffs gradually increasing in height from 50 feet to the south of the village to 120 feet at the back of it, falling again further northwards. The back of the hamlet, consequently, consists of a natural wall rising to its greatest height about the centre of the hamlet itself, and gradually falling off to right and left, whilst above this natural wall a rapid incline of grassy glacis leads the eye up to a very near horizon, having an average height of about 300 feet, and forming the backbone of the Start peninsula. The hamlet of Hallsands itself looks as if it properly belonged to the sea, and had only been borrowed from it for a time. The whole of the platform on which the hamlet stands is only from thirty to forty feet wide, with a single row of cottages just under the cliffs, and a narrow road along which a van can pass until about the middle of the village, where it abruptly ends in the gravel. Hallsands is pure and simple the abode of fishermen. Out of thirty houses, only the residents in two follow different occupations, and those are the tavern and the village shop, where comfortable lodgings may be obtained. The fishing, however, is of a peculiar character, inasmuch as all the real fish is brought into the place instead of being carried away from it, and is used as bait for the crab and lobster pots. The crab fishery is the real industry of the place. Once a week a smack comes in and lies off the shore; the result of the week's fishery is transferred to her and she is off again to Hamble, near Southampton, and that week's harvesting for the men of Hallsands is done. The smack is built for this particular trade. Her hold is formed into deep wells, into which is admitted a supply of sea water. The living crabs are put into these wells. Each crab as it is passed from the boat into the smack is carefully measured to see that it has attained the regulation size across the back.

The sister smack which puts into Beesands, about a mile further up the shore, has its well fitted mainly for the reception of lobsters, though why there should be this difference between the products of the two places whose positions are so similar is difficult to understand. A good deal of bait is required for crab fishing, and the life of a Hallsands fisherman is pretty evenly divided between examining his crab-pots and getting bait, which consists to a large extent of skate and ray, supplemented as far as possible by red gurnard which is most agreeable to the crabs when perfectly fresh, but can only be obtained in very limited quantities. Some of this bait is purchased from trawlers which happen to pass in the offing, but for the greater part of it the fishermen are obliged to make continual trips along the bay and round Berry Head to Brixham, a voyage of about forty miles in going and returning. Most of the boats club together and make up a crew to go to Brixham and obtain the necessary supply. This causes the boat-load to be often very heavy, and in dirty weather portions of the bait are frequently thrown overboard, and buoyed until the weather permits its recovery. The difficulties of landing at these beaches are so great at times, that the help of Newfoundland dogs has been secured.

A good instance of the hardship of the fisherman's life, and also of the use of the famous Hallsands dogs, will be best illustrated by the following instance that occurred on a July night, during a severe thunderstorm, that was very general over the whole country, described by a visitor to the village:—

The day had been gloriously fine, but in the evening the weather changed and promised a wild night. In a short time the thunderstorm burst, and golden sheets of lightning shot forth on three sides, as if from three distinct storms, in the centre of which Hallsands appeared to lie without feeling the full force of any one of them. Burning wires of most intense depth of colour seemed to hang from the dark clouds above and flash down to the dark sea below, whilst the peals of thunder rolled in the distance. An anxiety, deeper than the blackness of the clouds could cause, was, however, hanging over the place, and was increased rather than dispelled by the vivid lightning. A boat with four men had gone away early that morning to Brixham for bait, and was now several hours overdue. Everyone was gazing out in vain before the darkness came on to distinguish her form, and now heavy rain as well as wind had come on. Suddenly there was heard a shrill whistle. It was the signal from the crew of the boat, and its purpose was evidently to collect all the neighbours together for the difficult task of beaching the boat and taking the crew ashore. Dark as it was everybody was out in an instant. There was the boat at no

216 SALCOMBE AND NEIGHBOURHOOD.

great distance from the shore. But how was she to reach the gravel beach? Unlike one of sand it is exceedingly steep, and if the boat came on "broadside to" the chances were very strong of her capsizing and all four hands perishing before the eyes of those ashore, and in very sight of home. The difficulty seemed to be as to how communication was to be established between her and the shore. A rope could not be cast out or in. But here it was that two black Newfoundland dogs shewed their true value. They had been down in the crowd all the time in a state of great excite-

HALLSANDS.

ment, evidently knowing that their time for work had come. Plunging into the sea, and battling bravely with the surf, they soon reached the boat, where one of them eagerly seized a stick thrown overboard from the boat. To the stick was made fast the end of a thin line, which the dog carried safely to the shore. Communication between the boat and the shore was thus established, and a strong line passing through the sternpost of the boat, quickly followed. Everybody on shore lent a hand, and soon the boat touched the shore, and all danger was at an end.

The only road to the Start is a high footway leading southward along the cliffs, a walk deeply embowered with clematis and brambles, and gradually rising from the general level of the village to the private path leading to the lighthouse. Just at the highest point we look down upon the hamlet of Hallsands, just left behind, and further still the village of Beesands, to which apparently there runs no definite path by land, so much more sensible does it seem to the hardy population of fishermen to take the wide road of the sea than to trouble themselves to cut out a road along the umbrageous wall of cliff above them.

The Start, with its long tongue of rock, closes the coast of Devon on the south-east. The great point pushes very suddenly out into the sea due east, and from all the coast to the north of it forms a very remarkable object, a long dark line upon the southern horizon. The Start bends very slowly to the sea, and at short intervals groups of broken and wildly fantastic rock divide the tongue of high, steep land into stations, from the summits or sides of each of which the traveller has a wide view over the sea to the north, east, and south. On a bright day the view from such an altitude is most fascinating. The dark point at our feet, shelving to north and south like a steep roof, only serves to emphasise by its sombre colour the luminous stretch of sea.

To the north, from Dartmouth harbour down to our very feet, is the great sweep of Start Bay, a gleaming arc of shingle, broken here and there by a low green promontory that scarcely finds the water's edge, and under each such cape nestles a fishing village. Inland, the blue line of Dartmoor lies like a cloud upon the north-western sky, those peaks that are seen being Haytor and Rippon Tor.

The Start is a place for observation rather than for meditation; it is a place where those who have their "eyeballs vexed and tired, may feast them upon the wilderness of the sea," and watch with infinite composure the courses of all the ships that with their various burdens of anxiety or regret move up or down the Channel that is the high road between our world and the West. The clusters of rock that gather along the backbone of the point, at intervals of a dozen yards or so, seem more like cromlechs than any chance arrangement of natural structure; the light grass that grows elsewhere finds no home in their precipitous crannies and dwarf cliffs, but their surface is richly dyed with the smooth orange litchen and the tufted moss of a blanched green colour that compose so much of the harmony of effect in all this country. If Polwhele is to be trusted, there once were to be seen remnants of a temple to the Syrian Astoreth upon the Start Point, and standing on that fantastic headland, with the cry of the sea around one, it seems not hard to recall in fancy the time, long past, when the Phœnicians may have gathered there from their tin-works at the day appointed for the Wailing for Adonis, and while they mingled their cries with those of the ocean, were dreaming of the wizard head then floating into the haven of Byblos. At least we cannot think a rock so grim and tortured unapt to witness the mysteries of a worship devoted to the winds and sea.

The lighthouse situated on the point is a handsome stone tower, 110 feet high, including the lantern, from which is exhibited a powerful revolving light, elevated 204 feet above the level of the sea, showing a bright flash every minute, visible 20 miles. In addition to this, a fixed light is exhibited in the same tower, in the direction of the Skerries Bank. Visitors are allowed to inspect the lighthouse. The light is that known as the dioptric, which consists of a single lamp with six wicks, placed in the middle of the lantern, the oil being supplied to the burner by the automatic action of a weighted plunger, the oil being forced up to the wicks from a reservoir being placed underneath the burner. The wicks used are concentric, that is ring within ring. The value of a light given by a six-inch burner is said to be equal to that of 722 sperm candles. The diameter of the flame in its broadest part near the top of the burner is 5 inches, but it is narrowed in the upper part to 3½ inches by the glass chimney. The height of flame usually maintained is about six inches, and the quantity of oil consumed is about 1,750 gallons per annum. In the dioptric method of lighting all the rays emitted by one large flame are intercepted by glass lenses or prisms at a short distance from the flame, and are bent or refracted so that they issue from the lighthouse lantern in a compact beam. The light is enclosed in what may be described as a glass hive. The internal surface of this glass hive intercepts nearly all the rays proceeding from the lamp. The hive is composed of three parts—the dome, the central belt, and the lower belt. For a revolving light, such as the Start, the hive is divided into vertical panels or segments, of which the divisions of an orange will give an approximate idea, in each of which a section of the incident rays is condensed so as to yield a separate beam. Between the vertical points or segments divisions occur through which no light passes. On the hive being made to revolve, the beams from the different panels, separated by intervals of darkness, successively come round like the spokes of a wheel, and the mariner sees the waxing and waning flashes of a revolving light.

The light at the Start is not required to show all round, as on one side of the tower is the land, and so the form of the hive is incomplete, and the greater part of the rear or landward rays from the lamp, which under ordinary circumstances would be wasted, are by an ingenious arrangement utilised in another way. At the back of the lamp a dioptric mirror is so adjusted as to reflect the rays falling upon it vertically downward through an opening in the floor on to another reflector, placed so as to re-reflect them out to sea through a lower window, situated in the tower twenty three feet below the actual light, and is shewn over the Skerries Bank near the Start, between the bearings S. W. ¾ W., and W. ½ N. In 1862 a fog bell was erected here, and it was

START POINT.

situated a little way down the cliffs, but it did not answer the purpose for which it was erected, as the fog intercepted the passage of sound. It was sometime since superseded by the powerful fog siren, erected near the lighthouse. The instrument is sounded with compressed air, made to pass through a fixed flat disc, fitted into the throat of a long cast-iron trumpet, connected with the air-pipe. This disc has twelve radial slits, and behind it is a rotating disc, with twelve similar slits, the rotation being effected by separate mechanism. With one disc fixed, and the other rotating, it will be understood that the slits in each frequently coincide—in fact, the twelve slits in one revolution coincide twelve times, and at each coincidence a puff of air, at great pressure, escapes through into the trumpet. It is the rapid succession of these puffs which forms the sound of the siren. The disc is caused to make 2,400 rotations in a minute, and, as there are twelve coincidences in a revolution, it follows that the number of puffs passing through in a minute would be 2,400 multiplied by $12=28,800$. The instrument is sounded with air compressed by means of caloric engines of great power, which also rotates the siren disc. It can readily be understood that a sound of surpassing power is thus generated, and, as the vibrations produced are not taken up by the cast-iron trumpet, the sound issues from the mouth in a condensed beam of great intensity. In foggy weather the Start fog-siren is frequently heard at Salcombe. Every fog-signal established on our coast has been made to particularly indicate itself by some distinguishing feature, and the necessary distinctions for siren fog-signals are obtained by employing combinations of high and low notes, the mechanism of the siren being adapted for producing the required sounds. The siren at the Start gives three blasts—high, low, high—quickly every three minutes. Near the Start Point and in the Bay, are a dangerous ledge of rocks and gravel called the Skerries, having on the south-west end only nine feet of water at low tide

Off the Start Point lie the Peartree Rocks, and about a quarter of a mile outside of them is a dangerous sunken rock.

On the night of May 11th, 1861, the keeper on duty at the Start lighthouse was surprised at discovering a great number of birds flying around and against the lantern of that building, and dropping either dead or much exhausted. The wind at the time was blowing strong from the north-east, with rain; after some time it became much calmer, the birds continuing to rush against the lantern, increasing in numbers as the gale went down, and finally reaching the immense number of 692; and the keeper had the curiosity to weigh them, and they amounted to about 34 lbs, consisting chiefly of skylarks, house sparrows, and several varieties of the smaller kinds of birds, amongst which was a cuckoo.

On the 9th and 10th of March, 1891, a fearful blizzard occurred throughout the whole of the South Hams district, causing serious destruction both at sea and on land. Roads were blocked with snow and impassable for many days, and during the height of the storm on Monday evening, the 9th March, the steamship *Marana*, 1692 tons register, from London for Colombo, went on shore in a blinding snowstorm on the Blackstone Rocks just off Start Point, and out of a crew of 28 hands all told, three only were saved. The barque *Dryad*, of Liverpool, 1,035 tons register, with 21 hands, was wrecked with the loss of all the crew just after midnight, on the eastern side of the Start, and on the next morning scarcely a vestige of the vessel could be seen. Other vessels were wrecked in Start Bay about the same time, and the total loss of life was 52 lives, the greatest number ever known to have occurred on this coast at one time. What the storm was like the following account, referring to the wreck of the *Dryad*, will give some idea:—

The head keeper of the Start lighthouse says, I was standing in my yard under the shelter of my house, a little after midnight, looking in the direction of the Bay, when I saw right under the headland, and close to the Start, what I considered to be a ship's lights. I called the other keepers, and as well as we were able we proceeded down the cliffs in the direction from which I saw the lights. It was at the risk of our lives we proceeded, and it was only by holding on to each other that we were prevented from being blown away. When we got down we could not discover a vestige of anything, neither did we hear a cry of any sort.

The coastguard in charge of Hallsands station says, at the same time as the lights were noticed by the lighthouse keeper, we also saw the lights just in the same position We proceeded to the Start and strained our eyes to try and see if anything could be discovered. But we neither saw or heard anything but the roar of the tempest. We did our utmost to keep our eyes open, and strained them in the face of the storm, but the effort was so painful that we had to desist. The force of the storm was so great that our eyes seemed as if they were being pricked with needles, and they were bloodshot the next morning as the result of the strain they had been put to. No sign of the *Dryad* or any other vessel could be discovered.

The most interesting way to return to Salcombe from the Start will be round by the coast, following the coastguard track for most of the way. The distance is about eight miles, and in consequence of the rough nature of the road, will take fully three hours to traverse it. From the Start, that sees so much of the ocean, the prominent neighbouring headlands are concealed by Peartree Point and a high field that rises on the south-west. But by crossing this, the pedestrian suddenly gains a superb view in an entirely different direction. Before him, across the bay, he sees the Prawle, and far beyond it the grander double buttress of Bolt Head. He may proceed at once to the Prawle; the distance is about four miles as the crow flies, but the best of walkers will do well to give two hours to the transit. There is no path whatever until we reach the mill and sandy cove of Lannacombe, and after this the briars and the brooklets have much more than their share of the adventure. There is a large and ancient elder tree adjacent to the mill-house at Lannacombe Cove, and no person, old or young, living in the neighbourhood, ever dares to injure it by taking from it a twig, or a flower, or a berry, or even a leaf.

PRAWLE POINT.

During the last war with France, a French privateer, hovering on the coast, sent at nightfall a boat's crew ashore, who took from the miller who then lived there, everything they could find, even the bed under his wife, who had recently given birth to a child. Having by him a considerable sum of money in a purse or small bag, he, without being observed, flung it out at the window, hoping that it might thus escape the privateers, and that he might recover it in the morning. At day-break there was no trace of the privateer; and on proceeding to that part of his premises where, if anywhere, his money would be found, he had the good fortune to see his purse with all its contents hanging in the elder tree. From that time it has been free from every kind of molestation on the part of those who know the story; and parents still point it out to their children as "the tree which saved the miller's money."

A long walk through the lanes of South Devon is not an exciting excursion, and requires for its thorough appreciation a cheerful spirit and the Wordsworthian "quiet eye." Between hedges ten feet high the traveller rises swiftly to no view, and descends apparently for no reason but to give a delicate streamlet occasion to gush out of a ferny wall and cross the road in a limpid and serpentine confusion. But the hedges are a study in themselves, with their foxgloves and mullens, their fairy pennons of ferns, the odourous garlands of their honeysuckles waving high up among the hazels. And if the view be shut out, so much the better; with an unwearied gaze we catch the line of azure sea cutting across the hedgerows at the summit of a decline, and lean on each gate to enjoy the trim-framed landscape of old farm-buildings, golden with lichen, embowered in a delicious land of orchards, with the soft outlines of the folding hills beyond.

It is rather on the wayward and indolent side of genius that these glowing villages and soft sequestered valleys seem to find their utterance; and there is especially one view, over a certain gate, which all travellers must pass on their way to the Prawle, which is well worth noting. Breaking the soft, faint outline of the hills, dividing rhythmically to left and right, the church of St. Sylvester, in Chivelstone, stands huge against the sky, starting from the middle distance, with a cluster of lichened cottages clinging about its feet. No other house is to be seen, until far away on the lofty horizon the eye just catches the steeple of Malborough. The scene is at once without form and vividly distinct, weak and brilliant, equally unique in what it possesses and in what it lacks. As we approach the sea, the hedges become lower, the land more barren and open, and the coast line to Prawle Point is somewhat tame and flat. Inland is the village of East Prawle, cultivated fields, apparently upon a raised beach left ages since by the receding sea, intervening between the village and the sea. Prawle is the most southerly inhabited place in the county, the abode chiefly of fishermen. There is a Bible Christian Chapel, but the church is at Chivelstone, more than a mile distant, to which parish Prawle belongs. The farmstead of West Prawle, about a mile inland, is one of the estates with which Blundell endowed his school at Tiverton. Just beyond the inn at Prawle the lanes descend toward the sea, and the sober headland comes slowly into view. There is a coastguard station situated here, and a life-saving apparatus belonging to the Board of Trade is attached to the station. Following the guidance of a meandering rivulet, which has taken advantage of the existence of a steep lane to adopt it as its watercourse, we arrive at a meadow, sloping gently to the beach. On our right hand the extreme south point of Devonshire rises in a rounded bluff of no great altitude, a broad and solitary headland, covered with wild thyme and grass. There is a strange legend that records that, in the Middle Ages, pilgrims from Scandinavia to the Holy Land were wont to break their voyage in a little cove beside the Prawle. If they landed anywhere near the Prawle, it must have been, however, on the further, or western side, for the reefs are unbroken from the point as far east as Lannacombe: long flakes of dark rock, one against the other, with pools and shallow channels laid bare at low tide, over which the broad leaves of brown sea-weed lie so thickly as to exclude all light. Turn these aside and a beautiful view is presented; each pool is thickly paved with a coloured mosaic of sea-anemones, *crassicornis* of every shade, from the warmest orange to the coldest lilac, spreading their banded disks to the damp face of the sea-weed, and intertwining lazily their distended tentacles.

Prawle Point does not appear so evenly rounded when we scale the height, for there we find the gneiss broken into crags, and drawn, as if violently bent, towards the west. The final rock, pierced with a hole, is insulated at low water, and a boat in very smooth weather, may creep under its eaves, between it and the mainland. Here is a Lloyds signal station for reporting vessels passing up Channel, and is largely used.

The next cape, westward from the Prawle, Gammon Head, would be the finest headland on the coast were it built upon a larger scale. Confine your vision closely to the form of its precipitous sides, vaulted back, and sharp tumultuous point, and it is of a rare sublimity. Near the head a mighty mass of rock has fallen from the cliffs above, slid a little way down the hill, and been propped as regularly as any builder would prop a gigantic mass of stone, with three supports; and here it lies in perfect form as a giant sarcophagus, awaiting for ages past its burial. Below it curves Maceley Cove, a little bay of pure sand. Here it must have been that the Norwegian dromonds pushed their thin prows into the shore; it might hold, with circumspection and in fine weather, one such casual visitor. One can but wonder whether, if a pilgrim of the eleventh century climbed the hog's back above the cove, and gazed westward over such a radiant sea as every fine morning brings, he would be moved to any delight at the soft violet reticulation on the misty buttress of Bolt Head, at the blue line of the long down by Malborough, or by the brick-coloured lichen burning through the wild thyme at his feet. If not, we have one great pleasure more than he, the satisfaction that the daily beauty of common things brings with it. At this spot awhile since one of the Chinese clippers, the *Lala Rhook*, homeward bound with a cargo of tea, was wrecked.

GAMMON HEAD.

The coastguard track is continued, past the Gammon Head, toward Rickham coastguard station, where another little cove is passed, Moor Sand Bay, a strange name to a wondrous bay, for it has not a fraction of sand in it. Its floor is formed of tiny spar and quartz pebbles, on the east side worn as fine as sand, and on the west the pebbles are larger. The rocks around are most lovely in hue, of quartz, slate, and green sandstone, the quartz forming serpentine wavy lines, in great lying slabs of rock.

The path touches the remains of an old disused iron mine at Deckler's Island. There is a quantity of iron in the whole of this coast line, and many a ship has had her compass affected by it when sailing past, and been drawn to destruction. An attempt was made some years ago to work an iron mine at Deckler's Island, but had after

THE COAST BETWEEN PRAWLE AND RICKHAM.

a time to be abandoned, the working expenses being too great. From Seacome Sand the path rises to Rickham station, where is kept a Board of Trade rocket apparatus, which has often been used in the past. Leaving the station Limbury Point is soon reached, and then the path leads by the side of the harbour, past a little inlet, named Millbay, and on to the ferry at Portlemouth.

SALCOMBE to TORCROSS and SLAPTON SANDS.

THESE places are situated in Start Bay, and are a great attraction, another such a stretch of sand and shingle being scarcely found in England. The distance is about seven miles, and an interesting route is by boat up the creek to Frogmore, choosing a state of tide when it will be convenient to go in the morning and return in the evening. From Frogmore the distance is a little over three miles, along a nearly level and pleasant road, the villages of Chillington and Stokenham being passed on the way.

Stokenham Church, dedicated to St. Michael the Archangel, takes rank among the largest and finest in the country, and consists of a spacious and lofty nave with aisles, transept, and south porch, a chancel, which retains its piscina, with south and north Chapels, and a tall western tower, containing an excellent peal of six bells. It was consecrated in 1431. The screen, which extends across the entire width of the nave and its aisles, is of unusual dignity and beauty, and has been not merely most minutely and admirably restored in all the details of its richly carven adornments, but (with the exception of a small portion, which loudly demands the same treatment), its ancient glories of gold and colour have been renewed, at the cost of a late Vicar and his friends, and with lavish munificence. The pulpit which is of stone, and is also resplendent with gold and colour, was the offering of the "Free Masons," and is, of course, adorned by illuminated representation of the symbols of the craft. A beautiful window of stained-glass has been placed in the tower. The church once belonged to the Priory of Brisham, in Somerset.

There is a curious and interesting entry in Bishop Stafford's Register. At Sherford, which is called in it "Schyreford, within the bounds and limits of the parish church of Stokenham," the banns of John Hals, and Agnes, relict of John Gongs (or Govys), belonging to the said parish, had been duly published in the chapel of Sherford once; but they were in a great hurry to be married, and the Bishop granted a special license, addressed to John Dene, the parochial chaplain of Sherford, to celebrate the marriage forthwith: he was to publish the banns for the second time on the very next Sunday, and then and there to marry the couple, "the Constitution as to threefold publication of banns notwithstanding." This license was issued on October 6th, 1412. As the 6th was a Thursday, they must have been married on October 9th. Sherford manor was part of the estates of St. Nicholas Priory, Exeter. Kennedon, in this parish, in the 15th century, became a seat of the family of Hals. Here lived John Hals, Justice of the Common Pleas in 1423, and here was born his son, of the same name, who, in 1450, was made Bishop of Lichfield and Coventry.

After leaving Stokenham, Stokeley House is passed on the left, and Widdicombe House, the residence of Mr. Holdsworth, on the right. On approaching Torcross the road forms a slight curve, with Slapton Ley on one side. One of the finest beaches in the country unquestionably is that at Torcross. Upwards of three miles of undulating sand and shingle, bounded on one side by the sounding waves of the English Channel, as they chase each other pell-mell up the steep slope, and on the other by the placid waters of Slapton Ley, with its patches of waving rushes, its flocks of water fowl and shoals of carefully preserved fish. It is a fine sight to stand on the verge of the quaint and sandy hamlet of Torcross, and glance along the yellow belt of shingle gradually narrowing to a thin white line in the distance; on still further among rugged rocks and brown coast vegetation, and beyond clearly facing us, we see Blackpool, where in 1403, after its more successful raids upon Tenby and Plymouth, the French squadron landed, only to be repulsed by the prompt Devonian women, who sallying out of many a thatched cottage heavy with house-leek and ivy, smote

START BAY FISHWIVES.

those invaders hip and thigh, slew their captain, and boldly bade them depart the way they came. The beach at Torcross is unquestionably very fine, and far, far from the madding crowd. The village is built, one might almost say, on the beach, and it is no uncommon thing during exceptionally high tides and easterly gales to find the gudewife humbly imitating Mrs Partington, and trying with a coier broom to brush the English Channel out of the front parlour. In greater straits it becomes necessary to "caulk" the door with clay; but, happily, this is not of frequent occurrence. Coaches call there three and four times daily, enroute between Dartmouth and Kingsbridge; a hotel boasting forty rooms, stands snugly under the cliff, and a card in the window of almost every house and cottage, bearing the legend, "Furnished Apartments," shews that the fisher folk are already alive to the pecuniary advantages of catering for lodgers. The visitor may constantly see five or six groups of hardy men and bronzed women with their rough shallow boats, stationing themselves on the verge of the water, and preparing to shoot their nets. These dwellers in the sand form the bulk of the inhabitants of Torcross, and fine, honest, homely, hearty-looking people they are. The women, who take an active part in the fishing operations, are of all ages, from ruddy, bright-eyed lasses to old dames of seventy years and upwards, whose bleached hair escapes from the great flapping sun-bonnets which cover their heads. They all wear painted canvas skirts, and stand holding a rope while their husbands, fathers, or sons start off in the boat, and paying out the nets as they go, describe a semi-circle, and land at a point a hundred yards or so along the beach with another rope. Both parties then commence to drag the net ashore, and one feels almost excited at the anticipations of a good haul—an excitement which is fully shared by the cloud of gulls wheeling and screaming overhead, and following the course of the net with as much interest as the crows follow a new-turned furrow. The air is simply delicious, and any worn-out "breadwinner" may come down here and enjoy the finest air, the profoundest quiet, enough exercise for health, a prodigious appetite, any amount of sleep, and no desire whatever to go away again. Excellent carriages and horses can be obtained at the hotel for those who want to excursionise. For lovers of sea-bathing, there is a noble beach, with fine gravelly sands, and machines attached to the hotel. A new ley, covering nearly forty acres, has been made to the south of the hotel, and stocked with fish. This fresh water lake is rented with the hotel, visitors staying at the establishment can obtain fishing tickets. If sea-fishing is desired, there are good boats and skilful men, with plenty of bream, gurnets, flounders, bass and mackerel.

Between Torcross and Start Point, which is distant three-and-a-half miles, are the fishing hamlets of Beesands and Hallsands, which are easily reached by taking a road at the back of the hotel. Some attempt to walk on the beach, but this is most difficult and trying to the legs.

Slapton Sands stretches away in a continuous line towards Dartmouth for about three miles, with the Royal Sands Hotel about midway across. A writer in the *Field* newspaper has thus described a visit to this place, and his experiences of fishery on the Ley:—

"The ride along the coast from Exeter to Dartmouth is a thing to see and experience. What a lovely ride it is! No railway in England can equal it. And then the drive from Dartmouth to Torcross, all along the cliffs, sometimes high up in the air, far above the sea, and anon down along the crest of the pebbly sand, with constant beautiful peeps of rocks and thickets, and hidden little sandy coves where luggers have whilom beached on moon-shiny nights, and hundreds of kegs of very bad brandy and worse hollands have come ashore to poison the natives. The pretty surf lined points, with foliage decked almost to the salt water's edge, sum up a ride which alone it is worth a long journey to make.

Slapton Ley is a huge sheet of fresh water, profusely studded with reeds in places, of which there are enormous patches— hundreds of acres, in fact. It is about a mile-and-a-half long, and probably half-a-mile wide at its widest. There is ample room for a dozen or more of boats to fish on it. There are, however, only seven, and these are attached to the Sands Hotel Visitors staying in any of the cottages can also hire a boat if there is one to spare, visitors at the hotel having the first claim. The Ley is divided from the sea by about one hundred yards or more of high beach, along the top of which runs the road, and in the immense waste of swash, reeds, and rushes the wildfowl find safe and secure harbour, for they are never allowed to be disturbed—two huge slices at the Torcross end and on the north shore being cut off and marked by posts, and on which no boat is allowed to trespass, and those two preserves comprise 200 acres of water and reeds at least. On these not a line is ever cast, and, as the Ley swarms with perch, eels, and rudd, it may well be assumed that there is a pike or two there, and of patriarchal age and size.

Besides pike, the Ley swarms with perch, rudd, and splendid eels, and a couple of hooks on a bottom line, and a bit of fish for bait, will always produce a dish of eels for dinner. As regards perch, ten, fifteen, or twenty dozen may be taken in a day, and a large portion of them will run three to the pound and up to one pound each. There are very large perch in the Ley, but they are not got every day. The rudd are something marvellous, and run up to a large size, and heaps of them may be had from 1 lb. to 2 lb. One of the most favourite ways of fishing for them is with a fly. Use a double-handed fly rod and a fragment of worm on the bend of the hook and a longish cast, as they are shy, and prefer, when taking fly, shallow water and sunny weather; and there in the shallows, two or three feet deep, crowds of big fellows, from 1 lb. to 2 lb. each, may be seen breaking the water and rolling about; and, with any luck you may fill a hamper with them, and rare fun it is, too, for they fight very ably, and are as strong and deep as a bream. Any sea-trout fly should fetch them. Such is the sport to be had on Slapton Ley, and I venture to say that there is no place in England like it.

The hotel is situated on the road that separates the sea from the fresh-water lake. That ivy-mantled building, with its stone-mullioned windows, scrupulously clean, the boats ranged in a row, and the fishermen, all look delightfully "fishy," in the highest acceptation of the word. The method adopted for engaging the fishermen is by roster. They are all equal, and no favouritism is allowed. This is as fair to the men themselves as it is convenient to visitors, who are thereby saved the nuisance of being touted, and the sometimes invidious task of making a selection. Nor is the visitor in direct *rapport*, as regards payment, with the fisherman. The charge for boat and man, 4s. a day, with bait and tackle

TORCROSS AND SLAPTON SANDS.

if required, is made by the proprietor of the hotel, and appears in the bill. Of this sum the man gets half a-crown. He expects you to give him his beer, but no lunch or dinner. The successful angler, in the generosity of his heart, engendered by unwonted exploits, may offer him some bread and cheese, but there is none of the greedy anxiety of the Thames puntsman about the worthy fellows. The air is very fine and bracing, and the invalid will rejoice at its invigorating qualities, even if he gets no fish. He has, moreover, excellent living at the hotel, with every comfort and civility, and the most luxurious beds that it probably was ever his fate to sleep in."

At Torcross there is a Congregational chapel, erected in 1884, which will seat 150 persons, but the church is at Stokenham, one mile distant inland. There is also a reading room in the village, whilst at Beesands there is a Mission Room belonging to the Church of England. There is a post office at Torcross, with money order and telegraph facilities attached.

SLAPTON.—The village of Slapton lies about a quarter of a mile inland from the Sands Hotel. Once a place of considerable importance, this quiet village is remarkable for little now, save indeed for the memories of the past, and for its venerable parish church, and some scanty relics of its once famous Collegiate Chantry. The manor of Slapton belonged for nearly three hundred years to the family of Bryan, whose heirs-male were always called Guy, and at length terminated with the celebrated Sir Guy de Bryan, who was standard-bearer to Edward III. at the battle of Cressy, and one of the first Knights of the Garter. He lived to the great age of 90 years, and dying in 1391. was buried in the north aisle of the choir at Tewkesbury, where a richly canopied monument was erected to his memory. A gaunt and ugly farm house, known as Poole Priory, occupies the site of the Chantry Chapel. In this house lived for several years, on his return from captivity in Spain, Sir Richard Hawkins, son of Sir John. from whom the Kingsbridge Hawkinses were descended. In the garden attached to the house stands the imposing tower of the Chantry

Chapel, in a tolerably perfect state, the very pure character of its details coinciding with the period of its erection, and grouping well with the spire of the church across the way.

The Chantry was founded by Sir Guy de Bryan, and dedicated to the Blessed Virgin, towards the close of the 14th century. Pope Clement VII granted his licence on the 22nd of December, 1372, and on the 10th of September in the following year, the College received its first endowment. The Community consisted of a Rector and several Priests, one of whom had charge of the parish Church and of the souls of the parishioners, and was called the "Minister." The Rectory of Poundstock, in Cornwall, was appropriated to the New Foundation on the 4th of July, 1379, and that of Loddiswell a few years later. The first Rector of the College, as distinguished from the parish, was Richard Bakewell, who was instituted on August 7th, 1373; and the names of most of his successors are to be found in the Episcopal Registers. Of these John Bouryng was presented by Robert Lovel, Lord of the Manor of Slapton, in right of his wife, Elizabeth de Bryan, a grand-daughter of the founder; and John Pawle (or Pawley) was instituted on the 24th of March, 1459, the patron being John Ormond, Earl of Wiltshire, as Lord of this Manor, which, a few years later, had passed to Henry, Earl of Northumberland, who presented Nicholas Morton in 1498. Morton's will, dated August the 26th, 1534, is of some interest. To "the College Church of our Lady of Slapton" he bequeathed a cross of silver, the sum of £40 sterling, a pair of organs valued at £12, a missal worth £4, a "tablement" of the same value, and a piece of silver worth 20s. To the Brethren he gave his kitchen utensils. He did not forget the parish church, leaving to "St James," i.e. to the altar dedicated in his name, 6s. 8d., to the High Cross— the "Rood"—6s. 8d., to "our lady of Pitie," 3s. 4d., to St. Michael, the same, and the like sum, also, to "our lady on the left side of the Altar." Richard Hals, Esquire, of Sherford, he appointed his " very hole and trew executor." The last Rector was John Morcombe, who surrendered his Chantry on November 17th, 1545; and so was destroyed not merely this ancient College of devoted clergy, but the parish itself, as well, which had so long been served by one of Sir Guy's priests.

William Couelle appears to have been the last "Minister" but one; he was appointed on the 21st July, 1530, and was buried—so he directed in his will, dated February 25th, 1544,—in the chancel of his church. To Morcombe was granted a yearly pension of £14, which was the exact amount of his endowment as Rector. The minister's income had been £7 a year; but he was granted a pension of £10, on account, no doubt, of his services being required by the parishioners still. In 1536, in addition to the Rector and the Minister, there were "three chaplains, two clerks, and four choristers, serving God" in this College, having an endowment of £37 8s. 4d. among them. The chaplains at the time of the Dissolution were John Jeffery, Robert Taylor, and William French, and to each of them was assigned a pension of £6 13s. 4d. The clerks were Arthur Featherston and Elizeus Lawry, each of whom had £4 13s. 4d.

The parish church of James the Greater is an edifice in the late Decorated and Early Perpendicular styles. It has in recent years been restored. It is, of course much older than the college, the tower and spire coming down to us from the 13th century; and there are traces of early work in other parts. But the church was greatly enlarged and improved in the 15th century, when the college was at the height of its prosperity.

Until recently the arms of Bryan—a specimen of heraldry of rare beauty—existed in one of the windows of the church, besides several shields displaying the same arms, with marks of cadency. The field of the shield and the surrounding foliations were beautifully diapered, with one or two exceptions, this was the finest example in the whole district, as it was by far the most interesting.

These shields are not now to be seen, but the parishioners were congratulated a few years ago in the Parish Magazine that the last window to be restored, namely, the one from which the heraldry had vanished, was now, like all the others, "sound and in good condition," but no one could tell what had become of the old glass.

Our work is finished; taking Salcombe for our starting place, we have traversed the whole of the district lying

SLAPTON VILLAGE AND PRIORY TOWER.

along the coast from the River Avon on one side to Slapton on the other, and have done our best to give a full and accurate description of every place visited, and we hope our ramblings up and down have not been in vain, but will prove of service, not to residents only, but also to the increasing number of visitors who find out this remote, yet lovely, part of beautiful Devonshire.

LIST OF PLANTS, &c.,

That have been found in the neighbourhood.

———:o:———

| Latin Name. | English Name. | Where found. |

RANUNCULUS TRIBE:—
Clematis vitalba ...... Traveller's joy .... Malborough road,
                                 near Kingsbridge, and Woolston
Anemone nemorosa .... Wood anemone ..... Bolt Head
Ranunculus aquatilis... Water crowfoot ....
  ,,   *hederaceus* Ivy-leaved crowfoot ....
  ,,   *lingua* .. Great spear-wort ...... South Sands
  ,,   *flammula*. Lesser spear-wort ......
  ,,   *sceleratus*. Marsh or celery-leaved crowfoot
  ,,   *bulbosus*.. Bulbous buttercup ....
  ,,   *repens*.... Common buttercup ....
  ,,   *acris* .... Meadow buttercup ....
  ,,   *parviflorus* Small flowered crowfoot Bolbury
  ,,   *ficaria* .. Pilewort or lesser celandine
Caltha palustris ...... Marsh marigold........
Helleborus viridis .... Green hellebore........ Maryknowle
Aquilegia vulgaris .... Common columbine.... Blank's Mill
Aconitum napellus .... Common monk's-hood.. West Alvington

WATER-LILY TRIBE:—
Nymphæa alba........ White water-lily ...... Slapton Ley

POPPY TRIBE:—
Papaver hybridum .... Round prickly headed poppy
  ,,   *argemone* .... Small pale red poppy ..
  ,,   *rhœas* ... . Common red poppy ....
  ,,   *somniferum* .. Common white poppy ... South Milton
  ,,   *Cambricum* .. Yellow Welsh poppy .. Portlemouth glebe
Chelidonium glaucium. Yellow horned poppy .. Between Start and
                                Prawle, Slapton Sands, and Bantham
Chelidonium majus .... Greater celandine ......

FUMITORY TRIBE:—
Fumaria capreolata .. Rampant fumitory ...
  ,,   *officinalis*.... Common fumitory ...
Corydalis claviculata .. White climbing corydalis Sharp Tors.

Latin Name.	English Name.	Where found.
CRUCIFEROUS TRIBE :—		
Cheiranthus cheiri	Common wallflower	
Nasturtium officinale	Common water cress	
Barbarea vulgaris	Yellow rocket	
Cardamine hirsuta	Hairy bitter cress	
,, *pratensis*	Cuckoo-flower	
,, ,,	Double variety	South Huish and Portlemouth churchyard
Sisymbrium trio	Common hedge mustard	
,, *alliaria*		
Brassica oleracea	Sea Cabbage	
Brassica sinapistrum		
Cochlearia Danica	Danish scurvy grass	
,, *armoracia*		
Capsella bursa pastoris	Common shepherd's purse	
Lepidium Smithii	Smooth field pepper cress	South Huish
Senebiera ruellii	Wart cress	
Thlaspi arvense	Field cress	
Draba verna	Vernal whitlow grass	
Cakile maritima	Purple sea rocket	Millbay
Raphanus raphanistrum	Wild radish	Rocks at Prawle
,, *maritimus*	Sea Wild Radish	
Arabis hirsuta	Hairy rock cress	Bantham Ham
Alliaria officinale	Garlic mustard	
Sinapis arvensis	Charlock	
ROCKET TRIBE :—		
Reseda luteola	Dyer's weed	
ROCK-ROSE TRIBE :—		
Helianthemum vulgare	Common rock-rose	
VIOLET TRIBE :—		
Viola odorata	Sweet violet	
,, *canina*	Dog violet	
,, *tricolor*	Pansy	
MILKWORT TRIBE :—		
Polygala vulgaris	Common milkwort	
CHICKWEED TRIBE :—		
Silena inflata	Bladder campion	
,, *maritima*	Sea campion	
,, *nocturna*	Night flowering catchfly	Coast west of Start
Lychnis flos-cuculi	Ragged robin	
,, *diurna*	Red campion	
,, *vespertina*	White campion	
Agrostemma Githargo	Corn campion	

PLANTS.

Latin Name.	English Name.	Where Found.
Stellaria holostea	Greater stitchwort	
,, *media*	Chickweed	
,, *graminea*	Lesser stitchwort	
Arenaria peploides	Sea-side sandwort	River Avon
,, *serpyllifolia*	Thyme-leaved sandwort	
,, *trinervia*	Plaintain-leaved chickweed	
Sagina procumbens	Procumbent peàrl-wort	Common
,, *apetala*	Small floweren pearlwort	Sharp Tors
,, *ciliata*	Pearlwort	ditto
,, *nodosa*		
,, *subulata*		ditto
Spergula arvensis	Corn spurrey	
Spergularia Rubra	Field sandwort spurrey	
,, *marina*	Seaside sandwort spurrey	
Cerastium viscosum	Viscid mouse-ear chickweed	
,, *triviale*	Narrow-leaved mouse-ear chickweed	

PURSLANE TRIBE :—

Montia fontana	Water chickweed	Starehole

SUNDEW TRIBE :—

Drosera rotundifolia	Sundew	Near Sewer Mill Cove

ST. JOHN'S WORT TRIBE ;—

Hypericum androsæmum	Common Tutsan	Cliff Road, also in lanes in various localities
,, *perforatum*	Perforated St. John's wort	
,, *quadrangulum*	Square-stalked St. John's wort	
,, *humifusum*	Trailing St. John's wort	South Huish, and Portlemouth
,, *pulchrum*	Small St. John's wort	Near Sharp Tors
,, *montanum*	Mountain St. Johns wort	Bantham Ham
,, *elodes*	Marsh St. John's wort	Starehole

MALLOW TRIBE :—

Malva sylvestris	Common mallow	
,, *rotundifolia*	Dwarf mallow	
,, *moschata*	Musk mallow	South Huish and at Bantham
Lavatera arborea	Tree mallow	Portlemouth

LINSEED TRIBE ;—

Linum catharticum	Purging linseed	
,, *angustifolium*	Narrow-leaved flax	
Kadiola millegrana		Fields near Thurlestone

MAPLE TRIBE :—

Acer campestre	Common maple	
,, *pseudoplatanus*	Sycamore	

Latin Name.	English Name.	Where found.
GERANIUM TRIBE :—		
Geranium sanguineum .	Bloody crane's bill	Sharp Tors and the coast between Portlemouth and Start
,, *phœum* . . .	Dusky crane's bill	Gerston & Fallapit
,, *pyrenaicum* .	Mountain crane's bill . .	A lane near Kerse
,, *molle*	Dove's foot crane's bill	Rickham Station
,, *rotundifolium*	Round leaved crane's bill	Kingsbridge road
,, *pusillum* . .	Small flowered cranesbill	Courtenay Wood
,, *columbinum* .	Long-stalked crane's bill	Salcombe
,, *dissectum* . .	Jagged leaf crane's bill . .	Common
,, *striatum*		One plant seen between Blank's Mill and West Alvington
,, *Robertianum*	Herb Robert . . . . . , ...	
,, ,,	White variety	Stithicombe Wood
. . *lucidum*	Shining crane's bill	Near Combe Royal
Erodium cicutarium . .	Hemlock stork's bill	Bolt Head
	White variety	at Borough Island
,, *maritimum* . .	Sea crane's bill	Bolt Head
WOOD-SORREL TRIBE :—		
Oxalis Acetosella	Common wood sorrel . . .	
HOLLY TRIBE :—		
Ilex aquifolium	Common holly	
SPINDLE TREE TRIBE :—		
Euonymus Europœus . .	Spindle tree	Near Woodville and Goodshelter
PEA AND BEAN TRIBE :—		
Ulex Europœus	Common furze or gorse	
Spartium scoparium . . .	Common broom	Bolt Head
Ononis arvensis	Common rest-harrow . .	
Medicago maculata	Spotted medick	Salcombe
,, *sativa*	Lucerne	Cemetery, Salcombe
Trifolium repens	White or Dutch clover	
,, *officinale* . . .	Melilot trefoil	
,, *subterraneum*	Subterraneous trefoil . .	
,, *arvense*	Haresfoot trefoil	Start & Bantham
,, *pratense*	Purple clover	
,, *medium*	Zigzag clover	
,, *striatum*	Knotted clover	Thurlestone
,, *scabrum*	Rough clover	Challaborough
,, *filiforme*	Lesser yellow trefoil	
,, *fragiferum* .	Strawberry clover	Thurlestone sands
,, *procumbens* .	Hop trefoil	
Anthyllis vulneraria . .	Kidney vetch	North Sands
,, ,,	Variety white and red flowered	Challaboro'

PLANTS.

Latin Name.	English Name.	Where found.
Lotus major	Greater bird's foot trefoil	South Huish
,, *corniculata*	Common bird's foot trefoil	
,, *maritimus*	Sea bird's foot trefoil	Common on coast
Ornithopus perpusillus	Common bird's foot	Prawle Point
Hedysarum onobrychis	Common saintfoin	
Vicia cracca	Tufted vetch	
,, *tetrasperma*	Slender vetch	Near Kingsbridge
,, *hirsutus*	Hairy tare	
,, *sepium*	Bush vetch	
,, *sativa*	Common vetch	
Lathyrus pratensis	Meadow vetch	
,, *sylvestris*	Everlasting pea	Bantham Ham also near Start Point
,, *macrorrhyzus*	Tuberous bitter vetch	Near Kingsbridge

FLAX TRIBE :—

Latin Name.	English Name.	Where found.
Linum angustifolium	Narrow-leaved flax	
,, *catharticum*	Purging flax	
Chenopodium polyspermum	Allseed	Starehole

ROSE TRIBE :—

Latin Name.	English Name.	Where found.
Prunus spinosa	Blackthorn	
,, *cerasus*	Common cherry	
,, *avium*	Wild cherry	Batson
Spiræa Ulmaria	Meadow sweet	
Rubus fruticosus	Blackberry	
,, *cæsius*	Dewberry	
Geum urbanum	Common avens	
Fragaria vesca	Wild strawberry	
Potentilla anserina	Silver weed	
,, *reptans*	Creeping cinquefoil	
Gragaria sterilio	Barren strawberry	
Tormentilla erecra	Common tormentil	
Alchemilla arvensis	Field ladies mantle	
Poterium sanguisorba	Salad burnet	
Rosa spinosissima	Burnet-leaved rose	Bolt Head road
,, *tomentosa*	Downy-leaved rose	Malborough road
,, *canina*	Dog rose	
,, *arvensis*	White dog rose	
Pyrus malus	Crab apple	
Sorbus aucupari	Mountain ash	River Avon, also in a Wood near North Sands
Crataegus oxyacantha	Hawthorn	
,, *aria*	White beam tree	

KNOT-GRASS TRIBE :—

Latin Name.	English Name.	Where found.
Polycarpon Tetraphyllum	Four-leaved allseed	Buckland

Latin Name.	English Name.	Where found.
Saxifrage Tribe :—		
Saxifraga tridactylites .	Rue-leaved saxifrage	Goodshelter
Chrysosplenium oppositifolium	Golden saxifrage	
Stonecrop Tribe :—		
Cotyledon umbilicus ..	Wall penny wort ..	....
Sedum anglicum	English stonecrop	
,, *album*	White stonecrop	Quarry near Sandhills
,, *dasyphyllum* ..	Thick-leaved stonecrop	Near Charleton
,, *acre*	Biting stonecrop	Bolbury
Semperivirum tectorum	Common houseleek	....
Starwort Tribe :..		
Aster trifolium	Sea starwort	Starehole & Rickham
Willow Herb Tribe :—		
Epilobium angustifolium	Narrow-leaved willow herb	
,, *hirsutum* ..	Great hairy willow herb	
,, *parviflorum*	Small-flowered willow herb	
,, *montanum* .	Smooth-leaved willow herb	
,, *tetragonum*	Square-stalked willow herb	
Ænothera odorata		On wall at Batson
Circœa lutetiana	Common enchanter's nightside	
Loosestrife Tribe :—		
Anagallis tenella	Purple loosestrife	Clannicombe
Lysimachia valgaris ..	Common loosestrife	....
Angalis arvensis	Scarlet pimpernel	
,, *tennella*	Bog pimpernel	Starehole Bay
Lysimachia nemorum ..	Yellow pimpernel	
Strapwort Tribe :—		
Corrigiola littoralis ..	Bastard knot grass......	Slapton Sands
Umbelliferous Tribe :—		
Hydrocotyle vulgaris ..	Marsh pennywort	Huish Marsh, &c.
Eryngium maritimum	Sea holly	Thurlestone sands
Sanicula Europœa	Common sanicle	
Conium maculatum ..	Common hemlock	Salcombe
Smyrnium olusatrum .	Common alexanders	.. Near Fort Charles
Cicuta virosa	Long-leaved water hemlock	
Apium graveolens	Celery	South Huish
,, *nodiflorum*		
Scandix pecten verens	Shepherd's needle	....
Anthriscus sylvestris ..	Wild beaked parsley	...
Petroselinum segetum .	Corn parsley	
Helosciadium nodifloru	Procumbent marsh wort	
Pimpinella saxifraga ..	Common burnet saxifrage	Woolston
Œnanthe crocata	Hemlock water dropwort	

Latin Name.	English Name.	Where found.
Œthusa cynapium	Fool's parsley	Shadycombe
Fœniculum vulgare	Common fennel	Salcombe
Crithmum maritimum	Sea samphire	Near Fort Charles
Pastinaca sativa	Common parsnip	
Heracleum sphondylium	Common cow parsnip	
Daucus carota	Wild carrot	
Torili santhriscus	Upright hedge parsley	

IVY TRIBE :—

Hedera helix	Common ivy	
Adoxa moschatellina	Common moschatel	Near South Sands

DOGWOOD TRIBE :—

Cornus sanguinea	Dogwood	

HONEYSUCKLE TRIBE :—

Sambucus nigra	Common elder	
Viburnum opulus	Guelder-rose	Blank's Mill
Lonicera periclymenum	Honeysuckle	

MADDER TRIBE :—

Rubia peregrina	Wild madder	Woodville road
Galium cruciatum	Crosswort	
,, verum	Yellow bed-straw	
,, palustre	Water bed-straw	Thurlestone Marsh
,, saxatile	Rock ladies bed-straw	Bolbury Down, &c
,, mollugo	Great hedge bed-straw	
,, aparine	Goose grass	
Asperula odorata	Sweet woodruff	
Sherardia arvensis	Field madder	

MISTLETOE TRIBE :—

Viscum album	Common mistletoe	
Orobanche Major	Common broom rape	Near Malboro' church

VALERIAN TRIBE :—

Centranthus ruber	Red valerian	
Valeriana officinalis		
,, olitoria	Lamb's lettuce	
,, dentata	Tooth corn salad	Near Start Point

TEAZLE TRIBE :—

Dipsacus sylvertris	Wild teazle	
Scabiosa succisa	Devil's-bit scabious	
,, Columbaria		
,, arvensis	Field scabious	

BELL-FLOWER TRIBE :—

Campanula rotundifolia	Common hair-bell	
Jasione montana	Sheep's scabious	Bolt Head

PURPLE FOXGLOVES IN COURTENAY WALK.

PLANTS.

Latin Name.	English Name.	Where found.
COMPOUND FLOWERS TRIBE :—		
Arctium lappa	Common burdock	
Carlina vulgaris	Common carline thistle	Bolt Head
Centaurea nigra	Black knap-weed	
,, *scabiosa*	Great knap-weed	White variety near Malborough
,, *cyanus*		
Serratula tinctoria	Common saw-wort	
Carduus nutans	Musk thistle	Bolt Head
,, *tenuiflorus*	Slender flowered thistle	Bantham Ham
,, *marianus*	Milk thistle	Bantham Ham
,, *lanceolatus*	Spear plume thistle	
,, *palustris*	Marsh plume thistle	
,, *arvensis*	Creeping plume thistle	
,, *acaulis*	Dwarf plume thistle	Bolt Head
Agrimonia Eupatoria	Agrimony	Ford
Eupatorium cannabinum	Common hemp agrimony	
Petasites fragrans	Winter heliotrope	Charleton
Tussilago farfara	Colt's-foot	
Bellis perennis	Common daisy	
Solidago virgaurea	Golden rod	Common on coast
Baccharis halmifolia	Ploughman's spikenard	Thurlestone
,, *dysenterica*	Common fleabane	
Anthemis nobilis	Common chamomile	Thurlestone Marsh
,, *cotula*	Stinking chamomile	Bantham
Achillea millefolium	Common milfoil	
Matricaria inodora	Silvery-leaved feverfew	
,, *parthenium*	Common feverfew	
Chrysanthemum leucanthemum	White ox-eye	
,, *segetum*	Corn marigold	Bury, Salcombe
Tanacetum vulgare	Common tansy	Kingsbridge road
Artemisia vulgaris	Mugwort	
,, *absinthium*	Wormwood	Slapton Sands
Gnaphalium uliginosum	Marsh everlasting, or cud-weed	
Senecio vulgaris	Common groundsel	
,, *sylvaticus*	Mountain groundsel	Thurlestone
,, *Jacobæa*	Common ragwort	
Lapsana communis	Common nipple-wort	
Cichorium intijbus	Chicory	Devon Road, and quarry near Sandhills
Hypochæris radicata	Long-rooted cat's ear	Thurlestone
Leontodon taraxacum	Dandelion	
Sonchus palustris	Marsh sow thistle	Sewers
,, *maritimus*	Sea sow thistle	Hope
Crepis virens	Smooth hawk's-beard	

Latin Name.	English Name.	Where found.
Sonchus oleraceus	Common sow thistle	
,, *a·vensis*	Corn sow thistle	Common
Hieracium pilosella	Mouse-ear hawk-weed	
Picis echioides	Bristly ox-tongue	
Picris hieracioides	Hawkweed ox-tongue	
Leontodon hispidus	Rough hawk-bit	
,, *autumnalis*	Autumnal hawk-bit	
Thrincia hirta	Hairy thrincia	
Pulicaria dysenterica	Common flea-bane	
Bidens tripartita	Bur-marigold	Slapton Sands
Onopordium acanthium	Cotton thistle	
Filago germanica	Common cud-weed	

HEATH TRIBE :—

Erica tetralix	Cross-leaved heath	
,, *cinerea*	Fine-leaved heath	
Calluna vulgaris	Common heather	
Vaccinium myrtillus	Bilberry	Blackdown

OLIVE TRIBE :—

Ligustrum vulgare	Common privet	
Fraxinus excelsior	Common ash	

PERIWINKLE TRIBE :—

Vinca major	Great periwinkle!	Batson
,, *minor*	Lesser periwinkle	Batson, &c.

BORAGE TRIBE :—

Echium vulgare	Common viper's bugloss	
Lithospermum officinale	Common Gromwell	West Alvington hill
Lycopsis arvensis	Small bugloss	Bantham
Symphytum officinale	Common comfrey	Woodville road
Anchusa sempervirens	Evergreen alkanet	Salcombe
Myosotis palustris	Forget-me-not	
,, *cæspitosa*	Tufted scorpion-grass	Common
,, *arvensis*	Field scorpion-grass	
,, *collina*	Early scorpion-grass	
,, *versicolor*	Yellow and blue scorpion grass	
Cynoglossum officinale	Common hound's tongue	Millbay & Prawle

NIGHTSHADE TRIBE :—

Solanum dulcamara	Woody Nightshade	
,, *nigrum*	Black nightshade	
Atropa belladonna	Deadly nightshade	Loddiswell
Hyoscyamus niger	Henbane	Portlemouth, on Beesands abundant, a few plants at Bantham

Latin Name.	English Name.	Where found.
GENTIAN TRIBE :—		
Gentiana centaurium...	Common centaury	....
Menyanthes trifoliata .	Buck-bean	Huish Marsh
BINDWEED TRIBE :—		
Convolvulus arvensis ...	Field bindweed	
,, sepium ...	Great bindweed	
,, soldanella .	Sea bindweed	Thurlestone
Cuscuta epithemum ...	Lesser dodder	Bolt Head and on the coast
FIGWORT TRIBE :—		
Digitalis purpurea	Foxglove	
Antirrhinum arvense ...	Yellow toad-flax	
,, elatine ...	Sharp pointed toad-flax	
,, cymbalarica	Ivy-leaved toad-flax ..	
Scrophularia nodosa ...	Knotted fig-wort	
,, aquatica .	Water fig-wort	
,, scorodonia	Balm-leaved fig-wort ..	Kingsbridge
Mimulus lutens	Monkey flower	River Avon near Hatch Bridge
Pedicularis sylvatica ...	Dwarf red rattle	
Rhinanthus crista-galli	Yellow rattle	
Bartsia viscosa	Yellow viscid bartsia..	Coast toward Prawle
,, coccinea	Red bartsia	
Euphrasia officinalis ...	Common eye-bright ..	
Sibthorpia Europæa ...	Cornish money-wort ..	Maryknowle and Buckland
Veronica serpyllifolia...	Smooth speedwell	
,, arvensis	Wall speedwell	
,, chamædrys ...	Germander speedwell ..	
,, montana	Mountain speedwell....	
,, beccabunga ...	Brooklime	
,, hederæfolia...	Ivy-leaved speedwell ...	
,, agrestis	Field speedwell	
,, buxbaumii ...	....	Common
Verbascum thapsus ...	Great mullein	Camperdown road
,, blattaria ...	Moth mullein	
,, ,, ...	White variety	Near Woodville
,, virgatum ...	Large flowered mullein	Portlemouth and Slapton Sands
VERVAIN TRIBE :—		
Verbena officinalis	Common vervain	Batson
BUTTERWORT TRIBE :—		
Pinguicula lusitanica .	Pale butterwort	Sewer Mill Cove
FOXGLOVE TRIBE :—		
Antirrhinum orontium	Small toad-flax	Blank's Mill
Melampyrum pratense	Cow wheat	Near Waterhead

Latin Name.	English Name.	Where found.
Labiate Tribe :—		
Salvia verbenaca	Clary or wild sage......	
Mentha hirsuta	Hairy mint	
,, *arvensis*	Corn mint	
,, *rotundifolia* ...	Round-leaved mint	Portlemouth
,, *pulegium*	....	Sewer Mill & Slapton
Thymus serpyllum	Common thyme........	
Origanum vulgare	Common marjoram	
Ajuga reptans	Common bugle	
,, ,, ...	White variety	
Lycopus Europæus	Gipsy wort	Slapton
Teucrium scorodonia ..	Wood germander	Near Salcombe
Ballota nigra	Black horehound	
Galeobdolon luteum ..	Yellow weasel snout ..	
Galeopsis tetrahit	Common hemp nettle ..	
,, *ladanum*	Red hemp nettle	Courtenay Wood
Lamium album	White dead nettle	
,, *purpureum*..	Purple dead nettle	
Betonica officinalis ..	Wood betony, white variety	
Stachys sylvatica	Hedge wound-wort	
Nepeta glechoma	Ground ivy	
Calamintha clinopodium	Wild basil	
,, *officinalis*.	Calamint	
,, *acinos* ...	Basil thyme	
Melittis melissophyllum	Wild balm	Near Kingsbridge and Portlemouth
Prunella vulgaris	Self heal	
Primrose Tribe :—		
Primula vulgaris	Common primrose	
Glaux maritima	Sea milkwort	Sewer Mill Cove
Samolus valerandi ..	Brook-weed	Ditto
Thrift Tribe —		
Armeria maritima	Common thrift	
Statice limonium	Sea lavender	Sewer Mill Cove
,, *spathulata*	Spathulate sea lavender	
Plantain Tribe :—		
Plantago major	Greater plantain	
,, *media*	Hoary plantain	
,, *lanceolata* ...	Ribwort plantain	
,, *maritima* ..	Sea-side plantain	
,, *coronopus* ..	Buck's horn plantain ..	
Littorella lacustris ..	Shore weed	Slapton Ley
Daphne Tribe :—		
Daphne laureola	Spurge laurel	Batson cliffs

Latin Name.	English Name.	Where Found.
Goose-foot Tribe :—		
Chenopodium Bonus Henricus	Good King Henry	
,, *album*	White goose-foot	
,, *murale*	Nettle leaved goose-foot	Salcombe
,, *polyspermum*	Round leaved goose-foot	Near the Start
Atriplex patula	Spreading fruited orache	
,, *laciniata*	Frosted sea orache	
Salsola kali	Prickly salt-wort	
Beta maritima	Sea beet	Common
Buckwheat Tribe :—		
Polygonum aviculare	Common knot grass	
,, *convolvulus*	Black bindweed	
,, *amphibium*	Amphibious bistort	
,, *persicaria*	Spotted persicaria	
,, *hydropiper*	Water pepper	
Rumex hydrolapathum	Great water dock	Thurlestone marsh
,, *obtusifolius*	Broad-leaved dock	
,, *crispus*	Curled dock	
,, *sanguineus*	Red-veined dock	
,, *acetosa*	Common sorrel	
,, *acetosella*	Sheep's sorrel	
Spurge Tribe :—		
Euphorbia peplus	Purple spurge	
,, *amygdaloides*	Wood spurge	
,, *exigua*	Dwarf spurge	
,, *paralias*	Sea spurge	Bolt Tail
,, *Portlandica*	Portland spurge	Bolt Head
,, *helioscopia*	Sun spurge	
,, *peplus*	Purple spurge	Slapton Sands
Mercurialis perennis	Dog's mercury	
Water Starwort Tribe :—		
Callitriche verna	Vernal water starwort	
Nettle Tribe :—		
Urtica dioica	Great nettle	
,, *urens*	Small nettle	
,, *pilulifera*	Roman nettle	Bantham
Parietaria officinalis	Common pellitory	
Humulus lupulus	Common hop	Batson
Iris Tribe :—		
Iris pseudacorus	Yellow iris	
,, *fœtidissima*	Stinking iris	Plantation Walk, and near Kingsbridge
Yam Tribe :—		
Tamus communis	Black bryony	

Latin Name.	English Name.	Where found.
ORCHIS TRIBE :—		
Orchis mascula	Early purple orchis	
„ *pyramidalis*	Pyramidal orchis	
„ *maculata*	Spotted orchis	
„ *latifolia*	Marsh orchis	
Spiranthes autumnalis	Lady's tresses	Salcombe, S. Huish
Listera ovata	Tway-blade	Collapit
AMARYLLIS TRIBE :—		
Narcissus pseudo-narcissus	Daffodil	Maryknowle
„ *biflorus*	Jonquil	Batson
„ *poeticus*	Poet's jonquil	South Huish
Galanthus nivalis	Snowdrop	Batson
FLOWERING RUSH TRIBE :—		
Triglochin maritimum	Sea arrow grass	Thurlestone beach
LILY TRIBE :—		
Ruscus aculeatus	Butcher's broom	South Sands, Bolt Head, and coast generally
Agraphis nutans	Blue bell	
Scilla verna	Vernal squill	Bolt Head
Scilla autumnalis	Autumnal squill	Bolt Head, &c.
Allium ursinum	Broad-leaved garlic	
„ *satirum*	Garlic	Woodville road
WATER PLANTAIN TRIBE :—		
Alisma plantago	Great water plantain	
REED-MACE TRIBE :—		
Typha latifolia	Reed-mace bulrush	Bantham
ARUM TRIBE :—		
Arum maculatum	Cuckoo-pint	
„ *Italicum*		Hope Cove
DUCKWEED TRIBE :—		
Lemna minor	Common duckweed	
POND-WEED TRIBE :—		
Potamogeton natans	Floating pond-weed	
Zostera marina	Single-ribbed grass-wrack	

FERNS.

Ophioglossum vulgatum	Adder's tongue	Prawle
Osmunda regalis	Royal fern	Ditto
Polypodium vulgare	Common polypody	
Polystichum aculeatum	Prickly shield-fern	
„ *angulare*	Soft shield-fern	
Lastrea oreopteris	Sweet mountain fern	
„ *spinulosum*	Crested shield-fern	
„ *fœnisecii*	Hay-scented-fern	Horsecombe

PLANTS.

Latin Name.	English Name.	Where found.
Lastrea filix-mas	Male-fern	
„ *borreri*		
„ *dilatata*	Broad prickly-toothed fern	
Athyrium filix fœmina	Lady fern	
Asplenium lanceolatum	Lanceolate spleenwort	Sharp Tors, &c.
„ *marinum*	Sea spleenwort	Starehole Bay
„ *trichomanes*	Maidenhair spleenwort	Coombe
„ *adiantum-nigrum*	Black spleenwort	
„ *ruta-muraria*	Wall-rue fern	Malborough
Scolopendrium vulgare	Hart's tongue fern	
Ceterach officinarum	Scaly fern	Blanks' Mill
Blechnum spicant	Hard fern	Coombe, Charleton
Pteris aquilina	Common braken	

BOAT FARES AT SALCOMBE.

FARE BY TIME.

	s.	d.
For a party not exceeding four persons for one hour	1	6
For every additional 30 minutes or portion of 30 minutes	0	6
For every person carried for each hour	0	6
For every 30 minutes or portion of 30 minutes	0	3

Provided that no boatman shall be compelled to take less than three passengers at one time at the above rates.

FARES BY DISTANCE.

For each person up to two persons from the place of embarkation to the place of disembarkation:—

	s.	d.
For a distance not exceeding two miles	1	0
Exceeding two miles and not exceeding five miles	2	6

For a distance exceeding five miles:—

	s.	d.
For every half mile beyond the first five miles	0	3

For each additional person beyond two persons, one half the fare for each person up two persons.

	s.	d.
Salcombe to Kingsbridge or Frogmore:—For one person	2	6
Salcombe to South Pool	2	0

For every additional person one half the fare.

	s.	d.
For landing or embarking passengers by Excursion steamers, for a distance not exceeding 200 yards from the landing place, for each passenger	0	1
For landing or embarking passengers by Excursion steamers to or from Splat Cove, for a distance not exceeding 200 yards from the landing place, for each passenger	0	2

For landing and embarking passengers by Excursion Steamers on Sunday double fares.

BIRDS that have bred in the District

Mistle Thrush
Song Thrush
Blackbird
Wheatear
Redstart
Redbreast
Whitethroat
Blackcap
Golden-crested Wren
Chiffchaff
Willow Wren
Reed Warbler
Sedge Warbler
Grasshopper Warbler
Hedge Sparrow
Dipper
British Long-tailed Titmouse
Great Titmouse
British Coal Titmouse
Marsh Titmouse
Blue Titmouse
Nuthatch
Wren
Tree Creeper
Pied Wagtail
Grey Wagtail
Tree Pipit
Meadow Pipit
Rock Pipit
Golden Oriole
Red-backed Shrike
Spotted Flycatcher
Swallow
House Martin
Sand Martin
Greenfinch
Hawfinch
Goldfinch
House Sparrow
Chaffinch
Linnet
Bullfinch
Corn Bunting
Yellow Bunting

Cirl Bunting
Reed Bunting
Starling
Jay
Magpie
Jackdaw
Raven
Carrion Crow
Rook
Sky-Lark
Wood-Lark
Swift
Nightjar
Green Woodpecker
Kingfisher
Cuckoo
White or Barn Owl
Tawny Owl
Buzzard
Sparrow Hawk
Peregrine Falcon
Kestrel
Cormorant
Shag
Common Heron
Mallard or Wild Duck
Teal
Ring Dove or Wood Pigeon
Stock Dove
Rock Dove
Turtle Dove
Pheasant
Partridge
Quail
Corn Crake or Land Rail
Water Rail
Moor Hen
Common Coot
Ringed Plover
Lapwing
Woodcock
Common Snipe
Common Sandpiper
Herring Gull

BIRDS that have visited the District

- Redwing
- Fieldfare
- Ring Ouzel
- Whinchat
- Black Redstart
- Nightingale
- Dartford Warbler
- Rufous Warbler
- White Wagtail
- Blue-headed Yellow Wagtail
- Yellow Wagtail
- Great Grey Shrike
- Woodchat Shrike
- Waxwing
- Siskin
- Tree Sparrow
- Brambling
- Lesser Redpoll
- Crossbill
- Snow Bunting
- Rose-coloured Starling
- Chough
- Hooded Crow
- Wryneck
- Great Spotted Woodpecker
- Lesser Spotted Woodpecker
- Bee-eater
- Hoopoe
- Long-eared Owl
- Short-eared Owl
- Marsh Harrier
- Hen Harrier
- Montagu's Harrier
- Rough-legged Buzzard
- White-tailed Eagle
- Kite
- Honey Buzzard
- Hobby
- Merlin
- Osprey
- Gannet
- Purple Heron
- Buff-backed Heron
- Night Heron
- Little Bittern
- Bittern
- Glossy Ibis
- Spoonbill
- Grey Lag-Goose
- White-fronted Goose
- Bean Goose
- Pink-footed Bean Goose
- Barnacle Goose
- Brent Goose
- Whooper Swan
- Bewick's Swan
- Mute Swan
- Common Sheld Duck
- Gadwall
- Shoveler
- Pintail
- American Green-winged Teal
- Garganey
- Wigeon
- Pochard
- Ferruginous or White-eyed Duck
- Tufted Duck
- Scaup Duck
- Goldeneye
- Long-tailed Duck
- Common Scoter
- Velvet Scoter
- Surf Scoter
- Goosander
- Red-breasted Merganser
- Smew
- Pallas's Sand Grouse
- Black Grouse
- Red-legged Partridge
- Spotted Crake
- Baillons Crake
- Crane

- Little Bustard
- Stone Curlew
- Dotterel
- Golden Plover
- Grey Plover
- Turnstone
- Oystercatcher
- Avocet
- Grey Phalarope
- Jack Snipe
- Red-breasted Snipe
- Dunlin
- Little Stint
- Curlew Sandpiper
- Purple Sandpiper
- Knot
- Sanderling
- Ruff
- Green Sandpiper
- Redshank
- Spotted Redshank
- Greenshank
- Bar-tailed Godwit
- Black-tailed Godwit
- Common Curlew
- Whimbrel
- Black Tern
- Common Tern
- Arctic Tern
- Little Tern
- Sabine's Gull
- Little Gull
- Black-headed Gull
- Common Gull
- Lesser Black-backed Gull
- Great Black-backed Gull
- Kittiwake Gull
- Pomatorhine Skua
- Arctic or Richardson's Skua
- Long-tailed or Buffon's Skua
- Razorbill
- Guillemot
- Little Auk
- Puffin
- Great Northern Diver
- Black-throated Diver
- Red-throated Diver
- Great Crested Grebe
- Red-necked Grebe
- Slavonian Grebe
- Eared Grebe
- Little Grebe
- Manx Shearwater
- Fork-tailed Petrel
- Storm Petrel

"According to Gilbert White's generalisation, June 21 marks the period of the maximum of bird-song, but from the beginning of the month there is no perceptible increase in its amount. Our native vocalists are reinforced by our summer visitors. There is the wren "with little quill" pouring forth such a volume of song from its tiny throat as to make one think with old Izaak Walton, that the age of miracles has not ceased. The rich flutings of the blackbird, the ouzel cock so black of hue with orange-tawny bill, and the cheery repetitions of the song thrush are still in full force. Sky larks "at heaven's gates sing," and scatter their loud notes around, while the less aspiring meadow-lark rises to less ambitious heights and warbles its simple song as it descends. And see, there is the tree-lark! It rises in the air above the tree top, turns and begins to sing as it descends with outspread wings. Reaching the tree top it there finishes with a few sweetly pathetic notes, "linked sweetness long drawn out."—*The Outlook*.

LOCAL DOMESDAY NAMES.

Modern Name.	Domesday Name.
Allington, Chivelstone	Alintone.
Alvington	Alvintone.
Alston, Malborough	Alwinestone.
Batson, Salcombe	Bachestane. / Badestane.
Bolberry, Malborough	Boltesberie. / Boteberie
Keynedon, Sherford	Chenighedone.
Charleton	Cherletone.
Chivelstone	Cheveletone.
Collaton, Malborough	Coletone.
Coleridge, Stokenham	Colrige.
Clotworthy, South Milton	Coltesworde.
Curtisknowle	Cortescanole.
Combe Royal	Cumbe Courte
Dodbrooke	Dodebroch.
Dunstone, Stokenham	Donestanstone.
Ilton, Malborough	Eddetone.
Galmpton	Galmentone.
Huish	Hewis-Twis.
Loddiswell	Lodeswille.
Malston, Sherford	Mellestone.
Milton	Mideltone.
Modbury	Mortberie.
Norton, Churchstow	Notone.
Woodleigh	Odelie.
Pool	Pole.
Sherford	Sireford.
Slapton	Sladone.
Stancombe, Sherford	Stancome.
Staunton, Loddiswell	Standone.
Stokeley, Stokenham	Stochelie.
Sewer, Malborough	Sure.
Sorley, Kingsbridge	Surlei.
Thurlestone	Torleston.
Widdicombe, Stokenham	Wodicombe.

TABLE OF DISTANCES

From Salcombe to the following Places:—

	Miles		Miles
Bantham	8	Plymouth	24
Batson	1	Prawle, by road	3
Bolt Head	3	Ditto by coast	4
Chivelstone	2¾	Rickham	1½
Dartmouth	14	Sewer Mill Cove	4½
Frogmore	4	Sharp Tors	2¼
Hallsands............	5½	South Milton	4½
Hope Cove, by coast..	7	South Pool	2¼
Ditto, via Malborough	4½	South Sands	1½
Ilton Castle	1½	Splat Cove	1½
Kingsbridge by old road	4½	Start Point	6
Ditto by Estuary	4	Ditto by the coast	8
Ditto main road	6	Thurlestone Sands ..	6
Malborough	2¼	Torcross via Frogmore	7½
North Sands	1	Waterhead	1½

Distances from Kingsbridge:—

	Miles		Miles
Aveton Gifford	3½	Highhouse Point	1
Avonwick	9	Loddiswell	3
Bantham	4¾	Modbury	8
Brent	12½	Sherford	4
Charleton	2	Slapton, via Torcross	8½
Churchstow	2	Stokenham	6
Collapit	1½	Totnes	12
East Allington	4	Torcross	7
Frogmore	3½	West Alvington	1
Gara Bridge	6	Woodleigh	3½

INDEX.

	PAGE.
Abbey, Buckfast	165
Admiralty Court	23
Regulations of	23
Copy of presentment	23
Ale, White	197
Allington, South	213
Aloes, American	35
First in Britain	35
Alvington, West	13 162
Amazons, South Devon	231
Astoreth, Syrian	218
Aveton Gifford	151
Avon, River	150 199
Bag, The	152
Bantham	147
Bar, Salcombe	78 110
Barrows	111
Bastard family	109 158
Bathing	83 234
Batson	127
Batson Hall	127
Beesands	214
Bickerton	213
Bigbury Bay	142
Birds, Rare	159
Bred in the district	256
Visited the district	257
Blackpool	231
Blank's Mill	158 164
Blizzard in South Hams	222
Boat Fares at Salcombe	255
Bolbury	11 113
Bolbury Down	123
Bolt, meaning of word	117
Bolt Head	98 114
Bolt Head Hotel	108

	PAGE.
Bolt Tail	126
Bowcombe Creek	162
Bowringsleigh	162
Brand, Rev. Mr.	155
Bryan, Sir Guy de	237
Buckfast Abbey	165
Buckland, Thurlestone	146
Bull-hole	110 114
Burdwood, Rev. J.	47 155
Burrow Island	126 150
Butterflies at the Bolt	115
Cadmus, stranding of	79
Cat-hole	123
Cavern, luminous	107
Starehole	114
Cemetery, Kingsbridge	162
Challaborough	150
Chalybeate spring	125
Charities, Malborough	132
Charleton	159
Charleton Marsh	159
Chantiloupe, wreck of	145
Chillington	230
China Clay, discovery of	178
Chivelstone	211 226
Churchstow	165
Clannacombe, Thurlestone	146
Civil Wars	129
Cliff House, Salcombe	35
Climate of Salcombe	57
Coaching Days, early	198
Collapit Creek	158 164
Courtenay Walk	107
Crab fishery	214
"Crossing the Bar"	80
Custom-house	41

	PAGE		PAGE
Danish Encampment	111	Galmpton	133
Distances, table of	260	Gammon Head	227
Death rate of Salcombe	65	Gerston	158
Devonshire fishing village	147	Giant's Grave	111
Dodbrooke, origin of	194	Gold, discovery of	125
Market	195	Goodshelter	211
Well House	195	Goss' Wall	123
Church, the	195	Graystone	125
Dogs, Hallsands	215-6	Gullet	201
Domesday names, local	259	Gutter Field	99
Dragon Bay	123		
Duncombe, William	179	Hallowe'en, wreck of	118
Durant Richard	107	Hallsands	213
Dutch galliott, wreck of	25	Hals, Bishop	231
		Halwell Wood	153
Early history of district	9	Hamstone Rock	118
Easton's Mine	125	Hawkins, Sir Richard	237
Eddystone Lighthouse	114	Hazel Tor	118
Elder Tree, Lannacombe	223	Hicks, Rev. Mr.	155 179
Epitaphs, curious	179 209	Highhouse Point	162
Estuary, Kingsbridge	152	Hope Cove	134
Exports from Salcombe	163	Huish, South	133
Fallapit	86	Ilbertstow Point	152
Ferns	115 254	Ilton Castle	17 127
Fisherman's life	214 233	Interdict, curious	206
Hardship of	215	Invalids, climate for	57
Fishing trade	17 134 139 214		
Flora of Salcombe	63	Jackson, William	103
Flowers, wild	115 135 164		
Folk-lore	147	Kelleton	10 213
Forests, submerged	102 145	Kingsale, Lord	29
Fort Charles	85	Hereditary right	30
Description of	86	Kingsbridge	13 165
Cost of victualling	86-89	Early history	165
Names of besieged	90	Origin of name	165
Siege of	91	Church, the	167 176
Articles of surrender	94	Right of burial	169
Ruins of	97	Market	170
Fortescue, Sir Edmund	86 97	Manor of	171 187
French-Atlantic cable	101	Old view of town	173
Friends, Society of	186	Description of	174 192
Frogmore	154 230	Seal, Original	182
Froude, Mr. J. A.	46 80 99 105	Places of Worship	183-6
		Trade	174 191

INDEX.

	PAGE
Kingsbridge, Town officers	187
Grammar School	186
Public Institutions	186
Portreeves, List of	189
Fair	191
Volunteers	191
Excursions from	192
Union	193
Kingsbridge Races	123
Lanes of South Devon	225
Lannacombe	223
Lantern Rock	123
Lawn Tennis Court	127
Lichens at the Bolt	115
Lifeboat, Salcombe	107
Hope Cove	136
Limpyer Rocks	99
Lincombe Hill	155
Lloyd's Signal Station	227
Lobster fishery	214
Luckner, Sir Christopher	90
Maceley Cove	227
Malborough	11 50 130
Marriage customs, curious	180
Marine Hotel, Salcombe	32
Merries, the	150
Mewstone	114
Moult, the	103
Montagu, Colonel	154 190
Moor Sand Bay	228
Nonconformists	156
North Sands	100
Oranges	60
Peartree Rocks	222
Persecutions, Religious	47
Pilchards, exportation of	18 150
Pilgrims in middle ages	226
Pindar, Peter	174
Pirates in Salcombe harbour	15

	PAGE
Pixies	123
Place names	10
Plants, list of	241
Porpoises	115
Portlemouth	11 89 207
Church, the	207
Ancient Rectors	209
Parsonage	210
Portlemouth ferry	38
Prawle	10 226
Prawle Point	227
Railway, Kingsbridge	198
Rain, signs of	147
Ralph's hole	125
Ramilies Cove	126
Loss of H. M. Ship	126
Range, Salcombe	78
Rickham	228
Rickham Common	93
Ringmore	10
Ringrone	29
Roden Point	118
Ruperra, wreck of	118
Salcombe, origin of name	10
Chapel-of-Ease	13 49
Leland's description	14
Infested with pirates	15
Early shipping	17
Fishing industry	17-8
Smuggling at	18
Fair	18
First Post	19
Description of	27
Pier, the	37
Postal arrangements	38
Shipbuilding	39
Water Supply	41 64
Public Institutions	42
Expansion of town	45
South Devon Land Co.	45
Cemetery	46
Places of Worship	50-55

Salcombe— PAGE	PAGE
As a Watering Place.. 55	South Sands 105
Its Climate 57	Spanish Armada 129 142
Visitor's description of 59	Splat Cove 109
Walks near the town 62	Stanborough 165
Flora, the 63	Starehole 12 111
Health of district 64	Start, the 217
Harbour, the 66 78	Lighthouse 218
What others have said 67	Fog-siren 221
Tennyson's Lord, visit 80	Start Bay 217
Bathing at 83	Start Bay fish-wives 233
Salstone Rock 154	Stokenham 230
Saint Peter the Great 129 142	Stone, Sally 19
Scobell 200	Strode, Mrs. 103
Sea-folk 11	Syrian Astoreth 218
Sea Villages, some 139	
Sewer Mill Cove 110 118	Tacket Wood 163
Camping out at 118	Thurlestone 146
Sewers, the 11	Thurlestone Rock 141 145
Sharp Tors 111	Thurlestone Sands........... 145
Sherford 130	Tides, the 83
Shippens, the 135	Torcross.... 231-7
Shipwrecks 25 118 126 145 222	Track, out of the beaten... 136
Shipwrights' yards 38 163	Turner, Sir George... 105 134-5
Shower of birds 222	Turks in the Channel 17
Siege of Fort Charles 86	Tyrwhitt, Sir Thomas 109
Skerries Bank 221	
Slapton 237	Volere, wreck of 118
Chantry and Church.. 237	
Ancient Rectors...... 238	Warriors, women 231
Slapton Sands 234	Waterhead 211
Hotel 234	Westercombe 200
Slapton Ley 231-4	White Ale 197
Fishery 235	Whorwood, Henry 103
Smuggling 18	Wide-gates 158
South Allington........ 213	Woodville, Salcombe 98
South Huish 13 133	Wolcot, Dr. 174
South Milton 13 145	Wreckage, right to 22
South Pool Creek 200	Wreckers 25
South Pool 201	
Church, the 202	Yarde, Malborough 130
Ancient monuments 202-3	Yeats, Mr 19 50 98
Interdict, relaxation of 206	Young, Rev. T. 21 51

A MAP
OF THE COUNTRY ROUND
KINGSBRIDGE & SALCOMBE
SCALE

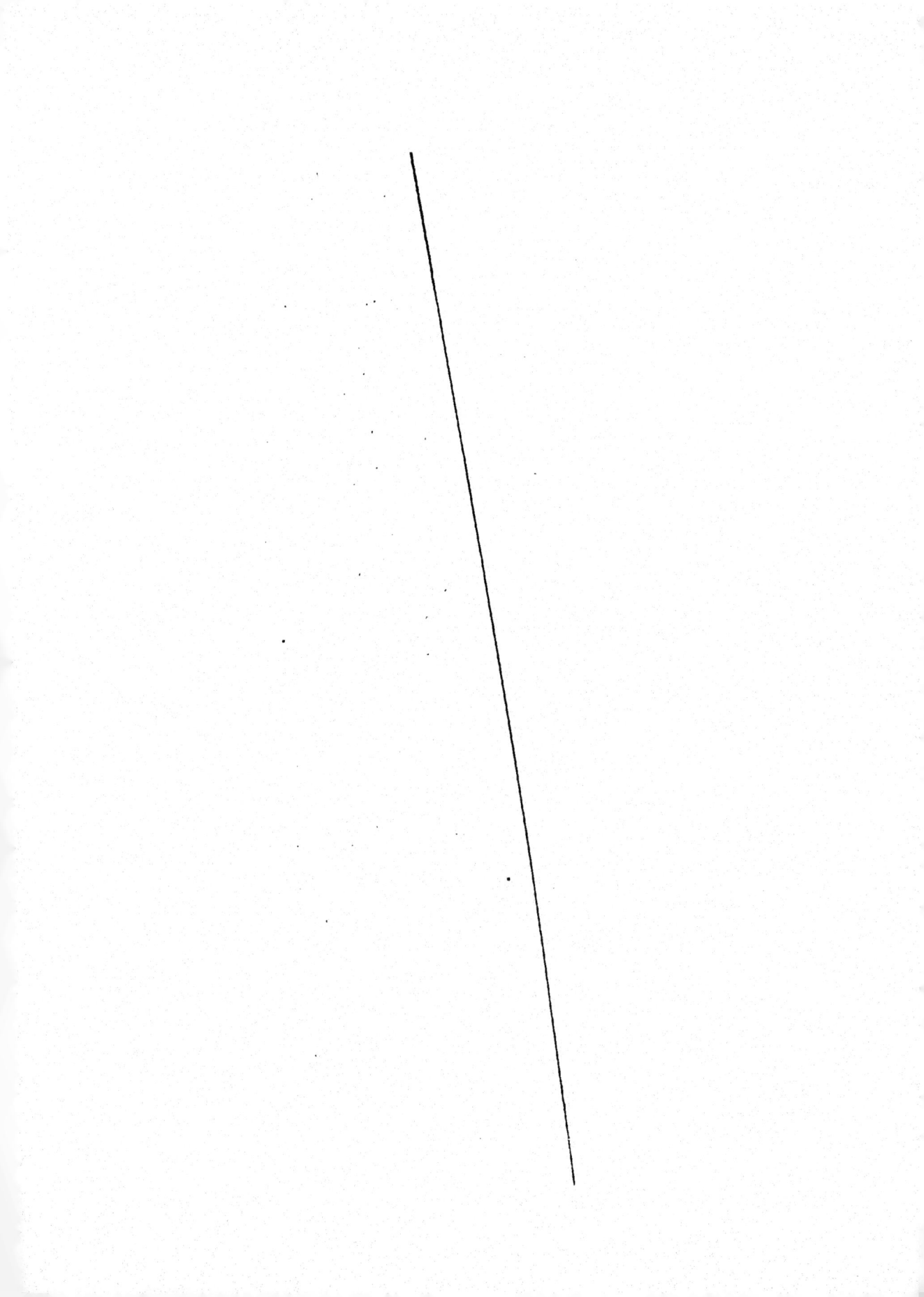